THE IMPLICATED SUBJECT

Cultural Memory
in
the
Present

Hent de Vries, Editor

THE IMPLICATED SUBJECT
Beyond Victims and Perpetrators

Michael Rothberg

STANFORD UNIVERSITY PRESS
STANFORD, CALIFORNIA

STANFORD UNIVERSITY PRESS
Stanford, California

© 2019 by the Board of Trustees of the Leland Stanford Junior University. All rights reserved.

Portions of Chapter 4 were originally published as "Progress, Progression, Procession: William Kentridge and the Narratology of Transitional Justice," *Narrative* 20.1 (2012): 1–24. Reprinted with the permission of Ohio State University Press. Portions of Chapter 4 were originally published as "Multidirectional Memory and the Implicated Subject: On Sebald and Kentridge," in *Performing Memory in Art and Popular Culture*, ed. Liedeke Plate and Anneke Smelik (New York: Routledge, 2013), 39–58. Reprinted with permission of Taylor and Francis Group LLC Books. Chapter 5 is reprinted from "From Gaza to Warsaw: Mapping Multidirectional Memory," *Criticism: A Quarterly Journal for Literature and the Arts* 53.4 (2011): 523–48. Copyright © 2011 Wayne State University Press, with the permission of Wayne State University Press. Portions of Chapter 6 were originally published as "The Witness as 'World-Traveller': Multidirectional Memory and Holocaust Internationalism before Human Rights," in *Probing the Ethics of Holocaust Culture*, ed. Claudio Fogu, Wulf Kansteiner, and Todd Presner (Cambridge, MA: Harvard University Press, 2016), 355–72. Copyright © by the President and Fellows of Harvard College. Excerpt from *Responsibility and Judgment* by Hannah Arendt, copyright © 2003 by The Literary Trust of Hannah Arendt and Jerome Kohn. Used by permission of Schocken Books, an imprint of the Knopf Doubleday Publishing Group, a division of Penguin Random House LLC. All rights reserved.

No part of this book may be reproduced or transmitted in any form or by any means, electronic or mechanical, including photocopying and recording, or in any information storage or retrieval system without the prior written permission of Stanford University Press.

Printed in the United States of America on acid-free, archival-quality paper

Library of Congress Cataloging-in-Publication Data
Names: Rothberg, Michael, author.
Title: The implicated subject : beyond victims and perpetrators / Michael Rothberg.
Other titles: Cultural memory in the present.
Description: Stanford, California : Stanford University Press, 2019. | Series: Cultural memory in the present | Includes bibliographical references and index.
Identifiers: LCCN 2018050186 | ISBN 9780804794114 (cloth : alk. paper) | ISBN 9781503609594 (pbk. : alk. paper) | ISBN 9781503609600 (epub)
Subjects: LCSH: Responsibility. | Agent (Philosophy) | Collective memory.
Classification: LCC BJ1451 .R68 2018 | DDC 303.6—dc23 LC record available at https://lccn.loc.gov/2018050186

Cover design: Rob Ehle
Cover art: William Kentridge, *Arc/Procession: Develop, Catch Up, Even Surpass*, 1990. Charcoal, pastel on paper. Courtesy of the artist and Marian Goodman Gallery.
Typeset by Kevin Barrett Kane in 11/13.5 Adobe Garamond

*For Benno and Elias,
and for Yasemin*

This vicarious responsibility for things we have not done, this taking upon ourselves the consequences for things we are entirely innocent of, is the price we pay for the fact that we live our lives not by ourselves but among our fellow men, and that the faculty of action, which, after all, is the political faculty par excellence, can be actualized only in one of the many and manifold forms of human community.

HANNAH ARENDT,
"Collective Responsibility"

Contents

List of Illustrations   xiii
Acknowledgments   xv

Introduction:
   From Victims and Perpetrators to Implicated Subjects   1

PART I: LONG-DISTANCE LEGACIES

1 The Transmission Belt of Domination:
   Theorizing the Implicated Subject   31
2 On (Not) Being a Descendant:
   Implicated Subjects and the Legacies of Slavery   59

PART II: COMPLEX IMPLICATION

3 Progress, Progression, Procession:
   William Kentridge's Implicated Aesthetic   87
4 From Gaza to Warsaw:
   Multidirectional Memory and the Perpetuator   119

PART III: LONG-DISTANCE SOLIDARITY

5 Under the Sign of Suitcases:
   The Holocaust Internationalism of Marceline Loridan-Ivens   149
6 "Germany Is in Kurdistan":
   Hito Steyerl's Images of Implication   171
Conclusion:
   Transfiguring Implication   199

Notes   205
Index   245

Illustrations

FIGURE 1. The logic of identification: "We Are All Trayvon" — 3
FIGURE 2. The logic of nonidentification: screenshot of "We Are Not Trayvon Martin" website — 5
FIGURE 3. William Kentridge, *Arc/Procession: Develop, Catch Up, Even Surpass* — 88
FIGURE 4. Looking on—the implicated subject. William Kentridge, video still from *Sobriety, Obesity and Growing Old* — 105
FIGURE 5. The coffee plunger. William Kentridge, video still from *Mine* — 107
FIGURE 6. The slave ship. William Kentridge, video still from *Mine* — 108
FIGURE 7. The barracks. William Kentridge, video still from *Mine* — 109
FIGURE 8. Mapping multidirectional memory — 125
FIGURE 9. Still image from *The Legacy of Abused Children*, Alan Schechner — 135
FIGURE 10. Still image from *The Legacy of Abused Children*, Alan Schechner — 136
FIGURE 11. "We will never forget." Still image from Joris Ivens and Marceline Loridan, *The Seventeenth Parallel: The People's War* — 165
FIGURE 12. An image of Andrea Wolf, Hito Steyerl, and an unnamed collaborator incorporated into *November*. Hito Steyerl, *November* — 177
FIGURE 13. An image of Andrea Wolf in a Kurdish demonstration in Germany incorporated into *November* as a "poster." Hito Steyerl, *November* — 182
FIGURE 14. An image of the artist as a "Kurdish protestor" incorporated into *November*. Hito Steyerl, *November* — 189
FIGURE 15. Footage of the mass grave near Van, Turkey, where Andrea Wolf's remains were reportedly found, and the artist with her mobile phone. Hito Steyerl, *Abstract* — 191

Acknowledgments

This is a book about our debts and responsibilities to people both near and far. It is also a book that holds out hope for new forms of solidarity across borders of identity and nation. Writing, for me, is one of the places where we experience such debts and such solidarity in tangible ways. To use a distinction key to my argument: the people acknowledged here are not *guilty* of the conceptual errors and other limitations that follow in this book, but they are definitely *responsible* for making it better than it would have been without them.

Two scholars I admire enormously, Robert Eaglestone and Amir Eshel, read the full manuscript for the press and provided useful, generous, and timely feedback. I am grateful for their advice, support, and professionalism. Various friends and colleagues read chapters from the book and offered consistently challenging and insightful responses: Stef Craps, David Glimp, Serhat Karakayali, Rosanne Kennedy, Neil Levi, William Maxwell, Ben Ratskoff, Robert Rushing, Gabriel Solis, Lyndsey Stonebridge, Naomi Taub, Jennifer Uleman, and Yasemin Yildiz. Other friends and colleagues also invited me to present talks that became chapters of this book, responded to earlier versions of the chapters when they were still in the form of essays and lectures, or discussed various aspects of the project with me: Ali Behdad, Kasia Bojarska, Lucy Bond, Matthew Boswell, Rosi Braidotti, Matti Bunzl, John Claborn, Richard Crownshaw, Zsuzsa Gille, Lauren Goodlad, Marianne Hirsch, Graham Huggan, Andreas Huyssen, Lilya Kaganovsky, Brett Kaplan, Eleanor Kaufman, Erica Lehrer, Philippe Mesnard, Brad Prager, Allyson Purpura, Susannah Radstone, Jessica Rapson, Ann Rigney, Debarati Sanyal, Irene Small, Sonali Thakkar, and Françoise Vergès. (I apologize for names I may have forgotten.) Nancy K. Miller has been a consistent and valued mentor throughout my career. Conversations with Saree Makdisi about the phenomenon of denial (and his own work on the topic) were also inspiring

xvi   *Acknowledgments*

in the latter phases of writing. A seminar organized by the Program in Jewish Studies at the University of Colorado, Boulder produced a lively and useful discussion of a draft of the book's introduction. Editors of journals and collections where earlier versions of some chapters appeared supported this work in various ways: many thanks to James Phelan, Jonathan Flatley, Liedeke Plate and Anneke Smelik, and Claudio Fogu, Wulf Kansteiner, and Todd Presner. I am also grateful to the artists who generously allowed their inspiring work to be reproduced here: William Kentridge, Alan Schechner, and Hito Steyerl.

This book is not only about memory, but the writing of it took place while I was immersed in the still-emerging field of memory studies. I owe great debts to my colleagues and students in this field for providing inspiration, feedback, and camaraderie over the last decade. I have been fortunate to be a member of the Network in Transnational Memory Studies, initiated by Ann Rigney and including Aleida Assmann, Astrid Erll, Rosanne Kennedy, and Barbara Törnquist-Plewa. I also feel privileged to be part of Mnemonics: Network for Memory Studies and received much inspiration from the emerging scholars who take part in each year's summer school. Like many others, I owe a debt to Jeffrey Olick, Aline Sierp, and Jenny Wüstenberg for founding the much-needed Memory Studies Association. Much of this book was written while I was directing the Initiative in Holocaust, Genocide, and Memory Studies at the University of Illinois. Working with colleagues and students in HGMS and the Program in Jewish Culture and Society, including Jennifer Baldwin, Jennifer Anderson Bliss, Estibalitz Ezkerra, Lauren Hansen, Brett Kaplan, Helen Makhdoumian, Harriet Murav, Matt Nelson, Priscilla Charrat Nelson, Bruce Rosenstock, Naomi Taub, and Jessica Young, was a great joy and privilege. Like many others, I miss the one-of-a-kind energy and brilliance of Okla Elliott. Students in my Illinois and UCLA graduate seminars on memory and the implicated subject helped me think through many of the issues addressed in these pages.

Over the many years of writing this book, I have been fortunate to benefit from the able research assistance of three graduate students who have also been invaluable interlocutors and are exemplary scholars in their own right: John Claborn and Jessica Young at the University of Illinois and Ben Ratskoff at UCLA. Funds associated with the 1939 Society Samuel Goetz Chair in Holocaust Studies were crucial to the late stages of the book's completion. I am indebted to—and honored to be associated with—the 1939 Society.

Emily-Jane Cohen, my editor at Stanford, has stuck with me over the course of two books and I am grateful to her for concrete and valuable advice about how to make this a better book. Also at the press, Faith Wilson Stein was a constant source of information and assistance as I was submitting the manuscript. Jessica Ling ably oversaw the production process, and Christine Gever was a sensitive copy editor. Derek Gottlieb prepared the index with great care.

This book has taken a long time to write. I can't blame that entirely on Benno and Elias, but they definitely deserve some of the credit. Although they are early in their reading careers, they already love books and I dedicate this one to them. It's also dedicated to Yasemin Yildiz. We've been through a lot together; it turns out that parenting requires the most intense and challenging forms of solidarity.

THE IMPLICATED SUBJECT

Introduction

From Victims and Perpetrators to Implicated Subjects

This book emerges from a belief that our understanding of power, privilege, violence, and injustice suffers from an underdeveloped vocabulary. In particular, we lack adequate concepts for describing what Hannah Arendt called "this vicarious responsibility for things we have not done": that is, for the manifold indirect, structural, and collective forms of agency that enable injury, exploitation, and domination but that frequently remain in the shadows.[1] As a contribution to such understanding, I offer here the category of the "implicated subject" and the related notion of "implication." Derived from the Latin stem *implicāre*, meaning to entangle, involve, or connect closely, "implication," like the proximate but not identical term "complicity," draws attention to how we are "folded into" (im-pli-cated in) events that at first seem beyond our agency as individual subjects.[2]

Implicated subjects occupy positions aligned with power and privilege without being themselves direct agents of harm; they contribute to, inhabit, inherit, or benefit from regimes of domination but do not originate or control such regimes. An implicated subject is neither a victim nor a perpetrator, but rather a participant in histories and social formations that generate the positions of victim and perpetrator, and yet in which most people do not occupy such clear-cut roles. Less "actively" involved than perpetrators, implicated subjects do not fit the mold of the "passive" bystander, either. Although indirect or belated, their actions and inactions help produce and reproduce the positions of victims and perpetrators. In other words, implicated subjects help propagate the legacies of historical violence and prop up the structures of inequality that mar the present; apparently direct forms of violence turn out to rely on indirection. Modes of implication—entanglement in historical and present-day injustices—are complex, multifaceted, and sometimes contradictory, but are nonetheless essential to confront in the pursuit of justice.

An approach based on implication and implicated subjects can help illuminate a wide range of social and political struggles, as this book will attempt to illustrate, but such an approach has a particular affinity to questions of race and racism, as many of the case studies below will also attest. Forms of violence and inequality premised on racial hierarchy take shape in small-scale encounters and large-scale structures; they are also instantiated repetitively in the present yet burdened with active historical resonances. Focusing on the position of the implicated subject allows us to address these different scales and temporalities of injustice. In order to demonstrate more concretely the conceptual specificity and analytical purchase of the implicated subject—in contradistinction from the perpetrator, the victim, and the bystander—I begin with responses to one of the most infamous recent cases of racial violence: the 2012 murder of Trayvon Martin in Florida. Together with an unfathomably long list of killings of black Americans by police officers, vigilantes, and white supremacists, the murder of Martin helped spark a major political movement: Black Lives Matter.[3] That long list of murders should also inspire thinking about collective responsibility among those positioned as implicated subjects—that is, those who occupy the histories and structures of racial privilege and white supremacy.

"We Are Not Trayvon Martin"

On the evening of February 26, 2012, Trayvon Martin, an African American teenager, was killed by a neighborhood watch vigilante while returning from a convenience store to the home of his father's fiancée in a gated community in Florida. A year and a half later, the killer, George Zimmerman, was acquitted on all charges in the death of the seventeen-year-old high school student on the grounds that he was acting in self-defense. Among those outraged by the killing and subsequent acquittal, a first response was to express solidarity with Martin through acts of identification. Since Martin was killed while wearing a hooded sweatshirt, the "hoodie" quickly became a symbol of the case and of the racist power dynamics that made both the killing and the acquittal possible. Thousands of people posed in hoodies and posted their images on the internet, frequently with an accompanying slogan that declared "I am Trayvon Martin" or "We are all Trayvon Martin" (fig. 1).[4]

Such expressions of solidarity-via-identification have an honorable history in political discourse. In May 1968, for instance, French students expressed their solidarity with the allegedly foreign activist Daniel Cohn-Bendit with the slogan "Nous sommes tous des juifs allemands" (We are all German Jews).[5] More recently, in a very different context, thousands of Turkish citizens adapted the slogan to the struggle against extreme nationalism and genocide denial by chanting the name of Hrant Dink, the murdered Armenian-Turkish journalist: "Hepimiz Hrantiz, hepimiz Ermeniyiz" (We are all Hrant, we are all Armenian). Meanwhile, the slogan "Je suis Charlie" (I am Charlie) swept the world after Islamists murdered journalists associated with the Parisian satirical weekly *Charlie Hebdo*, and many people in

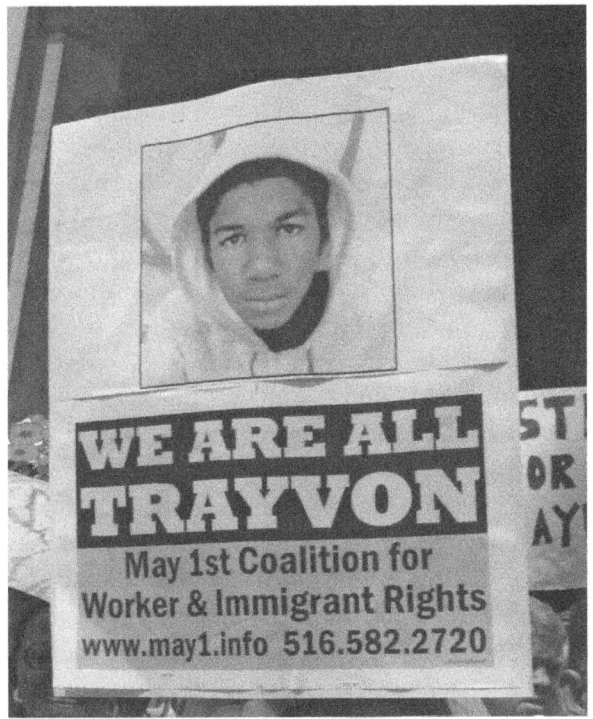

FIGURE 1. The logic of identification: "We Are All Trayvon." Trayvon Martin rally, July 20, 2013, Manhattan, New York. Photograph by The All Nite Images, retrieved from https://www.flickr.com/photos/otto-yamamoto/9361288107. Used under Creative Commons Attribution-ShareAlike 2.0 Generic license (https://creativecommons.org/licenses/by-sa/2.0/).

the US protested Donald Trump's 2017 executive order barring citizens of several Muslim-majority countries from entry into the country by declaring, "We are all immigrants!"

Such acts of solidarity-as-identification can successfully mobilize participation and attract attention, but they have limits and frequently come under criticism. The claim to universal immigrant status in the US, for instance, has been seen as erasing the presence of indigenous people and distorting the experience of Africans deported to the Americas in the slave trade. "No ban on stolen land," a counterslogan to "We are all immigrants," was coined by indigenous activists to mark the injustice of both Trump's "Muslim ban" and the ongoing fact of settler colonialism. When taken up, as it has been, by some nonindigenous speakers, the slogan tacitly acknowledges the speaker's own implication in settler colonial dispossessions. In the case of Trayvon Martin, it was not long before criticism arose regarding white Americans' identification with the murdered teen.[6] White people, the convincing argument ran, do not in fact experience the kind of profiling and "justified" violence to which black people are daily exposed, nor can they necessarily comprehend easily the history of racialization and unfreedom—including slavery, Jim Crow, and lynching—that many see as lying behind contemporary experiences.

Those who took this critique seriously sought other means of expressing their outrage and solidarity. In abandoning—or shifting away from—the discourse of identification with Trayvon Martin, such public rhetoric might have taken up another possible slogan: "We are all George Zimmerman." Such an articulation would have offered one means of taking responsibility for the murder of Martin and the widespread existence of racism. Although less common than alignment with victims, other examples exist of claiming identification with perpetrators as a mode of resistance and solidarity with the victims. In the wake of the Abu Ghraib revelations during the Iraq War, for instance, the journalist Mark Danner asserted, "We are all torturers now."[7] Such assertions stay within the logic of identification but shift its focus from victim to perpetrator. Yet, as Timothy Kaufman-Osborn argues in response to claims like Danner's, "such invocations of collective accountability" can end up granting legitimacy to what one seeks to criticize because they "help to manufacture the sort of popular sovereign, the 'we,' that is required in order to sustain the apparent legitimacy of [the] regime."[8] In any event, whether or not such an argument could also be made in the case of a racist murder, this option was not often taken up in the wake of Trayvon Martin's murder—at least not in antiracist discourse.[9]

Instead, in response to the critique of over-identification and appropriation in the claim "We are all Trayvon Martin," a new slogan appeared that briefly attained prominence: "We are not Trayvon Martin." This slogan, like "No ban on stolen land," starts to move us toward recognition of the position of the implicated subject. Over the course of the days and weeks following the acquittal of George Zimmerman in July 2013, a website named "We Are Not Trayvon Martin" published hundreds of short autobiographical texts, sometimes accompanied by photographs (fig. 2).[10] Those declaring themselves "not Trayvon Martin" were a diverse group: many of the texts and images came from white Americans recounting experiences of privilege or dawning awareness of being part of a racist society, but there were also posts by black women that drew attention to the gendered dimensions of racism and vulnerability and many posts that raised issues of class and geographical region.

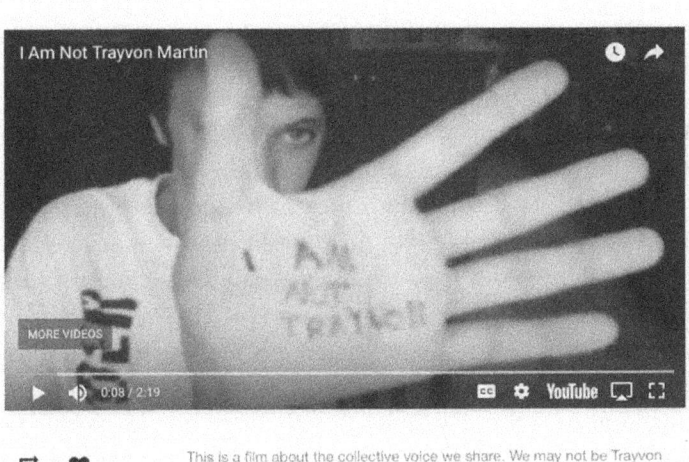

FIGURE 2. The logic of nonidentification: screenshot of "We Are Not Trayvon Martin" website. http://wearenottrayvonmartin.tumblr.com.

As a slogan, "We are not Trayvon Martin" seems at first to flirt with a discourse of disidentification that distances its speaker from the victimized teenager. Such a framing also risks keeping the concerns of white people at the center of attention instead of offering a space for people of color to share their experiences. But beyond the fact that the website created a platform for a range of voices and was not meant to displace other possible responses to the events, its mobilization of an explicitly antiracist rhetoric transformed the potential distancing from the victim into something else. Rather than understanding this enunciation as an act of disidentification, I read the slogan as a way of resisting appropriation that has the potential to open up a new political space for examining unwelcome forms of implication.[11] At least in this context, asserting "We are not Trayvon Martin" brings the speaker into proximity to both Martin and Zimmerman without stepping into the shoes of either.

This alternative strategy differs from acts of disidentification, which distance speakers from the murder and leave them floating in an unmarked position of privilege.[12] But it also diverges from acts of identification with either the victim or perpetrator that grant the speaker a clear, delimited location. Neither identification nor disidentification, the slogan "We are not Trayvon Martin" becomes an occasion to mark another kind of belonging: the speaker's implication in the conditions that contributed to Trayvon's murder. For instance, one post on the website declares, "I am not Trayvon Martin—I am the poster girl for White privilege."[13] This fairly typical contribution illustrates that "We are not Trayvon Martin" is not just a negative enunciation; rather, it creates the opportunity to claim a kind of responsibility for Martin's death and for the deaths of many others like him. Yet, it is a kind of responsibility that does not fit neatly into the victim/perpetrator binary that frames so much mainstream discussion of racist violence.[14] Indeed, contributions to the "We Are Not Trayvon Martin" website testify to how complexly situated many people are in relation to the racism and racial violence that killed Martin. Consider the comment of another woman on the website, who leads with "I am not Trayvon Martin because I pass": "My father's family is from the Caribbean. My grandmother is of mixed African Descent. I have the privilege of sharing my family history when it feels safe to do so. When it will make me seem interesting and exotic."[15] In this case—but especially for the many self-identified white contributors to the website, including the one cited above—the particular form of responsibility at stake involves enmeshment in the hierarchies of racial privilege and white supremacy.

Claiming that "we are not Trayvon Martin" can become an opportunity for acts of self-identification. Nevertheless, as the negative formulation under which those acts take place suggests, a clear vocabulary for describing political responsibility beyond that of the criminal perpetrator or direct agent of injustice does not come immediately to mind. Mainstream vocabulary remains limited by the individualist and legalistic assumptions of liberal culture and inadequate to the systemic forms of violence that surround us and become visible in cases such as that of Trayvon Martin—especially when his death is considered alongside those of Sandra Bland, Eric Garner, Freddie Gray, Tamir Rice, and a whole host of other black Americans championed by Black Lives Matter who have died at the hands of police, vigilantes, and white supremacists. As a slogan, "We are not Trayvon Martin" is an attempt to break with those liberal assumptions, but its act of negation also suggests the limits of political imagination and organization beyond a legalistic, individualist framework.

The Martin case—as well as the others that have preceded and followed it—indicates the need to reflect on modes of responsibility and justice that exceed the legal frames in which crimes are usually adjudicated. It also demands that we take into account legacies of violence that spread beyond the stable categories of what I call "the victim/perpetrator imaginary," a conceptual framework that anchors most explorations of traumatic violence.[16] The acquittal of George Zimmerman heightened the injustice done in the murder of Trayvon Martin. But even if Zimmerman had been convicted on criminal charges of murder or manslaughter, that conviction would in no way have addressed the scope of the problems of race and injustice in the US that Trayvon Martin's murder exposes. A limited focus on the trial and the criminal justice system fails to reflect on the figure of political responsibility brought to light by the "We are not Trayvon Martin" campaign, a figure who is neither the criminally responsible agent nor a mere innocent bystander to violence, namely, the implicated subject. This is not a subject who could be indicted by a court; rather, the implicated subject is an analytical category that can help us understand the kind of society that makes George Zimmerman and Trayvon Martin possible. As the historian and journalist Jelani Cobb wrote in a column reflecting on the causes of deadly police violence against African Americans, "The police [become] simply the final and most lethal vectors of a much broader public suspicion" of black people.[17] Within this broader, suspicious public can be found those who are neither Trayvon Martin nor George Zimmerman but whose "suspicion" and conscious or unconscious investment in white supremacy enabled the deadly scenario that unfolded on February 26, 2012, and continues to unfold daily. If there is a politics to "We are not Trayvon Martin," it begins here: in making visible the way implicated subjects reproduce the everyday conditions of possibility for systemic racism and thus enable the "lethal vectors" of perpetration.

To be sure, simply declaring "We are not Trayvon Martin" on a website does not constitute an adequate politics, but such a declaration can open up a space of reflection that exceeds what arises from a sole focus on victims and perpetrators (as important as those positions remain). Thinking about the case beyond the focus on its two most familiar protagonists leads us into the realm of implication: a realm where people are entangled in injustices that fall outside the purview of the law and where the categories into which we like to sort the innocent and the guilty become troubled. Indeed, implication consists precisely of those discomfiting forms of belonging to a context of injustice that cannot be grasped immediately or directly because they seem to involve spatial, temporal, or social distances or complex causal mechanisms. It goes without saying that contexts of injustice are multiple and often contradictory, and that categories such as "perpetrator," "victim," and "implicated subject" are abstractions that serve analytical purposes but do not describe human essences. That is, it is best to think of the implicated subject (not to mention the victim and the perpetrator) as a position that we occupy in particular, dynamic, and at times clashing structures and histories of power; it is not an ontological identity that freezes us forever in proximity to power and privilege.[18] In other contexts—with respect to other histories and other structures—we might also (or instead) be perpetrators or victims or descendants of victims. I call the coexistence of different relations to past and present injustices "complex implication" and focus on them especially in Part II of this book. Forms of implication are difficult to grasp not only because they are complex and shifting, however, but also because they are frequently rendered obscure by forms of psychic and social denial.[19] Implicated subjects need not be conscious of their implication.

The Trayvon Martin case illustrates in addition how the kind of entanglement implication names almost always has a diachronic (historical) dimension that intersects with a synchronic (contemporary) structure. I use the language of synchronic and diachronic implication throughout this book to signal an analytic distinction between forms of participation and responsibility that are keyed to present-day or to historical injustices, respectively. While this distinction clarifies the variety of ways in which implicated subjects find themselves entangled with power and violence in both past and present contexts, the two dimensions or axes are in reality inseparable. In Chapter 2 I introduce the concepts of "genealogical" and "structural implication" to name two different ways in which the past and present may entwine. Without a link to the present, historical injustices do not implicate us; they remain of strictly antiquarian interest. At the same time, what we consider the present is itself the outcome of historical processes that have created the world in which we live. As the theorist of history Berber Bevernage argues, how we think about the relation between past and present is the product of a politics of time: social practices that create different regimes of historicity, different relations between past, present, and future.[20] Bevernage's account of the "irrevocable" nature of certain violent histories—histories that remain unresolved and thus trouble the distinction between a fully "absent" past and a fully "present" present—influences my approach to the relation of the synchronic and the diachronic: there is neither strict continuity between past and present nor a clean break between the two temporal dimensions. Rather, implication emerges from the ongoing, uneven, and destabilizing intrusion of irrevocable pasts into an unredeemed present. Nowhere are such intrusions—and the consequent entanglement of the synchronic and diachronic that follows from them—more visible than in the differential vulnerability of racialized subjects such as Trayvon Martin.

Part of the reason that a legal approach to racist violence fails to bring out the full dimensions of such cases is that it can focus only on a discrete, recent act (the killing of Trayvon Martin) and cannot easily address the collective, historical legacies of racism that frame that singular event: the echoes of lynching and Jim Crow, for instance, that Martin's killing evoked. Indeed, debates about racism today have an unavoidable diachronic dimension to them. The resurgent interest in—and lively controversies around—reparations for trans-Atlantic slavery signals the burgeoning awareness of the historical dimensions of contemporary race politics.[21] A phenomenon that connects various locations across what Paul Gilroy has called "the Black Atlantic," the debate over reparations focuses attention on the problem of how to calibrate responsibility for a transnational system of chattel slavery that was eliminated more than a century ago but that—like the more recent histories of lynching and segregation—continues to shape today's unequal social relations.[22] An approach through the idea of implication allows these different temporal dimensions to come into focus by drawing attention to the simultaneously historical and contemporary production of the scene of racialization and racial violence.

In the wake of Trayvon Martin's murder and George Zimmerman's acquittal, there is a need for mourning and there is a need for accountability. Mourning involves the recognition and remembrance of victims—not just Trayvon but also the legions of others who have fallen victim to racist violence and the impunity that too frequently follows it. Accountability, for its part, demands reckoning with perpetrators, whether through courts, truth commissions, or other social and political mechanisms. Victims and perpetrators are rightly part of our vocabularies for responding to violence.

But beyond the unavoidable categories of victims and perpetrators there is the need for a larger reckoning with both the structures of power that undergird such cases and the histories that continue to resonate as afterlives. Such a reckoning with what Lauren Berlant calls "the ordinary of violence" cannot take place if the conversation remains limited to victims and perpetrators, to attitudes of mourning and indictment.[23] Those of us who are white residents of the US—but also many others—possess another kind of responsibility: a responsibility to reflect on and act against our implication in a system of racial hierarchy that we enable and a history of aborted justice that we benefit from in manifold ways. Such forms of implication rarely rise to the level of indictable offense, but confronting them constitutes one of the most urgent political tasks for our time.

Such insights about the relation between racism and implication are not new, although they have not yet been elaborated at length. The rhetoric of implication appears, for instance, in the *Report of the National Commission on Civil Disorders* (1968)—the so-called Kerner Commission Report, written in the wake of the urban uprisings among African Americans and others in the 1960s. In its opening assessment of the situation that led to the uprisings, the commission writes: "Segregation and poverty have created in the racial ghetto a destructive environment totally unknown to most white Americans. What white Americans have never fully understood—but what the Negro can never forget—is that white society is deeply implicated in the ghetto. White institutions created it, white institutions maintain it, and white society condones it."²⁴ The report brings into focus three dimensions of my argument in this book. First, as the authors stress, implication does not require consciousness of one's entanglement in injustice—in fact, implication is often unconscious or denied. Second, the report signals that implication is produced and reproduced diachronically and synchronically: segregation has a history, and overcoming it will require not just an end to policies of discrimination in the present, but also an active reconstruction of the historically sedimented layers of society. Third, in this struggle against the conditions that produce implication, memory can serve as a resource. African Americans' memories of victimization—what they "can never forget"—can help make implication visible, especially when they are embraced as well by those who are implicated in that victimization and usually disavow their responsibility.

The Kerner Commission Report did not achieve its ambitious goals—neither politicians nor most white Americans were ready to take up the report's recommendations or their own implication in the conditions that produced the unrest. For that very reason, a recent commentator notes, "some of the report's assessments could—eerily and depressingly—have been written yesterday to describe America's recent racial disturbances, in locales ranging from Ferguson, Missouri, to Baltimore, Maryland."²⁵ The unequal conditions that the Kerner Commission highlighted—and that recent cases such as those of Trayvon Martin, Rekia Boyd, Mike Brown, and Freddie Gray confirm still exist—call for an approach attuned both to the urgencies of the present and the way that the present preserves and reproduces injustices past.²⁶

At its core, then, this book argues that the category of the implicated subject can help us conceptualize and confront both the legacies of violent histories and the sociopolitical dynamics that create suffering and inequality in the present. The category can help us understand both slavery's ongoing impact and the systematic, structural racism brought to the fore by Martin's killing and the Kerner Commission Report, but the book is by no means limited to the hugely complicated problem of racial slavery and its aftermaths in the US. Instead, *The Implicated Subject* also addresses other situations where contemporary and historical problems of responsibility intersect, such as the legacies of the Holocaust, the experience and aftermath of South African apartheid, struggles for national liberation in Vietnam and Kurdistan, and the persistent crisis of Israel/Palestine.

The wager of this book is that an approach based on implication can illuminate heterogeneous cases of historical and contemporary violence and injustice, including many pressing cases that—due to limitations of space and expertise—only receive passing mention here. For example, the workings of contemporary capitalism at a global scale depend on relations of exploitation that systematically produce inequality as well as psychic and physical harm. Privileged consumers in the Global North are not, however, best described as "perpetrators" of exploitation, but rather as implicated subjects, participants in and beneficiaries of a system that generates dispersed and unequal experiences of trauma and well-being simultaneously. Such an approach also helps us conceptualize collective responsibility in the age of what many have called the Anthropocene: we citizens of the Global North are not precisely perpetrators of climate change, yet we certainly contribute disproportionately to current and future climate-based catastrophes and benefit in the here and now from the geographically and temporally uneven distribution of their catastrophic effects.[27] Many other current examples whose analysis would benefit from such an approach come to mind as well, including sexual harassment and gun violence—examples where there are, of course, victims and perpetrators, but where perpetration is often facilitated by a network of implicated subjects (co-workers, friends, family members, lobbyists, politicians, etc.). An engagement with implicated subjects alongside victims and perpetrators in these and other contexts can lead not only to a rethinking of the dynamics of violence and injustice, but also to new ways of thinking about political solidarity. Indeed, a notion of "long-distance solidarity"—that is, solidarity premised on difference rather than logics of sameness and identification—constitutes the horizon toward which this work tends.

Figures of Implication

Moving from a discourse of victims and perpetrators to one of implicated subjects helps open up a broad, worldly terrain for thinking about social and political responsibility in the shades of gray that Primo Levi identified even in the Nazis' "concentrationary universe" in his famous essay "The Gray Zone" (an essay I discuss in the first chapter). Within that terrain we find multiple implicated subject positions, multiple figures of implication. In the following chapters, several different avatars of implication will emerge—as they have already begun to do in this Introduction.

We will reflect on the descendant, the beneficiary, and the perpetuator, along with those who—like the internationalist—seek to overcome implication (if often with mixed results). The point is not to replace those other terms and roles (just as the point is not to do away with the categories of victims and perpetrators), but rather to demonstrate that common problems of (in)justice unite a disparate set of historical and contemporary concerns and that different modes of implication frequently converge and overlap. The implicated subject serves as an umbrella term that gathers a range of subject positions that sit uncomfortably in our familiar conceptual space of victims, perpetrators, and bystanders.

The term closest—semantically and etymologically—to implication is "complicity." Sharing implication's sense of folded-togetherness, complicity refers first to "being an accomplice" and to "partnership in an evil action" (*OED*). It carries with it a strong sense of legal wrongdoing, as in the *Merriam-Webster* definition, "helping to commit a crime or do wrong in some way." Complicity, in other words, operates in proximity to notions of criminal guilt. In recent years, however, scholars from a range of fields from law to literature have opened up the concept of complicity in ways more fitting to its second definition as "states of being complex or involved" (*OED*). In the field of memory studies, Debarati Sanyal makes an especially strong and nuanced case for this alternative understanding of complicity as a "structure of engagement that produces ethical and political reflection across proliferating frames of reference."[28] Kaufman-Osborn ably summarizes this recent work: complicity is not considered in the terms of "liberal legal doctrine" as "abetment and even collusion," but is rather "predicated on a relational understanding of conduct, one that reminds us that human action is always *implicated* with as well as conditioned by the actions of others."[29] As this quotation from Kaufman-Osborn suggests, various forms of the word "implication" appear frequently in contexts relevant to my concerns. All the same, however, in contrast to concepts such as complicity, "implication" generally remains an unmarked and thus untheorized term.[30] My use of this term shares the relational understanding of human action articulated by Sanyal and Kaufman-Osborn. Yet, despite the important work undertaken with the concept of complicity, I suggest that implication is both a more capacious and a more fundamental term for describing the forms of indirect participation illuminated here in this book. Complicity presupposes implication, but implication does not always involve complicity.

Two fundamental features distinguish complicity from implication, one relating to synchrony and the other to diachrony. First, complicity, as Iris Marion Young has remarked, remains too closely tied to legalistic models of responsibility in which causality functions in relatively direct ways. In this model, responsibility is understood as liability; but such an understanding is less illuminating for structural problems in which indirect agency and complex causality are at play. As Young writes, responsibility for structural injustices is not simply "an attenuated form of responsibility as complicity . . . but rather a different conception of responsibility altogether."[31] My concept of implication seeks to map that different conception of responsibility. But equally significant from my perspective is the diachronic issue: complicity works best as a term linked to unfolding processes and completed actions (such as the perpetration of a crime), but it works less well for describing the relationship of the past to the present. We are implicated in the past, I argue throughout this book, but we cannot be complicit in crimes that took place before our birth.[32]

To capture the diachronic transmission of implication I take inspiration from those such as Marianne Hirsch and Gabriele Schwab who have thought about the transgenerational impact of traumatic histories.[33] Hirsch's concept of "postmemory" has galvanized work across the humanities that focuses on the experience and cultural production of second (and subsequent) generations in the wake of a traumatic event. Hirsch focuses primarily on the legacies passed down, whether consciously or in more indirect, somatic ways, to the descendants of the victims (as well as to those who affiliate with the victims). Postmemory is not generally used to characterize the divergent experiences and memories of descendants of perpetrators, and I follow that convention here. While scholars have taken up the dilemmas of the heirs to and descendants of societies that have perpetrated genocide, colonization, expulsion, and other forms of extreme violence, these "haunting legacies," in Schwab's resonant phrase, demand further theorization. As with other modes of implication, we do not yet have an analytically illuminating name for those who occupy the position of the latecomer to histories of perpetration.

One way to capture diachronic implication is to speak of the beneficiary, a category that also illuminates synchronic contexts. The beneficiary profits from the historical suffering of others as well as from contemporary inequality in an age of global, neoliberal capitalism. In his vigorous critique of post–Cold War human rights discourse, Robert Meister argues that contemporary discussions of mass political violence have paid insufficient attention to the position of the beneficiary. Recent human rights discourse, in particular, "focuses especially on the relations between former victims and perpetrators after an evil regime has been defeated" and occasionally includes discussion of "the justifiable anger former victims feel toward bystanders," but it involves "very little discussion of the role of victims . . . in relation to the structural beneficiaries, those who received material and social advantage from the old regime and whose continuing well-being in the new order could not have withstood the victory of unreconciled victims."[34] The "omission of the victim/beneficiary relation," Meister suggests, "is not accidental" (26); to the contrary, it testifies to the antipolitical nature of contemporary human rights discourse. By privileging reconciliation over justice, human rights discourse demands that victims give up their claims on material redistribution and settle instead for a "moral victory" that declares that evil has already been overcome: "the cost of achieving a moral consensus that the past was evil is to reach a political consensus that the evil is past" (25).[35] Egregious perpetrators may be punished, but beneficiaries are given assurance that their inherited advantages will not be contested. For Meister, human rights discourse and the programs of transitional justice that accompany it thus represent "the continuation, by more benign means, of the counterrevolutionary project of the twentieth [century]—to assure that beneficiaries of past oppression will largely be permitted to keep the unjustly produced enrichment they presently enjoy" (31). In contrast, focus on the beneficiary can illuminate the nexus of past and present modes of implication and signal the need to resist closing the books on the past, instead keeping open questions of social justice.

Meister's critique of post–Cold War human rights and his focus on the beneficiary help us conceptualize the implicated subject, but Meister himself would almost certainly refuse this category, since it emerges from a distinction he finds suspect: human rights discourse, he observes, "reinstate[s] the distinction between perpetrators and beneficiaries that revolutionary politics denies" (24). For Meister, it is only by refusing this distinction that a possibility of redistributive justice can emerge: the association between perpetrators and beneficiaries keeps alive material claims that would otherwise be relegated to the moral sphere and to the past. It thus follows that, from Meister's perspective, insisting on a distinction between the two groups— one of the basic arguments of this book—entails taking part in a "counterrevolutionary" project.

Although I find Meister's critique of contemporary human rights discourse powerful and support his insistence on redistributive justice beyond the terms of truth and reconciliation commissions, I believe that his desire to collapse the distinctions between beneficiaries and perpetrators is wrongheaded and unnecessary for the formulation of radical political projects.[36] As Bruce Robbins writes in his account of the beneficiaries of global economic inequality, "If in a sense all of us are sinners, I'm not sure that 'perpetrator' is the most useful category in which to put us."[37] Mahmood Mamdani, whose work stands behind Meister's critique of reconciliation, also relies on the distinction between perpetrators and beneficiaries in reflecting on problems of justice. Adopting a comparative perspective on postapartheid South Africa and postgenocide Rwanda, he asks: "What would social justice mean in the South African context, where perpetrators are few but beneficiaries many, in contrast to Rwanda, where beneficiaries are few, but perpetrators many? Which is more difficult: to live with *past* perpetrators of an evil, or its *present* beneficiaries? If perpetrators and victims have a *past* to overcome, do not beneficiaries and victims have a *present* to come to terms with?"[38] As these questions suggest, Mamdani shares Meister's concern with the problem of beneficiaries, but by keeping the category of beneficiaries distinct from the category of perpetrators Mamdani is able to illuminate a number of postconflict dilemmas and the plurality of means necessary to achieve justice. In other words, historical violence and ongoing inequities demand a more differentiated analysis than that afforded by a collapse of beneficiaries into perpetrators; I open up a space for such analysis through the figure of the implicated subject.

The specificity of the beneficiary as a category is, as Robbins rightly notes, that it suggests a particular kind of causal relationship, a specificity that distinguishes it from humanitarian frameworks (a concern analogous to Meister's critique of human rights).[39] While humanitarian concern for the suffering of others need not involve reflection on one's own position in the story, Robbins argues, the "discourse of the beneficiary" fosters recognition that our well-being is contingent on others' suffering and impoverishment and that the world is connected by "causal and therefore moral relationships" (*Beneficiary* 6). In combining synchronic and diachronic dimensions, the category of the beneficiary provides a rich terrain for exploring the two intertwined axes of implication.[40] Yet, as with the case of complicity, I find that the semantic range of the concept does not cover all the cases that concern me as examples of implication. For instance, as much as acts of genocide can produce beneficiaries who profit from the dispossession and murder of others, I do not believe that, say, contemporary Germans are best understood as "beneficiaries" of the Shoah, even as they remain implicated subjects responsible for the deeds carried out in the name of their nation. Nor is the case of diasporic implication in long-distance nationalism (of the sort that I explore in relation to Israel in Chapter 5) best described through the category of the beneficiary, although, again, the category is not wholly irrelevant, either. Diasporic nationalist subjects don't (just) benefit from links to their homelands (or purported homelands). They help to *perpetuate* nationalist projects that are based on the subordination of others. The causal factors in these latter two cases diverge from those in the stricter case of beneficiary status—global inequality—that concerns Robbins.

The wager of putting forth a broad category like that of the implicated subject is that it will illuminate convergences—as well as contradictions—between different dilemmas: namely, the entanglement of the diachronic and synchronic, the impure positionings that render subjects fundamentally complex, and the way different forms of power interact and build on each other. Because it allows us to survey a large array of cases, using a broad category paradoxically enables a high degree of differentiation within an overarching force field of power.

The Stakes

The realm of implication is broad and deep, and the position of the implicated subject can help illuminate a range of historical, theoretical, and structural dilemmas and cases of injustice. But the stakes of this book are also deeply personal, even if my preferred mode of writing is not autobiography and I often choose to approach these questions from oblique angles. The matter of implication emerged for me decades ago—and long before I had a word to name it—when I contemplated what my position as a white Ashkenazi Jewish descendant of early twentieth-century immigrants to the US implied about my responsibility for the foundational crimes of genocide and slavery that had taken place on the North American continent, crimes perpetrated in the centuries before my ancestors arrived here fleeing poverty and antisemitism in Eastern Europe. I found myself arguing against peers with similar backgrounds—sometimes more recently arrived—who claimed what the German chancellor Helmut Kohl once described as the "mercy of late birth": a seeming exoneration from responsibility based on belated arrival at the scene of the crime.

Such responses, it seemed clear to me even then, confused two forms of responsibility: direct and indirect. When I later discovered the writings of Karl Jaspers and Hannah Arendt, it became easier to see that at stake was the difference between what Jaspers called "criminal guilt" and what Arendt called "collective responsibility" (see the discussion in Chapter 1). But not even the category of collective responsibility, premised as it is on mere membership in a polity, accurately captures the unevenness of our relations to the past and present, the differentiated nature of our social positions, and the ironies of belatedness that mark cases such as these. The racial hierarchies that define the contemporary US entail that even people fleeing from traumatic histories may find themselves implicated in the "distant" crimes of slavery and genocide, especially if they are able to benefit from inclusion in the category of whiteness. Such questions of responsibility are by no means limited to the US context, of course. The Turkish-German writer Zafer Şenocak, for instance, famously posed the dilemma of "guest workers" brought to post–National Socialist Germany by asking, "Doesn't immigrating to Germany also mean immigrating into Germany's recent past?"[41] Despite the fact that most such immigrants are not accepted into the ethnic and racial categories of the dominant majority, Şenocak still thought that a responsibility to acknowledge history came with the fact of being in Germany so soon after a genocide perpetrated in the name of the nation.[42]

My desire to confront what I would eventually call implication did not arise only from reflection on what it means to be white in a society still shaped by settler colonialism and the aftermaths of slavery. A very different question began to trouble me as well: what it means to be part of the Jewish diaspora in the face of the ongoing struggle over Israel and Palestine. My critical perspective on Israel will soon be apparent—especially in Chapter 5—but I also believe that Jews of opposed political persuasions (and of course many non-Jews) feel a similarly strong sense of implication in this political conflict. The sources of this implication are surely different from those noted above with respect to slavery and settler colonialism: here it is less a matter of being a beneficiary (though that is not entirely irrelevant given the Israeli "right of return") and more a matter of our ideological interpellation as Jews into relation with the State of Israel and of the affective bonds that accompany such interpellation. In addition, a more material form of implication characterizes those of us—of all religions, ethnicities, and political persuasions—who pay taxes to the government of the US and thus help to fund the Israeli army and its occupation. As taxpayers, we are indeed all implicated in the actions of our government, whatever our ideological opposition to or affective disengagement from particular policies. The powerful—or as it sometimes feels to me, uniquely powerful—affects that accompany the question of Israel and Palestine, especially but not only in the Jewish diaspora, also highlight one feature of implication's complexity: the fact that most of us feel torn by our relation to divergent, intersecting histories—in this case, histories of antisemitism, genocide, and occupation. A theory of implication allows us to retain our sense that situations of conflict position us in morally and emotionally complex ways and yet still call out for forms of political engagement that cut through complexity to remain on the side of justice.

Recognizing ourselves in the position of the implicated subject—even in the multiple positions of implication that many of us occupy—will not automatically make us better people; such self-reflexivity can indeed become a form of narcissism or solipsism that keeps the privileged subject at the center of analysis.[43] Self-reflexivity alone will not lead directly to a political movement that can dismantle the conditions of implication. The burden of history will not simply evaporate once we see our place in its long- and short-term legacies. Precisely because it involves negotiating with the past, the confrontation with historical violence is ongoing, its expiration date uncertain. Nor will systemic forms of violence and exploitation precipitously collapse because of a revolt of implicated subjects. Still, acknowledging one's implication is a necessary step in refusing "violent innocence," which Carrie Tirado Bramen describes as "the psychological mechanism necessary to create a white Christian settler nation, where innocence is regenerative and disavowal represents a habitual mode of thinking."[44] This book argues that the insights derived from the lens of implication outweigh the risks of narcissistic forms of self-reflexivity and that it is worth training our analytic powers on a terrain that too often remains invisible yet is central to the production of injustice.[45] Still, the most basic questions remain: What can a theory of implication provide? What does it offer to the theory of collective responsibility and the practice of politics?

The primary contribution I hope to make to a just politics is a reorientation of the conceptual vocabulary with which scholars and activists (and scholar-activists) approach injustice and historical and political responsibility. In place of a primarily binary design—perpetrators versus victims or similar terms—and in place of the weak triadic model that sometimes supplements it with the category of "bystanders," I expand the conceptual field by joining those who are theorizing figures such as beneficiaries and accomplices. I offer the new umbrella category of the implicated subject, the one who participates in injustice, but in indirect ways. Above all, this figure contributes to analysis and critique: it gives us a more complete picture of the workings of violence, exploitation, and domination by teaching us how "the things we are experiencing are 'still' possible" despite our collective memory of injustice.[46] That is to say, a fundamental argument of this book is that such things are "still" possible not because some restricted group of demonic individuals continues to perpetrate extreme evil, but because most people deny, look away from, or simply accept the benefits of evil in both its extreme and everyday forms. Implicated subjects are often versions of the obedient and complacent "mediocre" subjects theorized by the philosopher Simona Forti in *New Demons*.[47] The things we are experiencing are "still" possible as well because most people refuse to see how they are implicated in—have inherited and benefited from—historical injustices: synchronic and diachronic injustices are intertwined. Collective memory that avoids such a sense of implication tends toward empty rhetoric and platitude, but what I call the "multidirectionality" of memory can also facilitate awareness of implication in the present as well as the past. Multidirectional memory describes the way collective memories emerge in dialogue with each other and with the conditions of the present; such dialogue can create solidarity even as it reveals implication.[48]

I hope that the analytical clarity provided by a theory of implication can carry over into unresolved real-world scenarios of injustice. Besides providing an alternative footing for discussions that—in academic as well as nonacademic contexts—often turn on binarized identities and the victim/perpetrator imaginary, the framework of implicated subjects can open up a space for new coalitions across identities and groups. It has the potential to do this, I propose, because it does two things simultaneously that stand in tension with each other: it both draws attention to responsibilities for violence and injustice greater than most of us want to embrace and shifts questions of accountability from a discourse of guilt to a less legally and emotionally charged terrain of historical and political responsibility. If the former action seems to increase our ethical burden, the latter loosens the terms of that burden and detaches it from the ambiguous discourse of guilt, which often fosters denial and defensiveness in proximity to ongoing conflicts and the unearned benefits that accrue from injustice. By foregrounding the "impurities" that characterize all identities, the framework of implication de-moralizes politics and encourages affinities between those who are positioned as victims and those who have inherited and benefited from privileged positions. A politics of implicated subjects will necessarily take part in what Robbins has called "the paradox of empowered dissent." "The process of global democratization," Robbins writes, "cannot afford to do without the input of those who are empowered (that is, who *are* beneficiaries) and yet who also dissent from and even denounce the system that empowers them."[49] I would not argue that an implicated politics of "empowered dissent" is the only politics we need, but I agree with Robbins that by taking advantage of opportunities to redirect power against the systems that produce it, such dissent can serve as an important complement to more familiar and still necessary forms of politics from below. Recognizing collective responsibility, in other words, can lead to new versions of collective politics that build on alliances and assemblages of differently situated subjects.

If I identify the pursuit of justice as the aim of such collectivities, I do not seek to offer a fixed, unitary, or holistic definition of what justice would amount to; rather, I suspect that such aims need to emerge out of particular struggles and against the backdrop of particular conjunctures and histories. Still, I derive a few points from the theory of implication and implicated subjects. It should be clear by now that the particular angle such a theory offers is one primarily focused on neither perpetrators nor victims. Although it does not propose abandoning the field of criminal justice, the theory of implication does underline the radical insufficiency of that field and the consequent necessity of broadening justice beyond matters that can be laid to rest through a focus on indictable perpetrators. Additionally, as I discuss in the conclusion to Chapter 2, I follow Meister's proposal to shift from a "loss-based" to a "gain-based" theory of redress, that is, from a primary concern with how to compensate someone for loss to how to assess what beneficiaries and other implicated subjects *owe* (see Meister 234–35). Thus, without discounting either the claims of victims and their heirs or the need to reckon with perpetrators, an approach to justice derived from an account of implication foregrounds instead the responsibilities of more ambiguously situated participants and descendants.

Implication, however, comes in multiple forms, and even within any single scenario, injustices are rarely singular. Nancy Fraser—whose ideas will play a role in Chapters 2 and 3—provides a useful grid for mapping multiple forms of (in)justice: she distinguishes between injustices of distribution, recognition, and representation, and thus between realms of material well-being, culture and identity, and political organization, respectively. Like the distinction between the synchronic and the diachronic, these are analytic distinctions that lend clarity to what the Combahee River Collective describes as interlocking systems of oppression (see Chapter 1). Framing implication broadly so as to encompass questions of race, exploitation, colonialism, ecological destruction, and more allows us to perceive the clashing, "abnormal" scenarios of injustice that Fraser identifies and to seek in response more "reflexive" modes of justice.

Outline of the Book

Foregrounding the role of implicated subjects does not mean reproducing an exclusive focus on privileged subjects who would then be kept at the center of concern to the detriment of those who typically remain out of view. First, as a relational methodology, the analytical lens of implication necessarily keeps in view differently situated subjects, including victims and perpetrators. Second, because implicated subjects are subjects who occupy particular positions at particular junctures in space and time, the implicated subject is not an ontological category and does not always or necessarily correspond to our stereotypical images of privilege (the "straight white cis-gendered man," for instance). The implicated subjects considered here include survivors of genocidal violence and artists and intellectuals of color along with more expected avatars of privilege. Even so, the theory of implication does not relativize structures and histories of power. Instead, it reveals the way power functions through complex and sometimes contradictory articulations, through the construction of what Primo Levi called "gray zones."

The Implicated Subject traces a conceptual arc from what Part I calls "Long-Distance Legacies" to what Part III calls "Long-Distance Solidarity," that is, from the varieties of implication to their self-conscious exploration in projects of internationalist activism. Throughout the book, the focus remains primarily on how we conceptualize different forms of implication and different figurations of the implicated subject. In a short conclusion meant to set the stage for further debate, I synthesize the argument of the book in eleven theses while reflecting on what it means to think of implicated subjects as "figures." This is not a sociological or historical study, but one grounded primarily in engagement with cultural materials—including philosophical reflections and aesthetic productions along with some activist projects (such as the "We are not Trayvon Martin" social media campaign). I do not treat these cultural materials as "evidence" of implication, but rather as implicit or explicit theoretical acts that help us advance thinking about political responsibility and solidarity.

Especially in the aesthetic realm, revealing the conceptual contributions of these materials entails reading them closely: their most powerful contributions to conceiving and responding to implication emerge not primarily from their content but from their form, whether it be a mode of literary address, a particular technique of animation or sound recording, the manipulation of still images, or a video montage. Although there is no single formal feature that dominates the explorations of implication I discuss throughout the book, several of the chapters focus on aesthetic projects whose political purchase emerges from the way the endeavor unfolds across a series of works and often across several media (see Chapters 3, 5, and 6 on William Kentridge, Marceline Loridan-Ivens, and Hito Steyerl, respectively). Exploring implication is a messy business, and the form of the serial project allows these artists to grapple with several things: historical change, the possibility of political error and the consequent need for recalibration, and the difficulty of unseating entrenched powers of state and capital.

Although I approach the question of implication from a cultural angle, *The Implicated Subject* draws on and is in dialogue with thinkers from a variety of fields—from legal studies and political theory to critical race studies and memory studies. Since the concepts I develop here are new ones—although growing out of and engaged with important precedents—I hope that the field of investigation I sketch will be taken up, revised, and advanced in further theoretical work as well as empirical case studies.

Part I begins with a theoretically oriented reflection that offers a genealogy of thinkers who have helped me give definition to the concept of the implicated subject. In Chapter 1, "The Transmission Belt of Domination: Theorizing the Implicated Subject," I draw on the black feminist theory of intersectionality (in particular the Combahee River Collective Statement) as well as several thinkers deeply influenced by the experience of National Socialism and the Holocaust (Primo Levi, Karl Jaspers, Hannah Arendt, and Simona Forti). A key role is also played by the political theorist Iris Marion Young, who, in her final book, *Responsibility for Justice*, developed a theory of responsibility for cases of structural injustice. This chapter argues that the concept of implication allows us to grasp the subject as a "transmission belt" of domination (to use Forti's term), and to respond to an apparent gap—identified by Mamdani, Meister, Robbins, and Samuel Moyn, among others—between movements for human rights and those for social and economic justice.[50]

Chapter 2, "On (Not) Being a Descendant: Implicated Subjects and the Legacies of Slavery," continues the theoretical exploration begun in the previous chapter by turning to the aftermaths of transatlantic slavery, a field of violence that powerfully condenses problems of historical and present-day implication. Here I explore what it means *not* to be the descendant of slaves but instead to "inherit" the legacies of slave ownership, whether one has genealogical ties to slavery or not. I work with the database of the innovative Legacies of British Slave Ownership project, spearheaded by historians Catherine Hall and Nicholas Draper, and I put that database into dialogue with Jamaica Kincaid's acerbic essay *A Small Place*. Usually read as a critique of tourism and neocolonial relations in Antigua (and, by extension, the formerly colonized world), *A Small Place* also forcefully addresses white readers in a way that mobilizes the discomforting memory of slavery. Kincaid offers a paradoxical account of what it means to be (and not to be) a descendant of slavery as she creates an awareness of implication that goes beyond cognitive models and encompasses bodily sensation. Read together, Kincaid's text and Hall and Draper's project help us reflect on—and distinguish between—the genealogical and structural forms of implication that constitute the legacies of slave-ownership. In my account, genealogy and structure name different "mixtures" of diachronic and synchronic implication.

The two chapters of Part II, "Complex Implication," focus on cases in which subjects implicated in histories of perpetration also possess genealogical connections to or postmemories of victimization. In Chapter 3, "Progress, Progression, Procession: William Kentridge's Implicated Aesthetic," I consider the provocative visual connections that emerge between slavery, apartheid, and the Holocaust in the work of the South African artist William Kentridge. These connections illuminate the ambiguous position of South African Jews caught between varieties of racism and vacillating between accommodation and resistance to the apartheid regime. Focusing especially on Kentridge's unusual, hand-drawn animated films, I trace how the artist's minimal narratives figure what it means to be implicated in the transition from an overtly racist state to a formally democratic but structurally unequal society. I read Kentridge's open-ended film series Drawings for Projection as simultaneously a reflection on the possibilities and limits of transitional justice in postapartheid South Africa and a grappling with deeper histories of violence, including slavery, the Holocaust, and structural racism. Besides reflecting on the phenomenon of simultaneous implication in historical and contemporary forms of injustice, Kentridge also explores the complexities of shifting modes of implication. Through the creation of dual alter egos, Kentridge addresses in an indirect but illuminating way what it means to be Jewish in twentieth-century South Africa. As with the "We are not Trayvon Martin" campaign, Kentridge's art does not occupy the position of the oppressed through identification, but rather marks the artist's privileged distance from the suffering of the masses. In his work of the last few decades, he often uses the form of the procession to stage the implicated subject in proximity to—but also at a distinct distance from—the mobilized masses.

Chapter 4, "From Gaza to Warsaw: Multidirectional Memory and the Perpetuator," further explores questions of complex implication by turning to the Israel/Palestine conflict zone. I argue that implication provides a productive framework for thinking especially about the relation of diasporic Jewish communities to the Israeli occupation of Palestine: the kind of "long-distance nationalism" (Benedict Anderson) often expressed in diaspora constitutes less an active perpetration than a form of indirect and distant participation. Many Jewish intellectuals, activists, and artists who are critical of such forms of implication engage with contemporary events against the memory of the Nazi genocide of European Jews—that is, like Kentridge, they make multidirectional links between a current crisis and a past trauma. In this chapter, I return to some of the material I explored in *Multidirectional Memory* and argue that there has been a persistent mnemonic connection between the Warsaw Ghetto as a site of memory and other histories of racialized violence. I then zero in on more recent connections made between Nazi-occupied Warsaw and the occupation of Palestine. Critically engaging with diverse articulations of the Warsaw/Palestine trope allows me to distinguish different reverberations of multidirectional memory on a grid that maps an axis of political affect (solidarity vs. competition) against an axis of comparison (equation vs. differentiation). In the hands of intellectuals and artists with a desire to intervene politically, multidirectional memory work of this sort can explore personal and communal implication from a "complex" perspective—one that recognizes both past victimization (a form of postmemory) as well as present affiliation with perpetration. Implication, I conclude, offers a more productive framework for confronting the Israeli occupation from a diasporic position than either that of shared "precarity" and "vulnerability" (as exemplified by the work of Judith Butler) or that of critical identification with the perpetrators (as in the work of Ariella Azoulay). The implicated subject, in this case, is a "perpetuator" of injustice rather than a perpetrator or precarious subject.

As Part II suggests, the multidirectionality of memory appears in *The Implicated Subject* as an arena of possibility, but also an arena of danger: the potential for creating a differentiated solidarity is buffeted by temptations to move toward antagonistic competition, toward facile equation between different experiences, or toward versions of politics that drown the ambiguities of memory in the dogmatism of a presentist program.[51] Thinking in terms of implication also helps draw further attention to how practices of memory—even multidirectional practices—intersect with power dynamics, forms of complicity and distancing, and risks of forgetting. Yet, tracking the multidirectionality of memory also illuminates the position of implicated subjects, because the border-crossing nature of remembrance alerts us to unexpected layerings of history and indirect forms of responsibility.

Without ignoring the difficulties of creating alliances in an uneven world, Part III, "Long-Distance Solidarity," explores possibilities for internationalist allegiance forged through activist aesthetics. In Chapter 5, "Under the Sign of Suitcases: The Holocaust Internationalism of Marceline Loridan-Ivens," I return to filmmaker and Holocaust survivor Loridan-Ivens (1928–2018), whose Algerian War–era testimony in Jean Rouch and Edgar Morin's *Chronicle of a Summer* inspired the concept of multidirectional memory. I follow Loridan-Ivens's trajectory as she leaves behind the position of surviving victim and fosters surprising new multidirectional forms of solidarity, though at some political and psychic cost. I focus in particular on one of the films she made with her partner, Joris Ivens, the Dutch communist documentarian, as well as on some later autobiographical writings. In *The 17th Parallel*, filmed under falling American bombs during the Vietnam War, Loridan-Ivens repurposes some of the cinematic techniques deployed in *Chronicle of a Summer* to serve as vehicles for the testimony of Vietnamese villagers fighting against the Americans. Although she came to cast retroactive doubt on some of her socialist commitments, the film represents an extraordinary attempt to shift positions from victim to ally in an internationalist struggle. In her memoir *Ma vie balagan*, Loridan-Ivens finds a nonredemptive metaphor through which to combine the various facets of her lifelong testimonial project. Describing her life as lived "under the sign of suitcases," she concatenates the deep imprint of trauma and the itinerancy of long-distance solidarity.

Remaining with the theme of internationalism as a form of self-conscious implication, the final chapter, "'Germany Is in Kurdistan': Hito Steyerl's Images of Implication," considers an ongoing, multimedia project by a leading contemporary artist and theorist from Germany. In 1998, Hito Steyerl's friend Andrea Wolf was murdered while fighting with Kurdish militants in southeastern Turkey. Renamed "Sehît Ronahî" (Martyr Ronahî), Wolf has been transformed into a *lieu de mémoire* of the Kurdish cause and of socialist internationalism through the production of books, posters, and videos and the dedication of a massive tomb to her memory in the region near Van where she died. In a series of videos, texts, and performances over the past decade and a half, the artist Steyerl has both participated in these acts of memorialization and created a countermemory of Wolf by interrogating the processes of remediation and heroization that followed her death. Simultaneously a personal act of mourning and the occasion for a complex reflection on internationalist politics and the contemporary regime of "traveling images," Steyerl's work illustrates how art and political violence are implicated in each other. In the Wolf series, both the artist and her friend are implicated subjects, and the interrogation of their implication leads Steyerl to develop a critical internationalism that rigorously examines failed elements of the socialist project while committing to new forms of solidarity in Kurdistan and beyond.

The murder of Andrea Wolf by the Turkish state could not be more different from the murder of Trayvon Martin by George Zimmerman, but I use these two cases to frame my discussion of the implicated subject because both cases expose the complexities of historical and political responsibility. Like the "We are not Trayvon Martin" campaign, Steyerl's Wolf series exemplifies how the possibility of solidarity can accompany the exploration of ongoing implication along with the recognition of some subjects' radical vulnerability in the face of violence. The Kurdish cause for which Andrea Wolf fought—and the geography in which she fought for it—remains contested to this day. The ongoing nature of the conflict is primarily of human and political concern, but it also raises methodological questions about how to think about and respond to implication amid rapidly changing, still-unfolding events. The as yet unanswered Kurdish question provides an appropriate terminus for this book excavating the implicated subject. Caught between various secular nationalist and religious projects of domination, the Kurds remain among the largest populations of people without a state. Yet, despite a recent romance with the autonomous zone of Rojava and the struggle against ISIS, the international public remains mostly silent about their predicament. I thus cannot suppose that most of my readers will be deeply knowledgeable or concerned about the Kurdish cause. Nor is the history of the Kurds a history of pure innocence and permanent victim status—consider, for instance, the complicity of Kurdish perpetrators in the Armenian genocide or the violent and dogmatic leftism of the older PKK (Kurdistan Workers' Party). At the same time, the Euro-American world is not innocent of implication in the plight of the Kurds, either: to the contrary, US and European policies continue to exacerbate the Kurds' vulnerability. It is out of such political complexity, with which we may be intertwined even without knowing it, that a new politics must emerge: one that admits implication in collective scenarios of violence, recognizes the asymmetry of vulnerability, and builds differentiated solidarities across and beyond nation-states.

PART I

Long-Distance Legacies

1

The Transmission Belt of Domination
Theorizing the Implicated Subject

In a critical reckoning with the rise of the international human rights movement, Samuel Moyn charts how a concern for the lives of distant others became detached from a concern for social and economic justice. Despite the terms of the 1948 Universal Declaration of Human Rights, which was "chock-full of economic and social rights"—albeit "only for those with citizenship"—the triumph of "globally minded organizations like Amnesty International" thirty years later "focused not on a broad set of economic and social rights but on human survival."[1] In this paradoxical situation, increasing cosmopolitan sentiment came to coexist with growing inequality: "As the notion of human rights spread, people found it easier to identify with strangers across borders. Yet at the same time, the liberalization of markets, the reliance on free trade, and the mission of governance to institutionalize both created vast gulfs of inequality. Human rights became our highest moral language even as the rich seized ever more power and wealth" ("Human Rights" n.p.). Moyn's historicizing account points to the possibilities and limits of cosmopolitan solidarity within the framework of human rights: "the ideal of human rights . . . has left the globe more humane but enduringly unequal" (*Not Enough* 11).

Moyn confirms the skepticism of Robert Meister and Bruce Robbins, who focus attention on beneficiaries in order to counter the inability of contemporary human rights and humanitarian movements to address economic inequality.[2] Although I agree with Moyn, Meister, and Robbins on the need to relink questions of social and economic justice with humanitarian and human rights concerns, the question of how to make such a link remains fraught. While Meister seeks to collapse the beneficiary with the perpetrator in order to bring inequality back into view, Robbins seeks to foreground the specificity of the beneficiary as a key category of analysis and potential political mobilization. Through the beneficiary, Robbins wants to extend and expand what he sees as a "concern for global justice [that] is in fact anchored in ordinary moral intuitions" regarding "causal linkages between the lucky and the unlucky" (25). My perspective rejects the conceptual collapse Meister proposes while building on the kinds of intuitions toward which Robbins directs our attention.

Yet, if the category of the beneficiary helps considerably in clarifying questions of economic inequality, it alone cannot bridge the divide that Moyn describes, because of the multiplicity of factors at stake in the striving for global justice. Robbins seeks to narrow his concerns to economic inequality between "the lucky and the unlucky" in the present; he thus largely eliminates the diachronic axis of beneficiary status, polarizes and homogenizes North/South relations, and excludes other markers of difference and inequality beyond the economic. Moyn, in contrast, calls for activists and thinkers to "*supplement* human rights with other ideals and projects" ("Human Rights" n.p.; my emphasis)—a formulation that leaves more room for a nuanced approach to intersecting forms of injustice and for alternative political visions, even as his focus remains, like Robbins's, on re-centering economic (in)equality.

Because it does not submit to the either/or logic of the zero-sum game, an approach based on implication and the implicated subject keeps questions of economic inequality in view without sidelining other struggles and dilemmas. Such an approach reveals that the divergence Moyn maps between human rights and social justice derives, at least in part, from the implicit investment of human rights and humanitarian discourses in an "un-implicated" subject of concern who confronts a binary field of victims and perpetrators. That is, there is a difference between those proponents of human rights and humanitarianism in the Global North who see themselves as "disinterested spectators" of acts of victimization and those who recognize that they may be implicated in events that are happening to others (a point made powerfully in the work of William Kentridge, which I discuss in Chapter 3 and contrast to narratives of transitional justice). Implicated subjects possess multiple political, economic, and moral linkages to allegedly faraway injustices (as well as those closer to home). Positing an implicated subject thus opens up the possibility of understanding injustice and claims to justice from a multidimensional perspective. This chapter theorizes such a perspective by working through a genealogy of thinking on intersectionality, complicity, and responsibility. In offering that genealogy, I focus especially on work that brings questions of subjectivity, structural inequality, and histories of violence into conversation. While my approach is primarily analytical and conceptual, the purpose of positing the category of the implicated subject is to open up possibilities for solidarity across social locations. A clear understanding of one's own implication in multileveled conditions of violence and injustice is not a sufficient condition for social change, but it may be a necessary step for the creation of alliances among differently situated subjects, an issue I return to especially in the last section of the book.

Although many of the cases I consider throughout can certainly be classified as responses to human rights violations—including genocide, slavery, colonial occupation, and the persecution of minority populations by nation-states—my focus is not primarily on human rights as such. I do, however, return to that topic explicitly in the final two chapters of the book. In Chapters 5 and 6, on Marceline Loridan-Ivens and Hito Steyerl, respectively, I suggest that human rights discourse constitutes an important form of internationalism, but also clarify its limits by contrasting it with socialist and anticolonial internationalisms and by putting forward an alternative framework based on implication. By shifting from human rights to implication, I move beyond approaches based on mere "human survival." Those latter approaches tend to posit innocent victims, demonic perpetrators, and "caring" but detached bystanders. My intervention does not discount those subject positions (or the real gains that a human rights perspective offers), but rather involves placing a predominant focus on implicated subjects—a focus that does not rely on positing innocence, demonic evil, or detachment. In contrast to the ideal victims, perpetrators, and bystanders of humanitarian and human rights dramas, implicated subjects are morally compromised and most definitely attached—often without their conscious knowledge and in the absence of evil intent—to consequential political and economic dynamics. Because the position of the implicated subject has largely remained unnamed and unexplored, our accounts of trauma, violence, and power also remain incomplete; theorizing implication helps us explain how historical and contemporary forms of violence can be simultaneously pervasive and persistent, and yet so difficult to pin down and eradicate. Opening up the more ambiguous space of the implicated subject between and beyond the victim/perpetrator binary paradoxically provides a more precise picture of the production of damage and a better starting place for thinking about responsibility for historical and contemporary injustices than can clear-cut categories of guilt and innocence, not to mention detachment and disinterest.

My thinking on this ambiguous space has been shaped by a variety of thinkers who chart the zones of implication, even if they do not name them as such and generally have very different projects in mind. The heterogeneous genealogy that follows suggests that although the theory of implication illuminates the role of subjects who experience relative privilege in different contexts, the theoretical resources that help us formulate that account often derive from the experiences of relatively *un*privileged subjects and from those who seek to think from their standpoints. Indeed, far from being epistemologically privileged, implicated subjects suffer from what the philosopher Charles Mills calls "structural group-based misrecognition," that is, from forms of ignorance shaped by occupying privileged subject positions (according to race, gender, class, etc.) in unequal social systems.[3] For Mills, whose primary focus is "white ignorance," such forms of misrecognition are not "contingent," but that does not mean they are inevitable: "there are typical ways of going wrong that need to be adverted to in the light of social structure and specific group characteristics, and one has a better chance of getting things right through a self-conscious recognition of their existence and corresponding self-distancing from them" (59). In other words, interrogating the position of the implicated subject offers epistemological and, eventually, political advantages precisely because it helps us access realms of social ignorance that are built into systems of power and privilege. I do not assume that most implicated subjects will "get things right," in Mills's terms, but rather proceed from the assumption that liberatory political projects emerging from any social location will benefit from taking the logic of implication into account.

In theorizing implication, I draw extensively on a tradition of reflection on victimhood, perpetration, responsibility, and memory that has emerged in my primary area of research, Holocaust and genocide studies, and supplement it with recent philosophical approaches to structural injustice. An important first step comes, however, with the black feminist theory of multiple oppressions, now commonly known as intersectionality. Intersectional thinking does not itself focus on the implicated subject—in fact it tends to foreground a standpoint far from that position—but its account of the social reveals the political necessity of working through questions of implication. In the following section we will see how the fact of implication arises from what the Combahee River Collective calls the "interlocking" nature of "systems of oppression." Primo Levi makes that insight explicit by revealing how, even under the most extreme conditions of subjection imaginable, structures of power produce implicated subjects as a necessary effect. Reflecting on societies that give birth to such conditions reveals the need to think about responsibility beyond legalistic and individualist models, a task in which we are assisted by the German philosopher Karl Jaspers's typologies of guilt. Hannah Arendt's rethinking of guilt as collective responsibility then allows us to shift the temporal axis of analysis and grasp how unresolved historical injustices also reproduce implication and implicated subjects. Iris Marion Young illuminates the different forms of responsibility that attend structural and historical injustices, and Simona Forti reveals why the subject remains an essential category for thinking power even at the systemic scale and thus helps clarify why this book makes the category of the subject so central. What unites these very distinct thinkers is their commitment to thinking political and social dilemmas complexly—that is, beyond a monocausal frame—and to situating violence and injustice, even when it takes extreme forms, in shared institutions and everyday relations.

Drawing on these diverse sources allows me to formulate a theory of implication and the implicated subject that offers an alternative to the usual accounts of human rights violations and their aftermaths. Foregrounding implication instead of victimhood or perpetration allows us to emphasize the dynamic interplay between subjectivity, structural inequality, and historical violence; supplement absolutist moral ascriptions with more nuanced accounts of power; and above all, leave behind the detached and disinterested spectators who dominate discussions of distant suffering in favor of entangled, impure subjects of historical and political responsibility. The implicated subject, we will see, is a transmission belt of domination.

Intersectionality and the Problem of Coalition

Intersectional theory proves essential for theorizing implication because its account of the social helps us avoid the split between human rights and social equality that Moyn describes. Although the legal scholar Kimberlé Crenshaw coined the concept of intersectionality in the late 1980s, its genealogy goes back much further.[4] It has historical sources that date at least to the late nineteenth-century intellectual Anna Julia Cooper, but something close to what would later be called intersectionality received its first full articulation in "The Combahee River Collective Statement," drafted by Barbara Smith, Beverly Smith, and Demita Frazier in 1977.[5] Central to the statement is the insight—now widely shared, but revolutionary at the time—that "the major systems of oppression are interlocking" and require "the development of integrated analysis and practice" (15). The need for such an analytical perspective stemmed, according to the authors, from a dramatic gap in knowledge: "No one before has ever examined the multilayered texture of Black women's lives" (20). Out of this analysis of the interlocking nature of oppression and the as yet unexplored texture of black women's lives, the authors derive a radical politics: "We might use our position at the bottom . . . to make a clear leap into revolutionary action. If Black women were free, it would mean that everyone else would have to be free since our freedom would necessitate the destruction of all the systems of oppression" (22–23). Here we arrive at the collective's most powerful insight, as well as a problem for political analysis and organization. The "position at the bottom" has proven essential to thinking the complexity of power and can be a springboard for politics from below, but it also necessitates an expansion of alliances beyond that particular position: "The fact that individual Black feminists are living in isolation all over the country, that our own numbers are small, and that we have some skills in writing, printing, and publishing makes us want to carry out these kinds of projects as a means of organizing Black feminists as we continue to do political work in coalition with other groups" (25–26). In other words, a position at the intersection of multiple forms of oppression represents both an epistemologically powerful standpoint and a location from which to conceive politics, but the practice of politics nevertheless requires translocal organizing and coalitions with differently situated subjects. As collective member Demita Frazier later wrote, "We understood that coalition building was crucial to our own survival."[6]

Such coalition building comes with intrinsic difficulties, however. As the statement details, solidarity with black men is essential to fighting racism, yet "we also struggle with Black men about sexism." Conversely, if feminist solidarity is essential for tackling sexism, white women are often bonded with white men in a "negative solidarity as racial oppressors" (19). Although the collective's statement originates the concept of identity politics—the idea that "the most profound and potentially most radical politics comes directly out of our own identity, as opposed to working to end somebody else's oppression" (19)—it also implies the need for a political vision that joins with others in the creation of politically effective alliances to confront one's own oppression. To translate back into my own terms: the forging of solidarity necessarily entails alliances between subjects who are differentially implicated in the interlocking systems of oppression that the Combahee River Collective identifies.

Precisely because systems of oppression are interlocking, most people do not occupy the isolated "position at the bottom" that the collective illuminates, but, rather, more ambiguous, mixed positions in proximity to different vectors of power. Thus, while holding on to the fundamentally intersectional vision that the statement articulates—which is then developed by Crenshaw and many others in the following decades—I find it necessary to supplement this theory with an approach that starts from a different position, that of the implicated subject. The impure position of implicated subjects does not provide grounds for a "clear leap" into revolutionary politics, but it can be analytically and politically productive: it offers a position through which to understand the kinds of "negative solidarity" that the Combahee River Collective finds in subjects who acquiesce to power, and it helps to clarify the unevenness that must be confronted in the creation of political coalitions of differently situated subjects. The negative solidarity of implicated subjects is the building block of white supremacy and patriarchy; confronting white supremacy and patriarchy thus also involves the coming to consciousness of at least some of those implicated subjects. As the Combahee River Collective writes, "Eliminating racism in the white women's movement is by definition work for white women to do, but we will continue to speak to and demand accountability on this issue" (27). In other words, confronting implication is the job of implicated subjects who need to be held accountable for their relations to histories of violence and current hierarchies of power.

In the Gray Zone

As the Combahee River Collective's brief references to the ambiguous positions of black men and white women imply, subjects who can in certain positions be termed victims can also in other contexts become enmeshed in hierarchies of power. A few years after the collective's statement first appeared, this insight received a significant elucidation in a very different context. In his final collection of essays, *The Drowned and the Saved* (orig. pub. 1986), Holocaust survivor and writer Primo Levi describes a space of complexity and ambiguity that bears an affinity to the space of implication and that he names "the gray zone." Like the authors of the

Combahee River Collective Statement, Levi was interested in the way degrees of privilege operate within starkly hierarchical relations of power. His primary focus was not the everyday, structural forms of oppression diagnosed by the Combahee River Collective, but the exceptional world of the "concentrationary universe." Yet, Levi's approach to that universe was one that put it in dialogue with more familiar operations of domination. As he wrote in the preface to *The Drowned and The Saved*, "The Lagers constituted a system that was widespread, complex, and deeply ingrained in the daily life of the country. This system has been described, correctly, as the '*univers concentrationnaire*,' but it was not a closed universe. Large and small industrial firms, farms, and weapons factories took advantage of the almost costless workforce provided by the camps."[7] In addition to describing how human rights violations are inscribed in larger economic relations, Levi's attention to the "open" nature of carceral spaces proves useful in thinking power in the context of implication.

Furthermore, Levi calls for an approach to the Nazi genocide and camp system that breaks with the simplified, moralistic framework that has defined the dominant cultural memory of the Holocaust. To this day, such conventional understandings seek "clarity and sharp distinctions," tend to "divide the field between 'us' and 'them,'" and "separate evil from good" (2431, 2430). In contrast, Levi points to the "incredibly complicated internal structure" (2435) of the Nazi-created camp world:

> The network of human relationships inside the concentration camps was not simple: it could not be reduced to two blocs, victims and persecutors.... What made the entry into the camps such a shock was, instead, the surprise that came with it. The world into which you felt you had fallen was indeed harrowing, but it was also indecipherable. It did not resemble any model. The enemy was outside but also inside. There was no clearly defined "us." There were more than two contenders, and, rather than one border, there were many blurred borders, perhaps countless, one between every person and every other. (2431)

Anatomizing the "indecipherable," "blurred" spaces of the Nazi camps, Levi's essay is concerned primarily, though not uniquely, with the impact on camp inmates of being *submerged* in a world of arbitrary but total violence (hence the Italian title of Levi's work, *I sommersi e i salvati*—which we could translate more literally as "The Submerged and the Saved"). The impact of that experience of the camps, as Levi repeatedly asserts, was not ennobling; it was instead corrupting. The camps were set up to make victims complicit in their own victimization and thus to blur the distinctions that have buttressed simplified understandings of the Nazi era—hence Levi's reference to "gray" as opposed to "black and white" as the emblematic color schema of the camp experience. To understand the gray zone is to understand that the process of victimization in the camps does not only produce victims who are clearly set against perpetrators, but, in addition, creates a whole cast of characters marked by shades or degrees of complicity who are not easy to place on either moral or juridical maps. In breaking with stereotypical notions of the "innocent victim," the gray zone troubles not only conventional morality but also legal judgment and historical understanding.

Dedicated "to explor[ing] the space that separates the victims from the tormentors (and not only in the Nazi Lagers)," Levi uses the gray zone to name a phenomenon grounded in the specificities of the Nazi camp system and to open up a field of inquiry whose relevance exceeds the twelve years of National Socialist terror (2433).[8] His essay anatomizes power and domination—not genocide as such—as they unfold in situations of "extreme duress."[9] In this sense, the concept of the gray zone can transcend the Holocaust and take on a broader reach related to the exploration of implication and implicated subjects. Yet, like all concepts, the gray zone has its limits, which derive in particular from the kinds of spaces and subjects Levi is dedicated to exploring.

Levi's imagination of space is multidimensional and characterized by heterogeneity. Yet, at the same time—and for obvious reasons having to do with his subject matter—Levi's primary concerns are with ostensibly exceptional spaces such as camps and ghettos and with the model (or perversion) of power that accompanies such spaces. To what extent does that spatial configuration remain pertinent today? On the one hand, it seems obvious that concentrationary structures continue to abound in our world and perhaps have become even more common: from the extensive prison system in the United States that locks up a breathtaking number of people of color to the refugee facilities around the world that hold millions of people in search of better living conditions. I would not call these situations genocidal (though some would), but they are certainly sites where highly policed spaces combine with "extreme duress" and the possibility of death; they are thus likely to produce versions of the gray zone despite their considerable differences from the Nazi camps Levi described.[10] On the other hand, despite continuities, systems of power have certainly changed since the construction (and destruction) of the *Lager* (the German word Levi favors for naming the camps). According to the philosopher Gilles Deleuze, we have moved from the dominance of disciplinary societies based on "vast spaces of enclosure"—like the factories, prisons, and schools considered in the path-breaking work of Michel Foucault—to the more fluid dominance of "societies of control."[11] In Deleuze's words, "Enclosures are *molds*, distinct castings, but controls are a *modulation*, like a self-deforming cast that will continuously change from one moment to the other" (4). Writing in 1990, Deleuze captures something important about the transformation of power in the late twentieth century, but today it is hard to overlook the fact that prisons have proliferated rather than disappeared. Thus, instead of relegating Levi's discussion of the *Lager* to an outmoded system of power, it might make more sense to suggest that Levi's model captures the overlap of discipline and control that we find in our world: he focuses on spaces of enclosure, but he talks about them in terms that suggest the modulations Deleuze associates with contemporary configurations of power.

A similar double-sidedness marks Levi's discussion of the figures or subjects who inhabit the gray zone. An important outcome of Levi's focus on enclosures is that the range of subjects he discusses seems to fall on a continuum between victims and perpetrators. On the one hand, this continuum is complex, and people can occupy multiple positions at the same time (as victims, perpetrators, and collaborators, for instance)—a multiplicity fundamental to what I call "complex implication." On the other hand, however, the focus on camps and ghettos almost inevitably leaves out individuals and groups who played key roles in the Nazi system and genocide, but were not so often found in the spaces of enclosure themselves and cannot necessarily be counted among either the victims or the perpetrators. We might expect those conventionally called bystanders, for instance, to be central to discussion of the kind of ambiguous morality that characterizes the gray zone—especially since Levi references such figures in the preface to his collection—but they remain outside his purview in the essay. Connecting the gray zone to contemporary problems of power and domination brings the issue into even greater relief: certainly today, power and domination function at scales well beyond the closed spaces Levi anatomized and increasingly without obvious, direct perpetrators. In this context, the category of bystanders is insufficient.

Because of its intensive nature as a highly concentrated space of duress, the gray zone does not map perfectly onto the space of implication. Yet, as with the Combahee River Collective, there is much we can take from Levi's investigations: we can hold on to the sense of moral ambiguity that does not fall into relativism; the recognition that subjects can occupy multiple positions simultaneously or in succession (a recognition also present in the collective's consideration of black men and white women); the insight that power and domination work precisely by co-opting their targets; the nonpurist approach to victimization, which does not require victims to remain innocent in order to claim justice; and the sense that different modes of power, such as discipline and control, build on each other. While Levi helps us especially to rethink the position of the victim, he does not explore in any detail the position of the dominant subject aligned with power who remains outside the direct lines of perpetration.[12] A theory of the implicated subject draws inspiration from Levi's nuanced vision of power, but puts those subjects aligned, however indirectly, with power at the center of analysis. Such a theory also supplements Levi's focus on the enclosed spaces of disciplinary society with attention to the modulations that connect dispersed subjects in a world where power does not require enclosures to produce its perverse effects of contamination. Systems of what Deleuze calls control produce implicated subjects in more subtle and far-reaching ways than do disciplinary systems. Finally, the theory of implication twists the temporal axis, so that the kinds of in-between spaces Levi finds in the *Lager* can be claimed for an approach to historical responsibility as well.

From Guilt to Responsibility:
Karl Jaspers and Hannah Arendt

Writing of the *Sonderkommandos*, those teams of mostly Jewish prisoners forced to work in and around the gas chambers and crematoria, Levi concludes: "I ask that the history of the 'crematorium crows' be pondered with compassion and rigor, but that any judgment of them be suspended" (2449). In the face of prisoners suffering the extreme circumstances that define the gray zone, it makes sense to suspend judgment and to bracket considerations of responsibility. Here lies yet another difference from the cases of implication explored in this book. Implicated subjects may of course experience degrees of coercion, but the realm of implication is above all a realm of conscious and unconscious consent, a place where privileges are enjoyed and historical legacies shunted aside, whether through deliberate denial or through what Eve Kosofsky Sedgwick calls "the privilege of unknowing."[13] The realm of implication is also a site from which to launch a new consideration of collective responsibility.

Although the concentration and extermination camps do not lend themselves to facile translation in matters of judgment, Nazi Germany, the society that created them, has served as a focal point for some of the past century's most important reflections on legal, moral, and political responsibility. Reflections on Nazi society travel more easily to other contexts than those focused uniquely on the camps because the former are forced to address the widespread everyday complicity and indifference that accompanied the Nazis' construction of a racial state along with the genocidal projects that followed from it. Such complicity and indifference do not constitute "unique" characteristics of German society. Indeed, histories of the Holocaust have now begun to use a wider lens to track the European dimensions of the moral and political collapse that enabled genocide. My concerns are even broader, however, for similar social dynamics accompany the production of suffering and death when the latter take less extreme—or simply different—forms than what the Nazis perpetrated. Some of these post-Holocaust reflections provide rich conceptual materials that can help orient explorations of implication farther afield, but they need to be supplemented as well by approaches that start from other historical and political scenes.

An important opening occurs in the series of lectures the German philosopher Karl Jaspers gave just a few months after the defeat of the National Socialist regime. In these lectures, which became the basis for his 1946 book *Die Schuldfrage* (*The Question of German Guilt*), Jaspers directly confronts his fellow countrymen's resistance to the Nuremberg trials being staged by the victorious Allies.[14] He partially acknowledges the grounds of that resistance when he argues against the notion that Germans share an undifferentiated "collective guilt" in the wake of the criminality of the Nazi period.[15] This notion was not the presupposition of the trials, although it was in the air and may have been fostered by other Allied policies. At the same time, however, Jaspers seeks to conceptualize the distinctive forms of guilt that attend the perpetration of collective violence in order to convince his compatriots that they do possess a share of responsibility for the catastrophic events that had just taken place. In order to "clarif[y] the meaning of the charges" being brought against Germany and Germans, Jaspers famously distinguishes between criminal guilt, political guilt, moral guilt, and metaphysical guilt. Criminal guilt refers to individually committed crimes that "violate unequivocal laws" and are "capable of objective proof." Because criminal guilt is tied to the identifiable actions of concrete individuals, it cannot be abstracted into a notion of all-encompassing collective guilt. Political guilt, in contrast, supposes that "everybody is co-responsible for the way he is governed," a form of responsibility that "results in my having to bear the consequences of the deeds of the state whose power governs me and under whose order I live." The concept of moral guilt returns us to the individual because it involves taking responsibility for "all my deeds, including the execution of political and military orders." Finally, metaphysical guilt derives from "a solidarity among men as human beings that makes each co-responsible for every wrong and every injustice in the world, especially for crimes committed in his presence or with his knowledge" (25–26). Such a metaphysical notion of guilt can be seen at play in the versions of human rights and humanitarianism explored critically by Moyn and Robbins; it opens up a cosmopolitan realm of concern without specifying the forms of social, political, and economic causality that materially link the "guilty" to those who are suffering.

These four forms of "guilt" can be grouped together in different ways.[16] We might say for the sake of clarity that in contrast to criminal *guilt*, the other three categories are best understood as forms of *responsibility* that extend beyond the jurisdiction of the law. Yet, moral and metaphysical responsibility resemble criminal guilt insofar as they concern individuals qua individuals; political guilt, in contrast, is Jaspers's only category that treats individuals as members of collectives, an important prerequisite for thinking about implication. If we distinguish how the four categories correspond to either public or private concerns, a different pattern emerges. Jaspers argues that criminal and political guilt involve charges brought "*from without*"—by courts or by the victorious powers—while moral and metaphysical guilt involve charges brought "*from within*, by [the guilty party's] own soul" (33). This public/private distinction has consequences for what follows from these charges. Accused individual criminals, such as those in the docks at Nuremberg, can be punished by imprisonment or even death. Those collectives marked by political guilt, such as German citizens at the time of the Nazi regime, are subject to "liability" (*Haftung*; also, accountability and responsibility); they may be obligated to make reparation (*Wiedergutmachung*) or find their "political power and political rights limited" in a version of what scholars of transitional justice call lustration (30). Instead of leading to punishment, reparation, or lustration, moral and metaphysical charges that come "from within" demand penance and self-transformation (30). Jaspers was most interested in these latter, internal forms of guilt, while my interest lies primarily with public and collective forms of responsibility, that is, with versions of "political guilt."

Jaspers's typology was an important counterpoint to apologetic German discourses of the early postwar period. As Anson Rabinbach comments, "Among German intellectuals [of the time] he was practically alone in publicly acknowledging" the extent and seriousness of National Socialist crimes (130). Although situated in the very particular climate of immediate postdefeat Germany, Jaspers's approach also remains a useful, if limited, resource for thinking about responsibility and implication in broader contexts. Negotiation of the forms of guilt enumerated by Jaspers characterizes the processes of transitional justice and postconflict reconciliation that have proliferated in recent decades but that received important impetus from the Nuremberg moment upon which the German philosopher was also reflecting. Simultaneously, by moving discussion of responsibility beyond the sole category of criminal guilt, Jaspers helps us understand the limits of the Nuremberg model, which, as Mahmood Mamdani argues, does not translate well to other situations of transition.[17] With its distinct but interacting categories, *The Question of German Guilt* draws attention to the problem of how to think about people who are implicated in events in which they may not be directly involved as active, criminally culpable participants.

Yet, numerous shortcomings characterize Jaspers's discussion, including his splitting of public and private responsibilities and his appeal to metaphysical, religious conceptions; together, these characteristics of his thought risk resulting in a depoliticized notion of guilt, as Hannah Arendt wrote to Jaspers in a well-known letter from 1946.[18] In that letter, Arendt points to other limits in the applicability of "criminal guilt" to the Nazi genocide, asserting that these "crimes . . . explode the limits of law": "this guilt, in contrast to all criminal guilt, oversteps and shatters any and all legal systems" (*Correspondence* 54). Whether or not a notion of criminal guilt is at all adequate to genocide, further questions of responsibility remain that apply equally to situations less obviously monstrous. A key limit of Jaspers's approach for understanding implicated subjects is the foreshortened nature of his conceptualization of guilt. That is, since he was writing in the immediate and overwhelming aftermath of the war, his analysis does not extend to the question of responsibility for events that are distant in time, although, as Rabinbach notes, he did believe that "any future German state would become responsible for the crimes of the former, and that political responsibility . . . would be an integral part of postwar Germany" (164).

Arendt, who was also interested in illuminating the problems of judgment and responsibility in the face of extremity, returned to these questions in the wake of the Eichmann trial.[19] At that point, she both shifted her perspective toward a greater emphasis on accountability and broadened her concerns by opening them onto more everyday matters. In the lectures "Personal Responsibility under Dictatorship" (1964) and "Collective Responsibility" (1968), she is at pains to distinguish something like what Jaspers called criminal guilt—which she now sees as essential to holding perpetrators responsible for their actions—from forms of collective, political responsibility (which are related to what Jaspers called "political guilt"). She writes, "There is such a thing as responsibility for things one has not done; one can be held liable for them. But there is no such thing as being or feeling guilty for things that happened without oneself actively participating in them."[20] Arendt is wrong from a psychological perspective: it is possible to feel guilty for things in which one has not actively participated. Indeed, the semantic ambiguity of "guilt," situated as it is between emotion and law, has consequences for coming to terms with implication, and analysts need to keep in mind the power of such "mistaken" emotions. Nevertheless, Arendt's responsibility/guilt distinction is useful in clarifying both synchronic and diachronic forms of implication.

On the synchronic side, Arendt's distinction illuminates people's relationship to events that are unfolding around them but in which they do not necessarily participate directly. Thus, in describing the "moral problems" posed by the National Socialist regime, Arendt writes of a situation that echoes the Combahee River Collective's notion of negative solidarity among black men and white women: "What disturbed us was the behavior not of our enemies but of our friends, who had done nothing to bring this situation about. They were not responsible for the Nazis, they were only impressed by the Nazi success and unable to pit their own judgment against the verdict of History, as they read it."[21] In other words, the "complex political problem" posed by

Nazism engendered a moral collapse that tore apart the preexisting solidarities and friendships of everyday life. In such a situation—the "intrusion of criminality into the public realm"—a broad form of implication arises: "whoever participates in public life at all, regardless of party membership or membership in the elite formations of the regime, is implicated in one way or another in the deeds of the regime as a whole" ("Personal Responsibility" 33). Arendt's opening up of this realm of implication complements the notion of "the gray zone" that Levi would later describe. While Levi's primary concern was the way that victims were incorporated into and contaminated by the construction of a concentrationary universe that sought to blur the distinctions between victims and perpetrators, Arendt inverts the angle of vision: she allows us to see how a dictatorship draws privileged subjects into forms of implication that differ from perpetration and criminal guilt but are nevertheless essential to the catastrophe of absolute power.

Although Arendt conceptualized these distinctions between different forms of guilt and responsibility by reflecting on life under dictatorship—and under National Socialism in particular—she also opened up a more general issue that has a diachronic, or historical, dimension as well. As her comment about "feeling guilty for *things that happened* without oneself actively participating in them" (my emphasis) already suggests, Arendt was not only thinking about everyday life *in* Nazi Germany, but was simultaneously confronting questions of responsibility in the *aftermath* of political violence. In her essay "Collective Responsibility," this line of thought starts from reflection on the confluence of a contemporary problem—the fact that "so many good white liberals confess to guilt feelings with respect to the Negro question"—and the historical problem of the legacies of extremity in a re-normalized political culture: "the cry 'We are all guilty'" by post-Holocaust Germans ("Collective Responsibility" 147). Arendt's discussion bears on all societies. Her worry is that by confusing guilt (something that can only pertain to one's own deeds) with responsibility (which can pertain to things one has not done), the claim that "we are all guilty" "only serve[s] to exculpate to a considerable degree those who actually were guilty. Where all are guilty, nobody is" (147). Guilt, then, is always contemporaneous with the life of the perpetrator of a deed. In contrast, responsibility not only encompasses those implicated at the time of the events without directly participating in them (the disappointing "friends" referenced above), but also political communities that are transgenerational in nature. Arendt's example is Napoleon Bonaparte, who on becoming ruler of France declared (in her words), "I assume responsibility for everything France has done from the time of Charlemagne to the terror of Robespierre" (150). In this political realm, we might indeed be called upon to say that "we are all responsible," but the "we" in this formulation differs from the "we" in "we are all guilty": in Jaspers's terms, we have shifted from (a misconstrued) criminal guilt to (a justly embraced) political guilt. With her example of Napoleon assuming France's history, Arendt specifies that responsibility is a diachronic as well as synchronic phenomenon: "We are always held responsible for the sins of our fathers as we reap the rewards of their merits; but we are of course not guilty of their misdeeds, either morally or legally, nor can we ascribe their deeds to our own merits" (150). Although not guilty of what precedes us, we remain captive to a communal responsibility by virtue of our participation in a collective way of life.

Arendt uses an ironic metaphor to describe misapplied political guilt: we inherit "the sins of our fathers." In doing so, she reveals the familial and ultimately ethnicizing tendencies of the model of collective guilt. The reason white liberals' claim that "we are all guilty" or "we are all George Zimmerman" fails as a response to structural racism is that it ends up reproducing the very racialized structure of society that lies behind the problem. In contrast, political responsibility understood as implication has the potential to break with such homogeneously imagined collectives. Indeed, Arendt's implicit example of how responsibility and guilt do not line up—and cannot be imagined along the lines of families or ethnicities—is the outsider or immigrant who joins a new national collective: "We can escape [our] political and strictly collective responsibility only by leaving the community, and since no man can live without belonging to some community, this would simply mean to exchange one community for another and hence one kind of responsibility for another" ("Collective Responsibility" 150).[22] Unlike guilt, which for Arendt is strictly individual, responsibility does not derive primarily from personal characteristics, but rather from our nature as social beings. Arendt makes this clear in the passage I have used as an epigraph to this book: "This vicarious responsibility for things we have not done, this taking upon ourselves the consequences for things we are entirely innocent of, is the price we pay for the fact that we live our lives not by ourselves but among our fellow men, and that the faculty of action, which, after all, is the political faculty par excellence, can be actualized only in one of the many and manifold forms of human community" (157–58). Since we live among others, our models of responsibility must leave behind the individualist assumptions of liberal legal culture and its emphasis on individualized guilt and consider instead what it means to act collectively—which also means indirectly and at a distance—both for good and for bad.

This distinction between guilt and responsibility allows us to see again, but in slightly different terms, the productivity of the enunciation "We are not Trayvon Martin," which we discussed at length in the Introduction. Defined negatively, the slogan acknowledges the force of racial categorization but does not reproduce its categories—hence, not only white Americans embraced the slogan, but also immigrants, women of color, and others. Arendt's discussion of the distinction between guilt and collective responsibility helps us see that in order for the category of implicated subjects to map injustices in a meaningful way it has to acknowledge the efficacy of dominant imaginations of group belonging (e.g., race) without simply repeating them. Implicated subjects neither possess an identity nor arise from a process of identification ("we are all X"). Rather, to be an implicated subject is to occupy a particular type of *subject position* in a history of injustice or structure of inequality—a history or structure one may enter, like an immigrant, long after the injustice at issue has been initiated or, like a beneficiary of global capitalism, far from its epicenter of exploitation. Just as the subject positions any given person occupies are necessarily multiple, the forms of implication in which people find themselves are frequently crosscutting. Although some people are consistently and systematically privileged (or deprivileged) by the intersectional nature of social categories (the focus of the Combahee River Collective), most people find themselves caught between legacies and actualities that project more complex and ambiguous patterns of power. To paraphrase Primo Levi, the zone of implication possesses an "incredibly complicated internal structure" (2435).

Attending to this complex structure requires tools such as those developed by feminists of color for the purposes of intersectional analysis; such analyses track the ways multiple categories, such as race and gender, inevitably interact and condition each other and thus cannot be thought in isolation. But the wide compass of Arendt's notion of collective responsibility and the particular internal structure of the *Lager* described by Levi—the hybrid positioning of some prisoners as implicated in the terrors of the camps—also highlight a potential pitfall of intersectional approaches. As Jasbir Puar has warned with respect to queer intersectional analyses, attending primarily to the concatenation of multiple forms of oppression may lead to the positing of "an impossible transcendent subject who is always already conscious of the normativizing forces of power and always able to subvert, resist, or transgress them." Such analyses "may fail to subject their own frames to the very critique they deploy." They may end up, in other words, denying their own implication in power: "It is precisely by denying culpability or assuming that one is not implicated in violent relations toward others, that one is outside them, that violence can be perpetuated. Violence, especially of the liberal varieties, is often most easily perpetrated in the spaces and places where its possibility is unequivocally denounced."[23] A theory of implication takes on board the complexity of social categories first articulated by intersectional feminism, but it follows Levi, Arendt, and Puar in drawing attention to the uneven intersection of those categories: the fact that—except for some fantasized ultimate victim or resistance fighter—most subjects find themselves enmeshed in histories and structures of violence they may not realize they inhabit and help prop up. In Arendt's terms, they may not be guilty of inaugurating those histories and structures, but by virtue of inhabiting them they are politically responsible. Analysis of implication refuses a moralization of politics by remaining skeptical of assertions of purity.

From Subject to Structure and Back

Arendt's notion of political responsibility helps open up a broad, worldly terrain for thinking a politics of implication in the shades of gray that Primo Levi identified in the more restricted space of the *Lager*. Arendt, however, leaves underdetermined the prerequisites for ascriptions of responsibility, because she focuses primarily, as did Jaspers in his discussion of political guilt, on the mere fact of membership in a nation-state. In Iris Marion Young's last, posthumously published book, *Responsibility for Justice*, the political theorist engages with the strengths and limits of Arendt's thought in order to make an argument for structure as the subject of justice and for a "social connection" model of responsibility.[24] By focusing on structural injustice, Young seeks to develop a way of thinking about the politics of justice that provides an alternative to a strict focus on individual responsibility—a framework in which Arendt largely remains, despite her emphasis on the importance of living in community. The theory of implication and the implicated subject foregrounds entanglements between subjects and social structures; Young provides essential resources for the movement from subject to structure.

Young draws fundamentally, but critically, on Arendt's distinction between guilt and responsibility (see esp. 75–93). For Arendt, as we have seen, guilt is always individual and imagined as direct criminal responsibility (or negligence) leading to a harm. In cases of guilt—as in Jaspers's "criminal guilt"—a linear mode of causality links a guilty agent to a crime or injustice. In cases of responsibility, Arendt posits, mere membership in a group already suffices to connect one to an injustice; one need not have taken any linear, causal action. (Note the phrase "things we have not done" in my epigraph passage.) Young builds on this distinction but argues against Arendt (and, I would add, Jaspers) that mere membership in a group, such as a nation-state, does not entail responsibility. Rather, responsibility (as opposed to guilt) arises in situations where one's actions contribute to structural injustices—a somewhat narrower range of situations than those that Arendt imagines with her more encompassing notion of membership as leading to responsibility. In the situations Young envisions, injustice derives not from distinct individual actions, however, but rather from the sum total of complexly interacting behaviors that indirectly and inadvertently produce some sort of harm.[25] One is responsible insofar as one contributes to that sum, not simply because one is a member of the polity in which the injustice takes place: "responsibility in relation to injustice thus derives not from living under a common constitution, but rather from participating in the diverse institutional processes that produce structural injustice" (105). An important corollary of Young's revision of Arendt is that it allows us to think beyond the nation-state when we think about participation in injustice, since "institutional processes" are not limited to such a narrowly defined terrain; this represents a necessary advance for dealing with the kinds of implication that characterize a globalized world without resorting to a metaphysical notion of guilt such as that offered by Jaspers or to the disinterested spectators of humanitarianism and human rights.

Young further distinguishes guilt from responsibility by virtue of their respective temporalities: guilt always points backwards toward a crime to which an agent is linked and for which that agent must be held accountable; responsibility involves commitment to transforming structural injustices in future-oriented actions: "one has the responsibility always now, in relation to current events and in relation to their future consequences" (92;

see 108–9). The types of remediating action necessary also distinguish guilt from responsibility; while retributive or restorative forms of justice in which individuals are held to account for their deeds characterize situations of guilt, responsibility always involves collective action, because the injustices it seeks to address are structural and not "event-like" deeds (109–13). In the final chapters of this book, on Loridan-Ivens and Hito Steyerl, I explore the possibilities and limits of internationalism as one future-oriented model for addressing injustice in collective forms.

The diffusion of agency in structural injustices calls for a shift in thinking about politics and morality away from the assignation of guilt and toward a broader conception of what it means to participate in and be responsible for injustices. Instead of isolating perpetrators via judgments about liability (which continues to be relevant in more straightforward cases), the social connection model of responsibility illuminates shared responsibility, brings "background conditions" into the conversation (instead of assuming that crimes are "deviations" from otherwise just conditions), and looks forward toward new kinds of collective action in the name of justice (see esp. 105–13). Young does not suggest that isolating guilty perpetrators as causal agents of injustice is never valid; rather, she argues that many pressing injustices involve structural conditions that we cannot adequately explain through reference to what I call the victim/perpetrator imaginary. Her approach thus opens up space for thinking the implicated subject. The social connection model helps move the discussion of justice beyond criminal guilt toward questions of structural injustice and the more complicated notions of causality that come with it. It also helps clarify the basis for the notion of implication and, as we have seen in the Introduction, allows us to distinguish implication from complicity, which, Young argues, is generally modeled on liability.[26]

Young focuses primarily on present-day injustices through examples such as vulnerability to homelessness and sweatshop labor. The former serves as an example of a nation-based injustice that may involve particular criminal acts (such as discriminatory landlords), but primarily results from an amalgam of structural features that would be present even if all relevant agents acted ethically. The example of sweatshops allows Young to parry claims that relations of justice must be restricted to the territory of the nation-state. Rather, the global apparel industry connects people and corporations across borders and—although certainly marked by unscrupulous actors at various levels—produces injustices for workers that cannot be explained simply by the liability model or individualized modes of guilt.

In addition to this focus on present-day injustices, *Responsibility for Justice* also includes a brief—and incomplete—discussion of historical injustices, which Young sees as equally illuminated by the social connection model. Here her primary example is the legacy of slavery in the United States, but she apparently intended to include further discussion of the legacies of colonialism in Africa and the dispossession of indigenous peoples in North America. Young argues convincingly that the liability model does not adequately describe historical injustices of these kinds because often the original victims and perpetrators are no longer alive, and thus no one exists who could be declared guilty. Yet, unlike those who draw the conclusion from this inaccessibility of the original agents that the past is therefore irrelevant to contemporary injustices, Young proposes that historical injustices contribute to the structural conditions of the present and seeks to apply the social connection model to these historical cases: "An account of the continuities of present with past injustices is important . . . for understanding how the present conditions are structural, how those structures have evolved, and where intervention to change them may be most effective" (181–82).

Thinking about historical injustices in terms of the social connection model instead of the liability model has consequential implications for the elimination of injustice. Young opposes reparations as a remedy for structural injustices such as slavery in which neither perpetrators nor victims remain alive because such a remedy relies on the liability model to attempt to correct what are today structural legacies of past policies and actions.[27] Shifting from liability to social connection in confronting historical injustices allows her to argue both that history matters—any "society aiming to transform present structures of injustice requires a reconstitution of its historical imaginary" (182)—and that politics involves a broadly shared societal responsibility to take collective action in the present to transform institutions and conditions that propagate the aftereffects of unjust histories. Historical injustice itself cannot be undone; but this "irrevocability of unrepaired past injustices makes those of us in the present responsible for facing up to its facticity." We must "*deal with* [that past] as memory" (182). Although predominantly focused on the present and the future, Young also echoes Bevernage's theorization of the "irrevocable" and makes the case for the entanglement of diachronic and synchronic axes. Yet, if Young offers one of the most powerful accounts of structural injustice and thus of both synchronic and diachronic implication, she does not have as much to say about the forms of subjectivity that accompany and enable implication.

Against the Dostoevsky Paradigm: Mediocre Demons and the Question of the Subject

In asking us to think about political responsibility in structural terms, Young helps fill in the political space between perpetrators and victims: she shows how the production of injustice and processes of victimization do not necessarily result from deliberate acts of evil or a particular will to violence, but rather from an accumulation of distinct, dispersed actions. In focusing our attention on the structural production of harm, she implicitly continues the work of the Combahee River Collective, which focused similarly on interlocking systems of power. She also moves us beyond what the philosopher Simona Forti calls the "Dostoevsky paradigm": a belief that evil happens in scenarios featuring absolutely diabolical perpetrators and absolutely innocent victims in which the "abyssal freedom of a subject who had taken the place of God" plays itself out in "the perverse jouissance of the death impulse."[28] Yet, if Young implicitly shares Forti's critique of radical evil, she does not go on to describe what kinds of subjects are necessary to the production of structural injustices. Although she is critical of Arendt for privileging "mere" membership in a nation-state as the basis of collective responsibility, Young leaves vague both the nature of those structures as well as the subjects who inhabit them. Forti helps to fill in the latter gap in Young's uncompleted argument. Urging readers to put aside the "demonic" account associated with the Russian novelist Dostoevsky, Forti focuses instead on "mediocre demons"—those normative subjects who contribute to the production of violence and the propagation of power through less dramatic, everyday behaviors. Although her examples come primarily from extreme historical experiences such as the Holocaust, Forti grounds these experiences in processes that echo Young's account of structural injustice and that take inspiration from Levi's account of the gray zone. Indeed, Forti describes the degradation in the Nazi camps as the result of "a dense but ordinary weave of intentions, actions, and objectives whose weft proved fatal" (308).

In addition to Levi, Forti draws significantly on Nietzsche's genealogy of morality and Foucault's exploration of biopower to put forward a theory of power and violence that focuses on obedience instead of transgression. Forti points to continuities between Christianity's pastoral power and modern systems of democratic government: "pastoral power establishes the value of passivity as a general rule of conduct, a value that becomes a universal virtue in a democracy" (227). Passivity, consent to authority, and the "normativity of nonjudgment"—all aspects of obedience—serve as the "carrier[s] of political evil, as its effective transmission belt" (179). Supplementing this focus on obedience with Foucault's work on biopower allows Forti to assert that the potential for evil resides not in a nihilistic death impulse but rather in the "maxim[ization] of the value of *life*—its preservation, the increase of its intensity, its duration, the optimization of its production capacity" (176; my emphasis). If obedience derives from a commitment to life, then power works through this commitment to enhance forms of domination. This provocative argument finds fulfillment in Forti's original analysis of the gray zone as the paradoxical site of such a commitment: Levi's essay investigates, she argues, "how, in certain circumstances, the thousand threads of the desire for life and the many faces of consent to authority provoked by the desire for life bind themselves together to the point of fusing into total domination of man over man" (308). In other words, because Levi's hybrid "prisoner-functionaries" are bound to life, they end up enlisted in the production of death.

Most important for the project at hand, Forti combines (in a way that Young does not) focus on the subjective dimension of desire and consent with attention to the structural level, the "dense but ordinary weave of intentions, actions, and objectives" (although her attention to structure is less sociologically grounded than Young's). The forms of domination that derive from the structural and subjective problem of obedience, as Levi already noted, cannot be submitted to "dualistic theories" of victims and perpetrators, even if that insight comes "at the painful, disturbing price of discovering that the status of victim does not in itself confer a certificate of innocence" (Forti 309). Crucial to the project of theorizing the implicated subject, however, Forti clarifies that the rejection of a binary schema of opposed figures does not lessen the importance of the subject, but rather heightens the need to take subjectivity into account. In Forti's words, "when dualism—both political and moral—is abandoned, it is subjectivity that calls out to be investigated: not only and not so much because it is the bearer of wicked dispositions, but because it very often serves as the involuntary support of domination" (310; my emphasis). We thus arrive at the position of what I call the implicated subject. Emerging from a densely woven zone of interaction, the implicated subject is a "support of domination" that cannot simply be identified as a bearer of wickedness or an agent of violence. In this scenario, as in Levi's account of the gray zone proper, ambiguity is productive: it is precisely the difficult-to-locate position between victims and perpetrators that makes implicated subjects useful to power, that makes them, in Forti's words, "transmission belts" of domination.

Conclusion: Implication, Memory, Human Rights

Forti's understanding of the subject as a support and transmission belt of domination is especially clarifying for forms of implication that are still unfolding in the present. Is it equally helpful in illuminating diachronic implication? Although each form of implication has its specificities, synchronic and diachronic forms are almost always entangled. On the one hand, diachronic implication involves what Robbins calls the "ongoing" relevance of the past in the present (148–49); a past that is cut off entirely from the present does not implicate contemporary subjects. On the other hand, contemporary structures are themselves always outcomes of diachronic processes; economic inequality is not simply a synchronic phenomenon, but the result of history. As we have already seen, Young proposes that "an account of the continuities of present with past injustices is important . . . for understanding how the present conditions are structural, how those structures have evolved, and where intervention to change them may be most effective" (181–82). Although I am not sure that recourse to "continuities" is the best way to describe this past-present relation—Bevernage's notion of the irrevocable suggests instead a more uneven form of "nonspatial proximity" (4)—I agree with Young that present conditions always possess (and are possessed by) a historical dimension. But does that mean, as Young implies, that reckoning with history is necessary to their solution? In his account of the beneficiary, Robbins is skeptical; he believes that too much of a focus on past atrocities can "sidetrack" the quest for justice in the present (146). Robbins is right that a risk exists of "inward-turning paralysis [following] all too naturally from seeing oneself as the beneficiary of atrocities in the past, atrocities that can never be erased" (147). But the opposite risk is equally pressing: that ignoring those past atrocities will only help contemporary structures stabilize themselves and accommodate superficial changes.

Here we return full circle to the intersectional approach forged by the Combahee River Collective. The interlocking nature of systems of oppression clearly involves very contemporary forms of domination, but those forms are built on historical legacies that extend back centuries in some cases. While addressing the kind of economic inequality that concerns Robbins in *The Beneficiary*, the Combahee River Collective also describes the need for a more encompassing approach to change: "We are socialists because we believe that work must be organized for the collective benefit of those who do the work and create the products, and not for the profit of the bosses. . . . We are not convinced, however, that a socialist revolution that is not also a feminist and antiracist revolution will guarantee our liberation" (19–20). Although the collective does not put it precisely in these terms, part of the reason that a socialist revolution would not guarantee the abolition of gendered and racialized oppression is that those forms of oppression would likely persist, and that persistence signals the historical nature of those wrongs. While certainly material and structural in their expression, gendered and racialized forms of domination also involve processes of meaning making and subject formation that sediment historical legacies—both for those who are disadvantaged by such legacies and for those who are advantaged by them (i.e., implicated subjects).

The persistent and historical nature of these processes does not entail that the structures and subjects they have produced are unchangeable (or that they are, in this sense, radically different from class relations). It does suggest, however, that part of what it will take to overcome structures and subjects that express relations of domination will be working through historical wrongs, even those that seem faraway or distant and especially those related to genocide, colonialism, and slavery. Genocide, colonialism, and slavery involve the destruction or disruption of collectives, societies, communities—groups of various types and scales—and they produce radical discontinuities that cannot simply or immediately be undone by the cessation of killing, formal independence, or emancipation from bondage (as much as those represent obvious and necessary steps). They also demand working with and through the past—a transformative version of remembrance, broadly understood, that would include aspects of reparation, restitution, commemoration, and historical education. The intimate link between race and collective forms of discontinuity helps explain why there seems to be an elective affinity—albeit not an exclusive one—between questions of race and questions of implication.

The field of memory and historical justice is a large one that has, in fact, occupied a great deal of the political and social space in recent decades—consider, for instance, the global commemoration of the Holocaust, the many truth and reconciliation commissions around the world, ongoing controversies in the US and elsewhere about the commemoration of difficult pasts, waves of state apologies, and claims for reparations in many different spheres. Yet, discussions of memory and historical justice have almost always revolved either around victims—mourning their deaths, working toward material and symbolic restitution—or around perpetrators whom one hopes to bring to justice in one way or another. However one evaluates this global movement for historical justice—and I would argue it has had both successes and shortcomings—one obvious lacuna stands out: it has not yet, in most cases, even attempted to address implication and implicated subjects. Here I side with Mamdani against Robbins: the beneficiary is (also) an important *diachronic* figure of implication whose illumination can open up new forms of memory work that are necessary to confronting the material and symbolic dimensions of inequality.

This hypothesis also takes us back to the paradox identified by Moyn with which we began this chapter: the growing inequality that has accompanied the takeoff of a human rights framework in the last several decades. The memory boom is surely an expression—or at least a parallel tributary—of the same forces that brought about the human rights boom.[29] Despite their global prominence and the many advances that accompany their rise, memory and human rights frameworks also share similar conceptual and political limits: each has largely remained within the victim/perpetrator imaginary and failed to put pressure on the position of implicated subjects. Nevertheless, even if dominant versions of the cultures of remembrance and human rights have avoided the problem of implication, this does not mean that the problem has simply remained in the dark, surrounded by a wall of silence. To the contrary, as this book illustrates: numerous significant artists, writers, and intellectuals have been investigating the problems of implication in recent decades in a variety of media and idioms. Grouping them together here—and reading them through the lens of implication—refocuses discussion of injustice and offers possibilities for a new politics beyond the victim/perpetrator binary that has shaped dominant discourses of memory and human rights.

In the next chapter, I turn to the complex problem of historical implication by considering one of its most controversial and consequential exemplars: the long-distance legacies of transatlantic slavery. Reflecting on redress for slavery will help us refine our understanding of the entanglement of the past and the present: for those of us who are not the descendants of slaves, the afterlife of slavery manifests itself in what I will call genealogical and structural implication.

2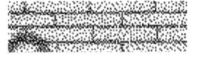

On (Not) Being a Descendant
Implicated Subjects and the Legacies of Slavery

How can violent histories find redress? All forms of restitution prove incommensurable before the brute facts of injury, death, and dispossession. As time passes, questions of responsibility also tend to grow more tenuous or more tangled. Despite such dilemmas of diachronic justice, however, redress remains imperative in cases where "irrevocable" traumatic pasts continue to echo in, imprint, and interrupt the present. Working through the example of transatlantic slavery, this chapter argues that, in addition to questions of commensurability and temporality, the aftermaths of violent histories demand that we address a third problem: the question of subjectivity. Like other traumatic histories, but with its own significant specificities, slavery poses fundamental challenges not only to the commensurability of trauma and justice and the temporality of redress, but also to the imaginary of victims and perpetrators that animates discussion of restitution and reparation.[1] Because it weaves subjectivity into structures and histories of power, the theory of the implicated subject can make an important contribution to thinking posttraumatic redress, both for the case of transatlantic slavery and for other histories of violence and expropriation.

Thus far, most discussions of redress for slavery have focused on the descendants of enslaved people. But, as Ta-Nehisi Coates argues, slavery is a "crime that implicates the entire American people"—and, we might add, many other peoples as well.[2] We need then to account for a diffuse and heterogeneous set of subjects when addressing slavery's legacies. The position of the implicated subject helps us broaden the focus to reflect also on questions of memory, justice, and responsibility in relation to those *not* descended from enslaved people.

This is an ethically and politically urgent field of inquiry, but intervening in it requires the kind of category of historical responsibility that I have been developing here: one that describes the implication of people in events that are temporally and/or spatially distant and in which they have not played or do not play a direct role as perpetrators or victims.

I begin this chapter by considering what the concept of the implicated subject can lend to the debates about historical redress, restitution, and reparations that have accompanied attempts to confront the long-distance legacies of slavery. Next, in order to assess those legacies, I reflect on the very word "legacy" along with its conceptual kin. Legacies have to be thought in the plural if we want to bring descendants and nondescendants of enslaved people into the same frame, because those legacies are asymmetrical. In a third section, I turn to a literary example, Jamaica Kincaid's *A Small Place*, in order to think further about how the category of descendant functions in the aftermath of traumatic histories. Kincaid's powerful polemic provides a visceral and affectively charged example of what implication might mean for the beneficiaries of slavery's legacies. Finally, I take inspiration both from Kincaid and from Catherine Hall and Nicholas Draper's Legacies of British Slave-Ownership project to distinguish between two forms of implication: the genealogical and the structural. Whatever justice for slavery means a century and a half after abolition, it will mean grappling with different forms of genealogical and structural implication. These two forms of implication are not discrete, however, and the overlapping nature of structural and genealogical implication renders the afterlife of slavery simultaneously diffuse and intimate. Redress in the face of that afterlife will need, in turn, to transform both the impersonal structures that make us who we are and the intimate subjectivities with which we confront those structures.[3] The theory of implicated subjects can help us account for the simultaneously structural and intimate conditions of possibility for injustice and its propagation in the aftermath.

Restitution and Implication

The debates and struggles that ensue over the terms of restitution and reparation in the wake of violence frequently take place in a context structured by a discourse of victims and perpetrators.[4] As Elazar Barkan writes at the beginning of *The Guilt of Nations*, his landmark exploration of the global dimensions of restitution, "the novelty of the discourse of restitution is that it is a discussion between the perpetrators and their victims. This interaction between perpetrator and victim is a new form of political negotiation that enables the rewriting of memory and historical identity in ways that both can share."[5] Although the discourse of restitution emerges necessarily out of a history defined by perpetrators and victims, however, that binary language of identity quickly reveals itself as inadequate. The inadequacy of the "victims and perpetrators" rubric is already signaled in Barkan's description when he characterizes the horizon of successful restitution processes as involving the negotiated creation of a "shared" memory and history. In others words, even as it draws upon those categories, restitution seeks precisely to move beyond them. Yet, even putting aside this essential horizon of restitution discourse, the rubric of victims and perpetrators is more critically limited in at least two other ways as well.

First, few collectives that could take part in the granting or receiving of restitution possess the homogenized membership implied by the term "victims and perpetrators." That is, the scope of restitution cases for collective historical injustice necessarily transgresses the limits of such simplified identity categories and comes to include subjects who are neither victims nor perpetrators, but still somehow caught up in the events. Societal participants who are not active perpetrators of human rights abuses, for instance, may still benefit from such abuses in direct or indirect ways or may have refrained from resisting abuses when they were in a position to do so. In drawing attention to such gray zones of restitution, I am naturally not implying that we should halt efforts at reparation or downplay the guilt of perpetrators, but rather that we should try to shift our efforts to a conceptual terrain in which participation and membership might join perpetration and victimization as the salient terms.

A second complication further troubles the discourse of perpetrators and victims: to the extent that a negotiated form of restitution is not achieved, an injustice persists across time, even across generations. There is a diachronic dimension to participation in a group that must be factored in. Since the contemporary category of restitution is a recent phenomenon—Barkan traces it to reparations for National Socialism and distinguishes it from earlier forms of war restitution—such a situation of unrepaired injustice has been the rule for most of human history (although it was probably not generally considered in those terms). The results of this common situation are paradoxical, especially once an international norm of restitution has been established. On the one hand, in the absence of some form of negotiated justice, injustice might be said to proliferate across eras, thus creating ongoing or additional future claims for restitution; this would certainly be the case in the US, where the abandonment of Reconstruction and the creation of subsequent forms of racial domination have propagated the injuries of slavery across the centuries (not to mention the dispossession and genocide of indigenous people). On the other hand, the future generations related genealogically to the original injustice are not easily categorized as victims and perpetrators in many cases. Even in the case of postslavery racial injustice to which I have just alluded, I am not sure that a discourse of victimization is the most historically accurate or politically efficacious; the discourse of victimization tends to re-objectify contemporary subjects and strip them of agency in the present. Furthermore, even the language of "future generations" can be misleading, since many contemporary subjects facing the legacies of the past have no genealogical connection to the events; this is true, for example, of immigrants and their descendants, including even black immigrants.

Marianne Hirsch's notion of postmemory has been influential in thinking about the transmission of trauma and memory to the children and grandchildren of victims of historical injustice, and more broadly to "future generations," but, with the exception of a fine essay by Nicole Immler, the relation between postmemory and claims of justice remains unexplored.[6] Immler highlights the importance of affect in the process of restitution and suggests that "being angry about the compensation [offered parents and grandparents] seems to be a fundamental element in the constitution of family memory regarding the Holocaust" on the part of the second and third generations (276). The performance of anger "grants the post-memory generation identification and solidarity with their parents," but it "may also prolong dichotomous thinking about the victim-perpetrator dialectic," thus thwarting processes of dialogue and reconciliation and eclipsing the specificity of the subject position of the postmemory generation (276, 278). While some scholars, including Erin McGlothlin, have brought the postmemory generation together with the second generation of perpetrator collectives, and others, including Gabriele Schwab, have focused on the "haunting legacies" of perpetration for children and grandchildren, the question of responsibility and restitution on the side of the descendants of the perpetrators also remains a knotty and controversial problem.[7] In popular discourse, that problem manifests itself in resentment (e.g., among young Germans) about being held responsible for events that preceded one's own birth. In both cases—later generations on the side of the victims and the perpetrators—the "dichotomous thinking" Immler references proves inadequate.

The aftermath of transatlantic slavery provides a particularly charged terrain for reflecting on these dilemmas of restitution and memory because it possesses two characteristics seemingly at odds with each other: significant temporal distance—since the end of the slave trade and the emancipation of slaves in Europe and the Americas took place across the nineteenth century and no living witnesses remain—and undeniable yet sometimes indirect legacies that mark former slave-holding and slave-trading societies across that distance, since questions of race, (un)freedom, and property remain unavoidable nodes of social stratification, producing both advantage and disadvantage.[8] Perhaps slavery's uncanny presence in contemporary Atlantic societies derives from this double temporality that combines distance and constant renewal, not to mention new and ongoing forms of racialization, enslavement, and exploitation.

Thinking through the categories of legacies and descendants can play a central role in addressing this context of implication. But what is a legacy, and who is a descendant?

Paradoxical Legacies

To speak of the legacies of slavery is to confront a tightly bound knot of concepts.[9] Indeed, some of the problems involved in addressing the aftereffects of slavery are already present in the words we use to assess those aftereffects. The English word "legacy" is derived from the Latin *legatus*, the past participle of *legare*, meaning to send as a deputy or to bequeath. The first meaning of the word establishes a link to the problematic of representation in the political sense—a legate is a representative, delegate, or stand-in. This now mostly obsolete usage of the word is relevant to my analysis, since it suggests a connection between legacy and implication: implicated subjects are in certain ways stand-ins for the perpetrators to whom some degree of responsibility has been delegated, yet the indirect nature of that standing-in and that delegation remains to be determined. The link between legacy and slavery is even more salient in the contemporary meaning of legacy, which involves, like slavery itself, the question of property. A legacy is a "sum of money, or a specified article, given to another by will," as well as a more generalized bequest: "anything handed down by an ancestor or predecessor." A legacy is then an inheritance, a concept that brings along its own semantic field involving "property, right, privilege, rank, and title" as well as a notion of "natural descent." Those who inherit legacies are descendants, and what they inherit are either the legacies of property, privilege, and right or the negation of those legacies.

The concepts of legacy, inheritance, and descent seem to promise direct lines of connection between past and present, but in practice the process of inheritance across generations rarely goes so smoothly. Not only are legacies and inheritances frequently contested at the level of the family, but at the level of society matters of descent become even more complex. Social legacies are rarely transmitted clearly or cleanly. Ubiquitous forms of social change, such as the demographic transformations catalyzed by migration, proliferate ambiguously situated implicated subjects. In the wake of trauma in general and slavery in particular, questions of familial and social inheritance become especially fraught.

Treating people as property, chattel slavery produced morally tainted legacies of wealth for some at the same time that it stripped other classes of people of property, privilege, and right. In *Slavery and Social Death*, Orlando Patterson conceptualizes what he calls "natal alienation" as a "constituent element of the slave relation."[10] Natal alienation describes the fact that slavery sought to turn the enslaved person into a "genealogical isolate" who is "socially dead": "Not only was the slave denied all claims on, and obligations to, his parents and living blood relations but, by extension, all such claims and obligations on his more remote ancestors and on his descendants. . . . Formally isolated in his social relations with those who lived, he was also culturally isolated from the social heritage of his ancestors" (5). While we know that enslaved people and their descendants have always struggled against this logic of depropriation and have re-created forms of kinship in defiance of it, Patterson's insight nonetheless helps us to think through one of the paradoxes of our topic. From the perspective of enslaved people, the legacies of slavery involve the impossibility of legacies: the attempted prevention of social inheritance through the enforcement of a radical, racialized notion of biological inheritance or "natural descent." This is the bifurcated legacy of slavery for descendants of the enslaved: the inheritance of a blocked inheritance. That paradoxical legacy manifests itself today in the persistent salience of race as a determining social category for both descendants and *nondescendants* of slavery, one that continues to distribute property, privilege, and right in radically unequal patterns. As Best and Hartman write, the descendants at stake here are not "the slave's potential heirs, but . . . the actual recipients of the slave's negative inheritance—the ongoing production of lives lived in intimate relation to premature death (whether civil, social, or literal)" (13n6).

This paradoxical situation has led to distinct strategies among those forced to confront the ongoing effects of this past. On the one hand, many members of the African diaspora have emphasized the continuities between the period of slavery and the postslavery present and have created movements meant to secure some form of redress in the form of reparations, apologies, and other forms of restitution. In the words of Marcus Garvey, "We are the descendants of men and women who suffered in this country for two hundred and fifty years under the barbarous, the brutal institution known as slavery. You who have not lost trace of your history will recall the fact that over three hundred years ago your fore-bearers were taken from the continent of Africa and brought here for the purposes of using them as slaves."[11] Embracing the position of descendant, Garvey asserts a strong mnemonic link both to slavery and to the preslavery geography of Africa, a link that had clear implications for the political movement he mobilized. At the cultural level, this perspective has led to works of art and literature—Toni Morrison's *Beloved* is exemplary—that depict slavery in a haunting present tense that lives on beyond its apparent death and continues to interpellate diasporic subjects.

On the other hand, some members of the African diaspora have sought to evade the paradoxical and negative inheritance of slavery through the assertion of a break with the past. The sociologist Ron Eyerman calls this the "progressive narrative" and cites a telling 1928 passage from the American writer and anthropologist Zora Neale Hurston: "Someone is always at my elbow reminding me that I am a granddaughter of slaves. . . . Slavery is sixty years past. The operation was successful and the patient is doing well, thank you" (qtd. in Eyerman 165). In light of the dire conditions in which many black people live in the US today—a situation the legal scholar Michelle Alexander calls "the New Jim Crow"—it may be difficult to maintain Hurston's optimistic assessment of such an operation.[12] Nevertheless, new versions of the discontinuity thesis have continued to emerge, even as they jettison the progressive narrative.

In a 2012 essay called "On Failing to Make the Past Present," Stephen Best writes explicitly against the "melancholic historicism" he associates with *Beloved* and finds widespread in contemporary African American intellectual culture. Instead of seeking explanations for contemporary problems in the mirror of slavery, he proposes to think about the "black political present" from the perspective of the "radical alterity of the past."[13] Turning to Morrison's 2008 novel *A Mercy*, Best finds a historical model that differs greatly from that of ghostly haunting: "Where *Beloved* calls us back to witness in the mode of melancholic historicism, *A Mercy* abandons us to a more baffled, cut-off, foreclosed position with regard to the slave past" (472). In this more recent work by Morrison, writes Best, abandonment takes the place of haunting and "throws into question the idea that the slave past provides a ready prism through which to apprehend and understand the black political present, by refusing to make the slave past the progenitor of the existential condition of black people, or of black people alone. Morrison invites us to think about what it means to be held in the grip of slavery but not of race" (473). Best does not by any means argue that we have reached the end of racism, but rather suggests that "the logic of racial slavery does not fully describe or capture racial injustice in the present" (474).

I can understand the value of Best's provocation as a challenge to thinking about the black political present. But what about the political present of non–African diaspora subjects, people who, for the most part, have been happy to abandon memory of the slave past? Best's critique of claims to continuity with slavery's past makes for a productive juxtaposition with historian Nicholas Draper's 2010 book *The Price of Emancipation* and Draper, Catherine Hall, and their colleagues' project Legacies of British Slave-Ownership, which, contrary to Best, do seek to trace potential lines of connection out of the past. An obvious and crucial difference between the object of Best's critique and the project of Hall and Draper, however, is that while Best focuses on the legacies of enslavement, Hall and Draper focus on the legacies of slave-ownership. Yet, the Hall-Draper project also does not operate in the mode of melancholic historicism and ghostly haunting to which Best objects. Rather, by attending to the financial compensation of slave-owners that took place in Britain at the moment of slavery's abolition—the only kind of compensation that has yet been granted!—their project seeks to make visible the material chains of transmission that connect profits from slavery to Britain's slavery-era and postabolition economy, politics, and culture. Perhaps a moment of connection also exists in Best's hesitant assertion that the shift from continuity to abandonment "refus[es] to make the slave past the progenitor of the existential condition of black people, or *of black people alone*" (my emphasis). This last qualification suggests that "what it means to be held in the grip of slavery but not of race" will have implications for people across racial categories and, in particular, for those who have inherited the cultural capital of whiteness (and non-blackness more generally), if not financial capital itself, from the slave-owners and their heirs.

A project on slave-ownership and its aftermath helps us to think of slavery's legacies as not just about "black people alone"—a possibility of the most urgent contemporary political importance. Hall and Draper make available an archive that can be the starting point for thinking empirically about the production of implicated subjects through the transmission of actual inheritances. As Draper writes, the slave system "was an economic system that continuously recruited new participants in the metropole through inheritance and legacies; almost invariably, those recruits retained rather than renounced their inheritance."[14] As this process of recruitment through inheritance and legacies took place, slavery was—paradoxically—both diffused through British society and rendered more intimate. According to Draper, "the abolition of the slave-trade in 1807 did not end Britain's intimate relationship with slavery. Slave-ownership had been converted into financial property and conveyed between generations and sexes by the full range of available techniques of management and control governing other types of property" (3). After the compensation program of the 1830s and the end of slavery in the British Empire, this process of conversion of property in human beings to other forms of capital continued. Although impossible to trace precisely, because of the fungible nature of currency, the process of conversion continued through the use of compensation capital to generate surplus from wage-laborers and financial markets, with obvious but uncertain implications for tracking slavery's ongoing legacies in the metropole.

The simultaneity of diffusion and intimacy that Draper and the Legacies of British Slave-Ownership project reveal can inspire reflection that moves beyond the immediate aftermath of emancipation as well as beyond the empirical transmission of slave-owning legacies. Their project can thus help us address the central dilemma of implicated subjects in this context:

What does it mean to inherit the legacies of slavery across significant distances of time? What does it mean to be implicated in slavery when you are not a descendant of those who were enslaved? Unlike the kinds of questions provoked by Legacies of British Slave-Ownership about the material forms of transmission, these questions directly call upon the work of the moral imagination. Because such inheritances and experiences of implication exceed those that are traceable in the archive, they must be given form through acts of representation in order to become perceptible. Literary narratives—and other forms of aesthetic production—provide avenues of access to legacies of slavery and questions of justice that intersect with but cannot be reduced to empirical history and material claims.

Just Human Beings

Rather than attempting to settle definitively the conundrum of how to think restitution for slavery, Jamaica Kincaid's *A Small Place* makes claims on white (and other implicated) readers by refusing to settle; that is, it refuses to put the past behind us or to offer a definitive answer about what would constitute proper restitution. Instead, Kincaid's 1988 work takes white readers directly into the moral and temporal confusions wrought by the histories of slavery and colonialism and their paradoxical legacies. In provocative and sometimes disturbing ways, Kincaid reveals—like Draper—the diffusion and intimacy of slavery's legacies in a globalized world. Yet, even as *A Small Place* brings us into proximity with the figure of the implicated subject, the deliberate contradictions and tensions Kincaid stages suggest that the conceptual vocabulary for mapping implication remains difficult to access. Instead, she provokes us to experience what implication *feels* like.

At the end of *A Small Place*, a generically hybrid, nonfictional work, Kincaid's narrator provides a condensed and provocative historical account of her homeland, Antigua. Generally—and correctly—read as a vitriolic indictment of tourism, colonialism, neocolonialism, and postcolonial corruption, *A Small Place* is also a reflection on the legacies of slavery in a nation that was a significant site of slave-based sugar cultivation starting in the seventeenth century. In the final paragraph of the text, Kincaid both reiterates many of the motifs that constitute the "argument" of *A Small Place* and seems radically to undo the very terms of that argument. Here is the full final paragraph:

> Again, Antigua is a small place, a small island. It is nine miles wide by twelve miles long. It was discovered by Christopher Columbus in 1493. Not too long after, it was settled by human rubbish from Europe, who used enslaved but noble and exalted human beings from Africa (all masters of every stripe are rubbish, and all slaves of every stripe are noble and exalted; there can be no question about this) to satisfy their desire for wealth and power, to feel better about their own miserable existence, so that they could be less lonely and empty—a European disease. Eventually, the masters left, in a kind of way; eventually, the slaves were freed, in a kind of way. The people in Antigua now, the people who really think of themselves as Antiguans (and the people who would immediately come to your mind when you think about what Antiguans might be like; I mean, supposing you were to think about it), are the descendants of those noble and exalted people, the slaves. Of course, the whole thing is, once you cease to be a master, once you throw off your master's yoke, you are no longer human rubbish, you are just a human being, and all the things that adds up to. So, too, with the slaves. Once they are no longer slaves, once they are free, they are no longer noble and exalted; they are just human beings.[15]

Like the entire text of *A Small Place*, and much of Kincaid's other work, this passage is characterized by deliberately hyperbolic claims, abrupt shifts in voice and address, and parenthetical reflections that disrupt the linear movement of the discourse. While the first few sentences mimic a European colonial narrative of discovery and its consequent rhetoric of condescension, Kincaid then quickly turns the tables and provides a morally polarized counterdiscourse that condemns the colonizer while idealizing the enslaved. The terms of this reversal are amplified by a parenthetical interruption, but the text also (inadvertently?) continues unvoiced aspects of the colonial narrative by glossing over the destruction of preexisting indigenous inhabitants of the island who "discovered" it—and indeed fought over it—long before Columbus or the slave trade. Kincaid's elision of that history—ironic or not—suggests the degree to which settler colonialism inevitably produces generations of implicated subjects. Next, the narrator's invocation of the ambivalences of emancipation and decolonization, which she deliberately conflates, partially displaces the discourses of colonialism and anticolonialism: "Eventually, the masters left, in a kind of way; eventually, the slaves were freed, in a kind of way." By describing decolonization as an experience of masters and slaves, Kincaid makes slavery the "master" code for understanding colonialism and its continuation "in a kind of way" into the era of formal independence.[16] In the passage's subsequent approach to the postemancipation, postindependence moment, however, a further and final reversal occurs: the anticolonial counterdiscourse of rubbish and nobility gives way to an apparent leveling in which both former slaves and former masters are redefined; now they are "just human beings."

In this concluding passage, Kincaid echoes Fanon's *Black Skin, White Masks*, a text that rethinks Hegel's master/slave dialectic in order to account for the end of slavery in Martinique from the perspective of the moment of (aborted) decolonization. Because the slave "was set free by his master" and "did not fight for his freedom"—and therefore gain recognition through struggle and work, as in the Hegelian dialectic—Fanon argues that emancipation has failed: "The Negro has not become a master. When there are no longer slaves, there are no longer masters."[17] Kincaid's account of postcolonial Antigua confirms Fanon's diagnosis of the failure of decolonization in the departmentalized French Caribbean colonies even as she also charts the emergence, decades later, of new domestic and foreign neocolonial masters.

In concluding *A Small Place* with this series of reversals and displacements, Kincaid situates the entire text in relation to a question about implicated subject positions that she never explicitly poses but is also central to Fanon's investigations thirty-five years earlier: What does it mean to be a *descendant* of slavery? This question addresses both those called here "the descendants of those noble and exalted people, the slaves" and those who would be the descendants of "human rubbish," the masters. At the same time, Kincaid's mode of address also encompasses those who would be the genealogical descendants of neither group while still living in slavery's shadow. Through the text's most evident rhetorical techniques—the expression of unbridled rage and the direct address to a reader explicitly evoked as a white European or North American tourist—Kincaid aggressively situates her audience among the descendants of human rubbish, while locating herself among the descendants of slaves: "we Antiguans," she writes several pages into the text, "for I am one" (8). Indeed, throughout *A Small Place*, the rhetoric of address serves as a powerful means of making implication in the racialized legacies of slavery a palpable experience for readers.[18] This mode of address continues into the text's last paragraph, where the implied—or better, implicated—white reader is imputed to have only a thoughtlessly casual relation to the existence of Antiguans.[19] But here the text's structure of address is unsettled, if not undermined, by Kincaid's final rhetorical twist: the suggestion that perhaps descent is an inadequate explanation for the sources of subjectivity in a postcolonial, postslavery world. How can we make sense of these twists and turns, and what do they tell us about being a descendant implicated in the legacies of slavery?

The contradictory ending of *A Small Place* and the retrospective rereading of the text as a whole that it provokes suggest the dilemmas of making sense of slavery and evoke the force of a double bind in confronting its legacies: either one foregrounds a particularistic identity premised on the I/we versus you distinction of the text's mode of address—a version of the victim/perpetrator discourse—or one moves in the direction of a universalizing liberal humanism (we are all "just human beings"). An instance of a much broader dilemma concerning how to confront stigmatized identities, neither of these options seems satisfactory: the particularistic version, because it risks reproducing what Wendy Brown has called "wounded attachments" that reify subordinate subject positions; the universalistic version, because it risks foreshortening history and thus prematurely foreclosing claims for justice made on behalf of legacies of suffering.[20] Kincaid, however, refuses the blackmail of the double bind, which also echoes the contrast between the continuity and abandonment perspectives I discussed earlier. Instead of choosing a side or seeking the articulation of a moderate middle ground, Kincaid's solution is to present both sides in equally overstated terms. Drawing on the resources of literature, which need not obey the logic of noncontradiction as must normative discourses of law or philosophy, this rhetorical strategy has the advantage of situating all descendants of slavery on the same moral plane while still demanding awareness of an unexpiated crime. At the same time, the need to resort to contradiction and paradox suggests the difficulty of addressing slavery's legacies when the category of the implicated subject is missing from our conceptual vocabulary.

The paradoxes of that reading of the text's conclusion can be supplemented by a further move. An alternative interpretation opens up if one emphasizes Kincaid's description of emancipation from both slavery and colonialism as having taken place "eventually . . . in a kind of way." The temporal and notional vagueness of Kincaid's phrasing here suggests that the final turn toward "just human beings" may describe not an achieved actuality but a future possibility—that horizon beyond victims and perpetrators toward which restitution discourse also gestures, in Barkan's account. Once the masters truly throw off the master's yoke they will no longer be "human rubbish," the narrator claims, but she supplies no evidence that such a divestment has actually taken place. Rather, she presents readers with a process of neocolonial "surrogation" that has ensured a quasi-continuous chain of mastery from the British colonizers to US hegemony and "foreign" (primarily Syrian and Lebanese) capital, which dominate postindependence Antiguan politics and economy together with corrupt local politicians.[21] As the text's focus on corruption suggests, the legacies of perpetration persist even as the descendants of slaves are no longer easily categorizable as mythic victims, as "noble and exalted human beings from Africa." An asymmetry has set in: the era of decolonization contains neither the clear-cut distinctions of the age of slavery and colonialism nor the erasure of race and class distinctions that a true emancipation would promise. *A Small Place* suggests that the histories of slavery and colonialism have produced a proliferation of rubbish that continues to characterize the actions of the powerful but also contaminates the relatively powerless.[22] Refusing to shelter descendants of victims from implication in the waste of neocolonialism, Kincaid offers an especially pessimistic view of history.[23] Indeed, in a reading of another passage in *A Small Place* to which I will soon turn, Bruce Robbins describes Kincaid herself as a kind of implicated subject, a beneficiary, in the terms of his argument: "Like her readers, she is herself a beneficiary. And that is why . . . she is unable to denounce without also denouncing herself."[24]

In the shifts, contradictions, and provocations of Kincaid's *A Small Place*, I want to locate both a dilemma and a possible step forward. The dilemma involves recognizing the paradoxical demands that histories of slavery and colonialism leave behind after formal emancipation: the need to recognize the persistence of tainted inheritances and legacies as well as the need to break the logic of natural descent that stands behind those inheritances. The step forward involves reading Kincaid's paradoxes as a contribution to theorizing a new kind of responsible subject out of the rubbish of the postslavery moment. The conceptualization of the implicated subject is a way of naming that in-between space evoked—but not yet named—by Kincaid, a space that is not adequately described by either the universalistic shedding of difficult pasts ("just human beings") or the maintenance of violence-determined subject positions inherited wholesale from history (the exalted vs. rubbish). Additionally, in blurring the differences between slavery, colonialism, and neocolonialism in *A Small Place*, Kincaid also blurs the relation between the temporal and spatial axes of implication, between the legacies of the past and the unequal relations of the present. While such a strategy provocatively jettisons claims to historical specificity (at a price that one must still reckon), it also allows us insight into cases such as slavery in which the original "protagonists" are no longer present even as their impact lives on and cases such as capitalist globalization in which the chain of what Paul Ricoeur calls "imputability" between agents and outcomes is rendered unimaginably complex.[25]

Through her address to an implicated reader, Kincaid seeks to make visible and visceral the "monstrous intimacies" that Christina Sharpe sees constituting the legacies of slavery. Sharpe is no doubt correct—if somewhat hyperbolic—when she argues that, "while all modern subjects are post-slavery subjects fully constituted by the discursive codes of slavery and post-slavery, post-slavery subjectivity is largely borne by and readable on the (New World) *black* subject."[26] Precisely because white people have not had to bear that burden, the bringing to consciousness of white implicated subjects after slavery requires fundamental anamnestic work. Sparking such work might be seen as Kincaid's project. She does not take for granted or abstractly theorize implicated subject positions; rather, even as the category of implicated subjects seems absent from her work, she evokes the category rhetorically through a mode of address that sometimes elicits an uncanny degree of embodied affect.

In a famous passage, Kincaid offers a vivid suggestion of what it might feel like to be an implicated subject caught between the currents of the past and the present. Early on, the narrator interrupts the white tourist's Caribbean idyll by speculating on the passage of human waste from the hotel toilet into the sea:

> You must not wonder what exactly happened to the contents of your lavatory when you flushed it. You must not wonder where your bath water went when you pulled out the stopper. You must not wonder what happened when you brushed your teeth. Oh, it might all end up in the water you are thinking of taking a swim in; the contents of your lavatory might, just might, graze gently against your ankle as you wade carefree in the water, for you see, in Antigua, there is no proper sewage disposal system. But the Caribbean Sea is very big and the Atlantic Ocean is even bigger; it would amaze you to know the number of black slaves this ocean has swallowed up. (13–14)[27]

This passage not only evokes one of the central tropes of Black Atlantic critique—"The Sea is History," in Derek Walcott's phrase—and confirms the sense of a society literally awash with refuse; it also produces a bodily frisson of implication in a present defined by neocolonial relations and ecological disaster.[28] In Timothy Morton's terms, Kincaid stages an encounter with earth and sea as "hyperobjects." Morton deploys the concept of hyperobjects in his philosophy of ecology to describe phenomena of overwhelming presence—like global warming—that seem distant but in which we are in fact already immersed.[29] At one point, he illustrates his concept by describing a scene that strongly resembles Kincaid's hotel lavatory:

> A baby vomits curdled milk. . . . The parent scoops up the mucky milk in a tissue and flushes the wadded package down the toilet. Now we know where it goes. . . . Instead of the mythical land Away, we know the waste goes to the Pacific Ocean or the wastewater treatment facility. Knowledge of the hyperobject Earth, and of the hyperobject biosphere, presents us with viscous surfaces from which nothing can be forcibly peeled. (31)

Writing a few decades after Kincaid, Morton describes the "viscosity" of hyperobjects as something we already know. In fact, however, despite that rhetorical move and similar to Kincaid, he ultimately writes against the fetishistic denial that marks humans' relation to waste. Morton seeks to decenter the human in a radical way and to situate human beings on the same flat plane as other objects; as he asserts, "the being of a paper cup is as profound as mine" (17). Like Kincaid, he imagines the toilet as part of a waste-removal system in order to provoke an acknowledgment of what I would call ecological implication.

If, in evoking the vastness of the "hyperobject" Atlantic, Kincaid pretends at first to minimize white subjects' implication in the dirt of the present, she then quickly changes course and ends up immersing them in further historical contamination. Perhaps because race remains a decidedly human experience of dehumanization in the aftermath of slavery, Kincaid's evocation of the implicated subject does not seek to decenter the human as radically as does Morton, nor does it stop at a present- and future-oriented indictment of ecological devastation: it also goes a step farther in linking this pollution to the history of slavery and thus to questions of diachronic justice. In moments like this, *A Small Place* charts the viscous, polluted terrain of memory and the diffused but intimate legacies of slavery beyond the certainties of victims and perpetrators. The graze of the ankle marks a bodily encounter between contemporary freedom (the tourist's "carefree" wading) and the waste of unfreedom—past, present, and future—that unsettles the reader and locates her in the position of the implicated subject.

Legacies of Slave-Ownership: Genealogical and Structural Implication

How can we think simultaneously about Kincaid's literary performance of implication and the sociohistorical question of redress? We can begin to answer this question by considering the one place where *A Small Place* and the Legacies of British Slave-Ownership project intersect.[30] In a particularly bitter passage, Kincaid recounts how a predatory and corrupt foreign capitalist has outbid the government of Antigua and bought the papers of the island's most historically significant slave-owners, the Codrington family.[31] The Codrington family papers would obviously be an important source for a project like Legacies of British Slave-Ownership, and sure enough, one Christopher Bethell-Codrington (1764–1843) figures in the project's database as a major recipient of compensation.[32] Son of a merchant in the West Indies and part of a family with long-standing links to the slave trade—and to the islands of Antigua and Barbuda—Bethell-Codrington inherited his family's Antiguan plantations along with estates in Gloucestershire when the only son of his uncle Sir William Codrington was disinherited. From another uncle, Christopher Bethell, he inherited additional property in the West Indies and in Yorkshire. Bethell-Codrington served as a member of Parliament between 1797 and 1812, as did his son Christopher Willliam Codrington between 1805 and 1864. Among the legacies of the Codringtons' implication in the slave trade is Dodington Park, the family's Gloucestershire estate, built for Bethell-Codrington between 1798 and 1817 and occupied by his descendants until 1980. In an account of how the Codringtons and other "famous heirs to slave fortunes . . . sought to remake their social standing through the patronage of art and the mastery of taste," Simon Gikandi writes that Dodington Park "reflected the neoclassical revival of the day. Here, as elsewhere, fashionability was enabled by the family's income from its West Indian sugar holdings."[33] As Gikandi's study makes clear, the legacies of slave-ownership filtered even—or especially—into realms like the aesthetic, seemingly at the furthest remove from the depredations of the chattel system.

The slave-owners' compensation process in 1835, which the Legacies of British Slave-Ownership project tracks, merely added to the benefits that had already accrued through the slave trade itself: Bethell-Codrington was awarded £30,000 for eight separate claims regarding the 1,916 human beings whom he had owned as slaves at the moment of emancipation. One of the claims for compensation involved the entire island of Barbuda, on which, according to project sources, two white overseers controlled 495 enslaved people. Another claim involved the plantation Betty's Hope, which was the original seventeenth-century site of sugar production in Antigua and which included 299 enslaved people in 1835. The plantation itself remained in the hands of the Codrington family for almost three hundred years, until 1944, at which point it was sold to Antigua Sugar Estates Ltd.[34]

As this brief and very incomplete summary makes clear, it is not difficult to trace the diffuse legacies of slave-ownership in Antigua and Barbuda well beyond the moment of emancipation. During the bicentenary commemorations of the abolition of the slave trade in 2007, a BBC documentary of the program *Inside Out West* titled "From Codrington to Codrington" established connections between two towns named after the slave-owning family: the Gloucestershire town of Codrington and Barbuda's sole town, also named Codrington. Yet, the short film made no apparent attempt to find current descendants of the Codrington family or to ask about their potential historical responsibility (although it did speak with one white Gloucestershire resident who may have had an ancestor who worked for the Codringtons on their plantations). To be sure, one can easily find detailed versions of the Codrington family tree in online genealogical sources that would allow us to identify particular individuals alive today related to this family of seventeenth- and eighteenth-century slave-owners. The goal should not be, as Catherine Hall made clear during a public presentation of the Legacies of British Slave-Ownership project, "to name and shame."[35] Still, there is a need to think through questions of accountability. What are we to make of the continuities that we can find? And what should we make of Best's argument that such apparent continuities distract from our abandonment by the past? While the Legacies of British Slave-Ownership project helps us understand the material chains of transmission connecting property in human beings to physical, cultural, political, and other legacies, it does not attempt to address the dilemmas of justice such chains of transmission raise, especially over the long run. For that, a final return to Kincaid may be illuminating.

Given its historical role in the Caribbean, it is not surprising that the Codrington family makes an appearance in *A Small Place*, most prominently in a passage where Kincaid refers to the efforts to build a museum and library in Antigua—a museum that was apparently founded in 1985, three years before *A Small Place* appeared.[36] Kincaid sets her brief narrative of these efforts in the context of one of the text's predominant motifs: the corruption of Antigua's postcolonial government and its links to exploitative foreign capital. Here she draws attention to the role of one unnamed foreign businessman who was allegedly "wanted in the Far East for swindling a government out of oil profits" (48) and subsequently was involved in the building of a failed oil refinery in Antigua (67). Kincaid writes:

> He has more plans. He wants to build for the people of Antigua a museum and a library. The papers of the slave-trading family from Barbuda (the Condringtons [sic]), the records of their traffic in human lives, were being auctioned. The government of Antigua made a bid for them. Someone else made a larger bid. He was the foreigner. His bid was the successful bid. He then made a gift of these papers to the people of Antigua. And what does it mean? The records of one set of enemies, bought by another enemy, given to the people who have been their victims as a gift. (67–68)

Kincaid's barbed commentary illustrates several things about the long-distance legacies of slavery. It certainly manifests some of the risks of all returns to past injury: the cultivation of resentments and the fall into nativism. Indeed, Kincaid seems deliberately to stage those two risks throughout much of the text. Without minimizing the risks, I would nevertheless hold that we can also read the passage as productively allegorizing the scene of slavery's inheritance in the contemporary moment. Besides the discussion of the family papers, the only other reference to the Codringtons comes earlier in the same chapter when Kincaid gives a capsule history of Barbuda: "Barbuda was settled originally by a family from England named Condrington [sic]; this family specialized in breeding special groups of black people, whom they then sold into slavery" (51). In these passages, Kincaid presents the Codringtons as linked to two kinds of historical legacies: on the one hand, they are the object of a tainted archival bequest transmitted to an institution of cultural memory (the museum) within the neocolonial circumstances of the present; on the other hand, they are the originators of a biopolitical project based on the manipulation of descent, a perverse variant of the already perverse production of natal alienation. (As far as I know, this latter history remains contested, but some documentary evidence for it does exist.)[37] Once again, Kincaid provides a vivid illustration of the paradoxical legacies of slavery in which the event of an inheritance—either cultural or biological—repeats an earlier disinheritance.

My interest in this story of the Antiguan museum—and in the story of the Codrington family—does not lie only with its meaning for contemporary Antiguans (Kincaid's concern) nor with what it might tell us about the responsibilities of descendants of Christopher Bethell-Codrington (relevant for questions of restitution and reparation), although these are both legitimate concerns. Rather, I am particularly interested in the broader allegory of implication Kincaid offers her readers, an allegory that once again reveals the entwinement of the spatial and temporal dimensions of implication. The historical burden of slavery, Kincaid shows us, is transmitted within the conditions of new crimes, and it is the moment of transmission that matters: the poisoned gift of the neocolonial present repeats the past with a difference. After Walter Benjamin makes his famous assertion that "there is no document of civilization which is not at the same time a document of barbarism," he continues: "And just as such a document is not free of barbarism, barbarism taints also the manner in which it was transmitted from one owner to another."[38] The problem of transmission equally concerns questions of legacy, cultural memory, and slavery because each involves matters of property and ownership.

The juxtaposition of Bethell-Codrington's Legacies entry and the fate of the Codrington family papers recounted by Kincaid illustrates the complementary contributions history and literature can make to thinking about the legacies of slavery. It also suggests the need to distinguish between two kinds of implicated subjects in relation to transatlantic slavery: those who are genealogically implicated and those who are structurally implicated.[39] Both of these versions entangle synchronic and diachronic implication, but in different modes and ratios. In cases of genealogical implication we can trace particular lines of transmission of the sort made available by the Legacies project. As I have mentioned, readily available genealogical sources allow us to identify particular individuals alive today who are related to this family of seventeenth-, eighteenth-, and nineteenth-century slave-owners. Those descendants are genealogically implicated subjects of transatlantic slavery: past injustice weighs heavily in this mode of implication, but its meaning for the present remains ambiguous. Kincaid's foreigner, in contrast, stands in for those of us with a nongenealogical relation to slavery who nevertheless find ourselves entwined in its aftermath, either because of our racial privilege, our financial interests, our migration into a postslavery situation, or because we too, as scholars, trade in the archives of slavery. We are, like the foreigner, structurally implicated subjects, and our implication concerns the way the deeds of the past continue to shape the relations of the present. In Tessa Morris-Suzuki's words, "We live enmeshed in structures, institutions and webs of ideas which are the product of history, formed by acts of imagination, courage, generosity, greed and brutality performed by previous generations. . . . Though we may not be responsible for such acts of aggression in the sense of having caused them, we are 'implicated' in them, in the sense that *they* cause *us*."[40] Structural implication implies that we are part of a society in which the legacies of slavery still matter, even if no continuous lines of transmission link us to that past.

The distinction between genealogical and structural implication brings with it a further paradox. To return to the terms provided by Nicholas Draper, genealogical implication is intimate, yet diffuse; structural implication, in contrast, is diffuse, yet intimate. On the one hand, in the case of genealogical implication, it is at least theoretically possible to use the family tree to trace precise links back to the event (of slave-ownership, of compensation for slave-ownership). In such cases, one can say "I am a descendant of slave-owners," but the significance of that statement and the responsibility that accrues to that fact is diffuse: after four or five generations (or more), I occupy one of many branches of the family tree. I am connected through family—thus, intimately—to the past, but in a way that does not yet suggest specific forms of redress in the present. In the case of structural implication, on the other hand, there may not be an intimate link to the history of slavery; my connection to the past is discontinuous and diffuse. Out of that diffusion, however, comes an even more intimate determination than the one that follows from (mere) genealogical implication: my very subjectivity as a social being derives from the impersonal structures that surround and support me. These forms of determination are diffuse in the sense that they emerge from all corners of the social world rather than from the intimate networks of family. However, although diffuse, such determinations create us: subjects occupy a differential position at the intersection of impersonal forces that nevertheless make them who they are. Lacan's concept of "extimacy"—in which the subject is defined by a Möbius-like continuity of inside and outside—captures the paradoxical diffuse intimacy of structural implication.[41]

It is likely that most of those who are genealogically implicated in a past such as transatlantic slavery will also be structurally implicated by virtue of race, class position, or geopolitical location in the present. The opposite is not necessarily true: one can occupy a structurally implicated position without a genealogical link to the events in question. Indeed, this latter possibility represents the most important contribution of a theory of the implicated subject: implication does not require the continuities of genealogy or the intimacies of the family. Implication derives from those continuities and intimacies in some cases, but also especially from a structural position in relation to groups, classes, and modes of production that makes some people the beneficiaries of histories "not their own" and disadvantages others regardless of their genealogical connection to the past.

Best and Hartman ask: "What is justice for the slave? What is justice for the slave's descendants? Does the slave even have descendants? Who are the slave's many descendants?" (3). A theory of the implicated subject does not provide a direct or easy answer to these questions, but it does suggest certain things about the descendants of *slavery* (as opposed to descendants of *the slave*) that can help us think through the question of justice. Rethinking descent as implication allows us to begin breaking with the logics of property and nature that continue to define the afterlives of slavery.[42] At the same time, it allows us to recognize that such logics remain powerful both for those with a genealogical connection to the past and those inserted discontinuously into structures that propagate the past by diffusing it into all areas of contemporary social life. A theory of implication can help bring out the gray zones of slavery's afterlife—complicity on the part of postcolonial states such as the Antigua indicted by Kincaid or collaboration by some Africans in the slave trade—but it also keeps the focus especially on those white beneficiaries of slavery and its aftermath, from the "compensated" slave-owners in the wake of abolition to those of us who benefit from the persistent hierarchies of the present.

Conclusion: Reframing Reparations

Although the theory of implication and implicated subjects does not provide easy answers to the problem of restitution, it can nevertheless help establish a framework for thinking about responsibility at a distance. What implicated subjects owe to those impacted by long-distance, transgenerational traumatic histories can never be as straightforward as cases in which easily identifiable perpetrators and victims survive—and even in these latter cases negotiating restitution is rarely a simple matter.

The threads of connection between the original events and implicated subjects genealogically connected to perpetrators of the past wear thin after a few generations, even if in some cases, such as that of the Codrington family, continuities can also be traced over decades and centuries (e.g., in the ownership of particular pieces of property). To the extent that the genealogically implicated maintain positions of privilege, that privilege probably derives as much from shared, structural conditions of inequality as from determinate links to the past. Sharing a name and family lineage with a historical perpetrator does not make one a perpetrator, but it may create moral demands for symbolic reparation. Ultimately, the more consequential and difficult question involves how to address structural legacies of past traumatic histories, such as slavery. Symbolic forms of restitution count here, as well, but there ought to be room for redistributive measures in addition.

Nancy Fraser's theory of justice, which attempts to take into account both symbolic and cultural forms of recognition and material forms of redistribution (along with political forms of representation), offers one way to address the long-term legacies of histories such as slavery.[43] Fraser identifies a paradox at the heart of certain efforts of recognition and redistribution: they can end up maintaining the very abjected identities they set out to redress. To counter that paradox, Fraser argues for a form of socialism (as opposed to liberal welfare state policy) in the realm of redistribution and for a deconstruction of identities in the realm of recognition. In this context, socialism entails "deep restructuring of relations of production," while deconstruction entails "deep restructuring of relations of recognition" (*Justice Interruptus* 27). The goal is to avoid reproducing structures of inequality in attempting to remediate them.

What would such a proposal mean for the aftermath of transatlantic slavery? Fraser's discussion is aimed primarily at those who have suffered from injustices of recognition and redistribution, and her proposals seek to eliminate material inequalities, while blurring the boundaries of group differentiation between victims and beneficiaries of those injustices. The concept of the implicated subject is a way to negotiate the "deconstruction" of the subject that Fraser calls for on the side of the beneficiaries of slavery without deconstructing responsibility. The absence of the perpetrators and victims of the initial crime means that identity has been "loosened" from its historical moorings, even if the crime, as in the case of slavery, continues to haunt and shape the present. If this "looser" identity means recognizing that the criminally responsible are no longer on the scene (and, in fact, have escaped being brought to justice in almost all cases), it also entails a more encompassing notion of responsibility at the same time: even those who are not criminally responsible are still responsible in other registers (including political, economic, and moral realms).

Redress for slavery is an example of what Fraser calls "abnormal justice"—situations, prevalent today, in which no agreement exists about the matter, subjects, and forums of justice.[44] Besides disagreement about how to render postslavery justice in the realms of recognition and redistribution, questions of political representation also arise. For Fraser, representation signifies the rules of membership that determine who gets a say about relations of justice and injustice with respect to recognition and redistribution: "*Who* counts as a subject of justice in a given matter? Whose interests and needs deserve consideration? Who belongs to the circle of those entitled to equal concern?" ("Abnormal Justice" 399). A situation of misrepresentation takes place when those who are impacted by a particular form of injustice do not have a voice to claim redress for the injustice—for instance, when corporate-caused environmental disaster has an impact in a region far from the "home" of the corporation.

Thinking about the aftermath of slavery in these terms allows us to expand Fraser's theory in a direction she does not address: historical injustice. Her examples of abnormality in the sphere of representation primarily concern questions of jurisdiction at different geographical scales—she mentions local, national, regional, and global spheres—but she does not address the question of temporal difference ("Abnormal Justice" 401).[45] In situations of historical injustice and diachronic implication such as slavery (or genocide), however, the initial victims are no longer alive and are thus a priori denied a voice in adjudicating the injustice they suffered; they have been "swallowed" by the ocean, in Kincaid's evocative words. Misrepresentation and abnormality are a given. Recognizing this abnormality has a positive side, as Fraser points out: "decentering" assumptions about justice allows for "an expansion of the field of contestation, [and] hence the chance to challenge injustices that the previous [normal] grammar elided" ("Abnormal Justice" 402). In our case, that means taking seriously claims about the need to redress the injustices of the past that continue to resonate in the present even when the original protagonists of the history are no longer around. And yet, as Fraser continues, "overcoming injustice requires at least two additional conditions: first, a relatively stable framework in which claims can be equitably vetted and, second, institutionalized agencies and means of redress" ("Abnormal Justice" 402).

My argument is that positing implicated subjects as a relevant category in addition to victims and perpetrators can help in creating the kind of framework Fraser calls for. In the aftermath of slavery, all forms of remediation must start from the assumption that "normal" forms of representation have already failed and that new forms of contestation and new institutionalized agencies are necessary. In such a situation, the concept of implication can provide a way to think about justice after "direct," "normal" representation is off the table. While the original victims and perpetrators are gone—and with them, "straightforward" solutions to the problem of reparations—groups remain who are implicated in that history. The question of redress involves determining the relation between differently situated groups—between those who have inherited or been otherwise denigrated by histories of victimization (postmemory generations) and those who have inherited or otherwise benefited from histories of perpetration (implicated subjects). Most disputes over reparations for slavery have centered on how to determine and assess the "loss" to African diaspora subjects by virtue of their ancestors' mistreatment and its long-term impact. An approach based on the concept of the implicated subject starts from the other side: it asks how we can address the "gain" that beneficiaries profit from by virtue of a history that, in Morris-Suzuki's terms, they have not caused, but which has caused them.[46]

Approaching reparations from the side of implication involves explaining—in terms borrowed from Arendt and Jaspers—how white subjects in former slave-holding and slave-trading societies are collectively responsible for the legacies of the past without being criminally guilty. It involves mobilizing both the historical lessons that a project such as Legacies of British Slave-Ownership can make available about the centrality of slave capital to capitalist society and the rhetorical power that Kincaid's *A Small Place* uses to produce feelings of discomfort. An approach based on implication suggests the need for work both in the realm of recognition—the deconstruction of a white identity founded on denial of implication in historical injustice—and in the realm of material well-being, where some form of redistribution in the direction of equality would offset the persistence of ongoing inequities.[47]

Finally, it involves keeping in mind one of the fundamental truths of post-traumatic justice: we are all in danger of misrepresenting the victims, who are no longer around to speak for themselves. An implicated approach to restitution involves reflexively marking the impossibility of complete redress and knowing that that impossibility only makes justice even more urgent.

PART II

Complex Implication

3

Progress, Progression, Procession
William Kentridge's Implicated Aesthetic

Living in the Interregnum

In 1990, the South African artist William Kentridge completed *Arc/Procession: Develop, Catch Up, Even Surpass*, a large drawing in charcoal and pastel created on eleven sheets of paper that together arch over an area of approximately 24½ x 9 feet (fig. 3). The work is typically installed high on a gallery wall, its shape recalling the triumphal arches of the Roman Empire. Indeed, Kentridge may have had in mind a famous instance of triumphalist architecture, the first-century Arch of Titus in Rome, which depicts the bearing away of the booty of imperial conquest, including a menorah and other spoils from the sack of Jerusalem. In an often-cited theorization of the link between "documents of civilization" and "documents of barbarism," Walter Benjamin implicitly evokes the same scene when he writes of "the triumphal procession [*Triumphzug*] in which the present rulers step over those who are lying prostrate."[1] Close in spirit to Benjamin's reflections on history, Kentridge's cryptic and decidedly nontriumphalist procession nonetheless involves not imperial booty, but rather the detritus of the dispossessed.

Most emblematically, on the far left-hand (or forward) side of *Arc/Procession*, the head and upper body of a hunched-over figure disappear beneath an indeterminate burden that includes cups and bowls, sacks and megaphones, all of which seem to be lashed around his body. A hobbling, one-legged man follows close behind. The feet of these two figures are hemmed in by low-lying barbed wire as they move toward a scarred landscape rendered in

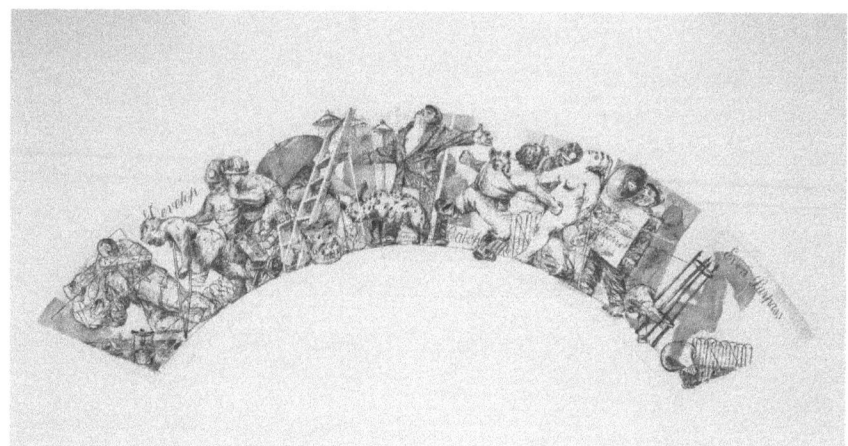

FIGURE 3. William Kentridge, *Arc/Procession: Develop, Catch Up, Even Surpass*, 1990. Charcoal, pastel on paper. Courtesy of the artist.

miniaturized, nonperspectival space at the left-bottom corner of the drawing. Following them in the procession we find a dense space populated by miners, a sandwich-board man, and male and female figures gesturing with despair, or perhaps imprecation, toward the heavens, along with abandoned cans, ladders, more megaphones, and two hyenas. Just to the left of center, three showerheads rain blue water on the proceedings—the only color in the drawing other than small triangles of green in the tiny landscapes at either corner of the arch. Meanwhile, imperfectly erased sketches at various points of the arch create an effect of layering, as do several human figures rendered in dark shadow.

In reworking the Roman triumph, *Arc/Procession* gives visual form to Benjamin's indictment of the violence embedded in progress narratives. Completed in the year in which the release of Nelson Mandela and the unbanning of political organizations such as the African National Congress and Communist Party officially inaugurated South Africa's transition from apartheid to an eventual nonracial democracy, Kentridge's drawing cites—in order to ironize and even violate—a series of tenets of the progressive narrative of nationalism in its classical and postcolonial variants. As critics frequently note, Kentridge has taken his subtitle, "Develop, Catch Up, Even Surpass"—incorporated into the drawing in neat, cursive hand—from the political vision of the modernizing Ethiopian leader,

Emperor Haile Selassie.² Selassie, who titled his autobiography *My Life and Ethiopia's Progress*, was an anticolonial hero and convener of the Organization of African Unity who believed that the country "must make progress slowly."³ At the same time, he sought to incorporate aspects of European modernity while holding on to traditional forms of hierarchical authority, a double game that ultimately failed and eventuated in his replacement by a military dictatorship in 1974.⁴ The production of *Arc/Procession* in the midst of a massive civil rights struggle may also contain an echo of Martin Luther King's oft-repeated dictum, "The arc of the moral universe is long but it bends toward justice," which continues to circulate in proximity to political change.

Yet, even as its title suggests an ambitious narrative of historical progress, *Arc/Procession*'s formal features complicate and undercut the progression at stake. Central to the piece's impact is the tension between the large-scale narrative suggested by its subtitle and the minimally narrative content of the drawing: if a procession is most certainly an event, the depiction seems to lack both an explicit causal agent setting the movement in motion and the sense of an ending. Tension derives in addition from the way the viewer's eye is pulled in two directions: while the procession moves from right to left, the drawn-in subtitle reinforces the tendency of Latin-alphabet users to "read" from left to right. Finally, the composition of imperfectly sutured panels give the arc a jagged line that doesn't simply "bend," as King's phrase would have it, but rather stutters—and thus fractures the seamless continuity promised by the notion of progress.

Working at a moment on the verge of massive social change, Kentridge explores what his compatriot Nadine Gordimer has called "living in the interregnum." In the 1980s, when she presciently saw change on the horizon, Gordimer twice cited Antonio Gramsci's famous sentence from the *Prison Notebooks*: "The old is dying, and the new cannot be born; in this interregnum there arises a great diversity of morbid symptoms."⁵ By staging progress as unresolved tension, *Arc/Procession* confirms what Gordimer also knows: that the crisis of the interregnum is also a problem of narrative and a challenge for implicated subjects. In this chapter, I explore some of the questions that arise from this conjunction of narrative form, subjectivity, and political transition. What challenges and opportunities attend narratives of historical responsibility from and in transition? What stories of collective transformation and improvement remain possible after the collapse of "grand narratives" of progress? If the old is indeed dying, how can its story still be told along with that of the emergent "new"?

In pursuing these questions, I turn not to more obvious purveyors of transitional narratives, such as Gordimer or the collective authors of the monumental *Truth and Reconciliation Commission of South Africa Report*, but to Kentridge, an artist who works the edges of narrativity. Kentridge, a globally prominent artist who comes from a Lithuanian- and German-Jewish Johannesburg family of lawyers involved in the antiapartheid struggle, makes art that is weighted with political implication, yet, for the most part, indirect in its political critique.[6] To be sure, Kentridge's innovative films, drawings, and prints—created throughout the transitional period of the late 1980s, 1990s, and early years of the twenty-first century—appear as illustrations of what "living in the interregnum" means. They help make visible the "morbid symptoms" of that moment of transformation: betrayal, violence, and complicity, to name some of the most important themes of his work. Seen from the present, much of this work seems prophetic: it seems to anticipate the failure of the "new" South Africa to confront structural inequality and transform the country's racialized political economy.[7]

Understanding Kentridge's exploration of implicated subjects in the moment of transition requires delving into the varied, media-specific techniques he employs as well as the form, content, and context of his heterogeneous oeuvre. In this chapter, I take the open-endedness, indirection, and outmodedness of Kentridge's implicated aesthetic as an inspiration for thinking more fundamentally about the narrative form embedded in what has come be called "transitional justice"—a politico-legal regime that has emerged in response to transformations like the one in South Africa.[8] I thus begin by providing a brief introduction to what we might call the "narratology" of transitional justice.[9] Drawing critically on the legal theorist Ruti Teitel, I suggest that transitional justice brings with it a fundamental narrative tension involving the negotiation between continuity and discontinuity, on the one hand, and implicated and disembedded subjects, on the other. This framework helps open up the narrative dimensions of Kentridge's experiments in animated filmmaking, where—along with *Arc/Procession*—he first begins to explore the minimally narrative genre of the procession.[10]

Reading Kentridge in the context of work on the narrative form of political transformation by theorists such as Benjamin, Benedict Anderson, and Eric Santner brings to light several keywords that orient this chapter's approach to implication: progress, progression, procession, and transition. This vocabulary is rich with narratological association, yet will appear here in defamiliarized form. To the extent that Kentridge creates a narrative of South Africa's transitional moment, it is a narrative that rewrites the conventional liberal narrative of change, which is founded on a vision of disencumbered subjects progressing through "homogenous, empty time" (Benjamin 261), and forges instead an alternative chronotope and a different, implicated kind of protagonist. In the two final sections of the chapter we will see how Kentridge's quasi-autobiographical exploration of implication opens up a deep, multidirectional history of race that is simultaneously postslavery and post-Holocaust. Moving from progression to procession in a transitional era, Kentridge provides resources for new forms of storytelling in the wake of racialized traumas and in the midst of a triumphalist capitalism.

Kentridge makes several linked contributions to the conceptualization of the implicated subject. His use of twin allegorical alter egos—Soho Eckstein and Felix Teitelbaum—helps craft an implicated alternative to the disembedded subject characteristic of human rights, humanitarianism, and transitional justice. Additionally, the "thick time" fostered by his aesthetic offers a formal correlate to the interlaced diachronic and synchronic axes of implication. Finally, through the multidirectional sensibility that some of his work exhibits, Kentridge provides an encounter with complex implication—the experience of occupying positions that align one both to histories of victimization and to histories of perpetration. While Kentridge's work always emerges from engagement with ethical, political, and aesthetic complexity, it falls neither into a facile relativism nor into a banal equation of histories: Kentridge's implicated aesthetic does recognize the artist's genealogical relation to Jewish suffering in the past—a version of postmemory—but it responds above all to the evidence of his ongoing structural implication in irrevocable violence and stubborn inequality.

Transitional Justice as Narrative

At the same time South Africa was making its dramatic political transition—and in dialogue with that process—a new way of responding to and thinking about what Gramsci called the interregnum was taking shape globally under the rubric of "transitional justice." Generally applied to states, such as South Africa, Argentina, and the former Soviet bloc, that have emerged from authoritarian or totalitarian rule into democracy, transitional justice involves the invention of contingent procedures and practices in the course of reckoning with particular past injustices. The institutionalized forms of transitional justice—often traced back to the Nuremberg trials and Germany's post-Nazi reconstruction—include truth commissions, the payment of reparations, and the practice of lustration (the banning of politically tainted politicians and civil servants from public office). The goal of transitional justice is the facilitation of new democratic regimes that break with the past yet maintain social peace; the attainment of such a goal proceeds necessarily from compromise (see Bickford; Teitel, *Transitional Justice*).

For all the importance of its institutional forms, transitional justice also entails a potent cultural logic. In the words of one of its leading theorists, the legal scholar Ruti Teitel, "Transitional law is above all symbolic—a secular ritual of political passage."[11] As a rite of passage, transitional justice possesses a strong narrative dimension. Narratives associated with regimes of transitional justice can appear in a variety of media that traverse the fiction/nonfiction divide—including courtroom testimony, truth commission reports, and literary and cinematic works. Regardless of the medium in which they appear, such narratives give form to political transformation by helping shape the transitional era's time consciousness, both its space of experience and its horizon of expectations.[12]

In her influential account, Teitel proposes that transitional narratives possess certain shared generic features. She emphasizes, in particular, their "contextualized and partial" nature: they are not "'meta'-narratives but 'mini'-narratives, always situated within the state's preexisting national story. They are not new beginnings but build upon preexisting political legacies" ("Liberal Narrative" 241, 255). In other words, transitional narratives do not stand alone, but only exist in relation to past narratives of violence and violation. They "recategorize" key events from a nation's past in the light of a new political dispensation (translating, for instance, "antiterrorist" measures into "crimes against humanity"), and they simultaneously "emplot" a vision of national history that projects from a tainted past into a different future (Teitel, *Transitional Justice* 85). As such, they combine continuity with discontinuity, recapitulation of a nation's history with a will to break with that history.

A fundamental tension in Teitel's account emerges, however, when she places transitional narratives under the sign of what she calls a "redemptive," "liberalizing" project ("Liberal Narrative" 257). Teitel's synthetic summary of the genre illustrates the risks of this subsumption:

Transitional narratives follow a distinct rhetorical form: beginning in tragedy, they end on a comic or romantic mode. In the classical understanding, tragedy implicates the catastrophic suffering of individuals, whose fate, due to their status, in turn implicates entire collectives. . . . In the convention of the transitional narrative, unlike that of tragedy, the revelation of knowledge actually makes a difference. The country's past suffering is somehow reversed, leading to a happy ending of peace and reconciliation. ("Liberal Narrative" 252)

Despite their contingent origins, transitional narratives, in Teitel's version, possess a strong teleological drive. The genre shift she identifies at their core—from tragedy to comic resolution—facilitates a parallel shift from contingency toward certainty: liberalizing transitional narratives become metanarratives or masterplots founded on a forgetful will to reconciliation.[13] As masterplots, transitional narratives shed their contingent connection to "preexisting political legacies" and become much more conventional stories that take for granted the direction of progress: in this case, toward the closure of liberal democracy. In Robert Meister's terms, such narratives risk slipping from the message that "the past was evil" to the consolation that "the evil is past."[14]

While committed to the masterplot of transition as liberalization, Teitel does show awareness of its dangers and acknowledges that, "despite its appeal, its entrenchment as a story of unity could undermine its potential for a more revolutionary project" ("Liberal Narrative" 257). Yet, insofar as she emphasizes "the potential of individual choice" as central to the "liberalizing function" of transitional "narratives of progress," her model becomes easily amenable to conventional, Hollywood-style plotting.[15] Take, for example, *Invictus*, Clint Eastwood's 2009 film about Nelson Mandela and the 1995 Rugby World Cup. There, the victory of the South African Springboks and the personal friendship between Mandela (played by Morgan Freeman) and the Afrikaner rugby captain Francois Pienaar (played by Matt Damon) become allegories of the "wholeness" and reconciliation transitional justice promises to the postapartheid nation (Teitel, "Liberal Narrative" 257). In this drive toward closure, well-meaning individualized stories triumph while structural implication in problems of race and class goes missing.[16] Indeed, the truth of the Springboks is more complicated than the film can admit. A decade and a half after their World Cup victory, the team remained almost entirely white, and success in the sport remained strongly correlated with ongoing economic inequalities.[17]

Invictus is, of course, a blatantly Americanized version of South Africa's transition. Yet, as such, it also emblematizes the transnational forces that are shaping the narrative of transitional justice today. As human rights scholar Paul Gready explains, "Globalisation as a whole is forging transitions and democracies characterised by continuity as well as change, by structures of inequality and patterns of conflict that are reconfigured rather than brought to an end" (*Era of Transitional Justice* 8). While predominantly a matter for political contestation, the limits of transitional justice in confronting such structures and patterns are also narrative limits, for, as Robert Cover has influentially argued, "no set of legal institutions or prescriptions exists apart from the narratives that locate it and give it meaning" (4). The generic conventions of the narrative of transition help install powerful ideological parameters that limit the field of possibility for new stories of transformation.

Although transitional eras are premised on a disruptive, qualitative break in political regime, liberal transitional narratives seek to install a more reassuring plot promising closure, as *Invictus* demonstrates. Central to the genre shift of transitional narrative, both Teitel and the film make clear, is a sense that closure is possible via a letting go of the past. While tragedy, in Teitel's account, "*implicates* the . . . suffering of individuals" and, through them, "entire collectives," the historical reversal that takes place in nontragic endings implicitly frees both individuals and collectives ("Liberal Narrative" 252; my emphasis). Disavowing the ongoing implication of individuals in collective contexts of suffering, such narratives take on not simply a liberal but a neoliberal guise and may become a form of what Eric Santner has called "narrative fetishism."[18] Writing about German attempts to "master" or overcome the Nazi past (known as *Vergangenheitsbewältigung*), Santner defines narrative fetishism as "the construction and deployment of a narrative consciously or unconsciously designed to expunge the traces of the trauma or loss that called that narrative into being in the first place" (144). A fetishistic narrative emerges out of a traumatic situation and may even, Santner proposes, "acknowledge the *fact*" of trauma, but it "disavow[s] the traumatizing impact of the same event" (150). In pointing to the need to preserve the traces of trauma's impact, Santner implies that the problem of fetishism lies not only in a past disavowal—or a disavowal of the past—but in the ongoing production of disavowal through narrative. The genre shift of transitional narrative from tragedy to comedy-romance constitutes a disavowal of two forms of implication. What is disavowed is not necessarily the past trauma, the "fact" of which may remain in view, but rather, first, the hold of the past on the present, and second, the ongoing inextricability of individuals from collective, social contexts. The sociologist Stanley Cohen describes this process of disavowal as "implicatory denial," a denial that the facts of the past continue to hold implications for the present.[19]

Regimes of transitional justice thus occupy a field of tension and remain poised at the intersection of conflicting demands. On the one hand, the drive for justice demands an account of subjects as implicated in histories of injustice and traumatic violence. On the other hand, the desire for social peace and progress diverts such a drive and seeks to create citizens for the new dispensation who are disembedded from past histories. Such contradictory demands play out in narrative form as a tension between continuity and discontinuity. The conventional transitional narrative seeks to deny continuities between past and present in order to forgo the need for a more fundamental break from previous social arrangements; it attempts to install moderate progress in place of qualitative transformation. At the limit, such a vision becomes a form of narrative fetishism, its version of progress built on disavowal of the ongoing production of trauma and inequality in the present—an ongoing production that is particularly marked in postapartheid South Africa, where a strong neoliberal turn accompanied the advent of nonracial democracy.

The thought of Walter Benjamin helps us to diagnose the problem of the liberal narrative at a more fundamental level—as a chronotope (Bakhtin)[20]— and to open up alternative possibilities for thinking transition as implication. Benjamin proposes in his reflections "on the concept of history" that the liberal (or in his time, social democratic) narrative of progress derives from an underlying gradualist temporality. As Benjamin famously argues, "the concept of the historical progress of mankind cannot be sundered from the concept of its progression through a homogeneous, empty time" (260–61). This same chronotope of progression lies at the heart of nationalist imaginings, as Benedict Anderson has demonstrated. For Anderson, the imagination of the modern nation becomes possible through the emergence of a new experience of temporal simultaneity, whose emblems are the novel and the newspaper, both of which present "the idea of a sociological organism [i.e., the nation] moving calendrically through homogeneous, empty time."[21] While the idea of the nation connects citizens to a horizontally conceived community as well as to that nation's canonical history, the homogeneous, empty time in which that community comes into being establishes a terrain purified of collective implication in traumas past and present. Combining

Benjamin and Anderson, we can propose that despite the peculiar, historically and socially heterogeneous circumstances in which the transitional nation necessarily emerges, the conventional transitional narrative that accompanies that emergence attempts to found the nation in this image of progression through homogeneous, empty time.

The notion of progression targeted by Benjamin is a much stripped-down version of the kind of progression that interests narrative theorists such as James Phelan.[22] In place of the dynamic organization of beginning, middle, and end that Phelan reveals in narrative, Benjamin finds in progressive thought a reduced temporal imagination with a dangerous political impact. For Benjamin, this concept of time stymied opposition to fascism because it led progressive thinkers of the era to grasp fascism as an outmoded aberration bound to disappear of its own accord (257). In the transitional context, the stakes are different and involve not fascism but rather the sense of inevitability that accompanies the assumed link between democratic nation-building and capitalist marketization—an inevitability that some versions of transitional justice help to produce and reproduce.

The liberal narrative offers one way of managing the tension at the heart of the transitional era between desires for stability and justice, yet counterforces are also at work in transitional contexts. Benjamin's critique of progress offers a framework for thinking about such counterforces. When he writes that "[a] critique of the concept of such a progression must be the basis of any criticism of the concept of progress itself" (261), he suggests the grounds on which an alternative narrative of transition might emerge, one that is not indebted to a gradualist vision but remains true to the other demand of transitional justice for a reckoning with ongoing implication in historical injustice. But what would such a narrative look like?

William Kentridge's Counternarratives

Just as South Africa's transitional process was getting under way, William Kentridge embarked on a remarkable period of productivity that would bring him to international prominence and would include, among other features, a sustained exploration of the problems of time, narrative, and progress that are at the heart of the transitional genre and fundamental to the thinking of implication. In highly mediated and indirect form, Kentridge's work depicts the contradictions and crises of narrative that accompany the long-wished-for moment of political change, a moment when the emancipatory possibilities of nonracial democracy run up against the persistence of entrenched privilege and material inequality. Well aware that the aesthetic production of one white South African artist could not possibly provide a totalizing overview of the era of change, Kentridge describes his approach as "trust in the inauthentic, the contingent, the practical as a way of arriving at meaning."[23] Infused with the contingent and the pragmatic, Kentridge's work operates on the same terrain as transitional justice, yet pushes back in at least two ways against the subsumption of contingency to the masterplot of progress: in place of the homogeneous, empty time of progression, Kentridge models a "thick time" and a dynamic, variable space; and in place of the disembedded liberal subject of the transition, Kentridge evokes an implicated, embodied subject.[24] In order to illustrate this alternative transitional chronotope, I will focus first on palimpsest and morphing—two techniques that emerge from what Rosalind Krauss calls Kentridge's "reinvention" of the medium of animation—and I will connect those techniques to a recurrent narrative function in Kentridge's films and other contemporaneous work: the procession of the crowd.[25]

These features (palimpsest, morphing, and procession) appear together for the first time in the Drawings for Projection series, an open-ended set of short animated films begun in 1989 and currently numbering ten.[26] The films reference early cinema, Weimar painters like Max Beckmann, and contemporary African artists like Dumile, among other sources. They include evocative extradiegetic music and nonsynchronous diegetic sound effects as well as occasional descriptive and narrative intertitles and bits of text, but no dialogue or voice-over narration. Despite minimal use of language—and an ambiguous, associative style—the films do offer both individual narratives and a collective story arc. In fragmentary form, they tell the tale of the industrialist Soho Eckstein and the artistic Felix Teitlebaum. These two men physically resemble the artist and serve as his alter egos in a simultaneously comical and serious reflection on contemporary South Africa. The inhabiting of seemingly opposed alter egos constitutes a crucial dimension of Kentridge's exploration of his own implication in apartheid and postapartheid South Africa.

The films recount a love triangle between the two men and Mrs. Eckstein, but also track the rise and fall of Soho's business empire while alluding to South Africa's history of racialized violence and the political struggles marking the transitional period. In coordinating intimate foibles with large-scale public events and transformations, Kentridge evokes certain conventions of the transitional narrative, as defined by Teitel. As she writes about the genre in general, "These tales of deceit and betrayal, often stories of longstanding affairs, appear to be allegories of the relation between citizen and state, shedding light on the structure and course of civic change" ("Liberal Narrative" 255). Like other transitional tales—including novels by the likes of Gordimer (*None to Accompany Me*), J. M. Coetzee (*Disgrace*), and Achmat Dangor (*Bitter Fruit*)—Kentridge's Drawings for Projection explicitly narrate the morbid symptoms that emblematize the interregnum through stories of interpersonal deceit and betrayal. Yet, acutely aware of the nonrepresentative status of his primarily white "cast," Kentridge also mediates the citizen/state allegory through the figure of the crowd, which appears in almost every film, albeit in different guises. As we will see later, he additionally includes an implicit reflection on his own implication as a Jewish South African.

Although the Drawings for Projection bear some obvious similarities to Teitel's account of the transitional genre—not only in their foregrounding of personal betrayal but also in their construction out of a series of microstories—they lack the overarching narrative progression from tragedy to comedy that the legal scholar finds in the genre and move instead in largely aleatory fashion between different subgenres and subplots. Unfolding simultaneously with the events of the transitional era, the series weaves in and out of relation to historical change. While Kentridge himself has voiced the opinion that apartheid constitutes a "rock" that cannot be confronted directly and thus needs to be approached with indirect and figurative means, in fact the series sometimes mobilizes quite literal references to issues of race, class, and violence.[27] Nevertheless, the "realist" and historically referential aspects of the Drawings for Projection still arrive mediated by experiments with form and aesthetic materiality. These experiments create the possibility of a new approach to transition by embracing the outmoded at the level of technique—Kentridge's reinvented handicraft version of animation.

The unusual drawing and filming technique Kentridge develops in the series resonates with the larger historical moment of the films' creation and constitutes his most original contribution to rethinking narration and implication in transitional times. Unlike traditional animation, in which the filming of a large series of images creates the illusion of movement, Kentridge works with a small number of drawings (typically between twenty and forty for an eight-minute-long film). His process of drawing for projection is based on marking, smudging, and erasure instead of the creation of an animated series.[28] That is, he draws an initial image on a white sheet with charcoal—occasionally supplemented with blue and red chalk—and then walks across his studio to his 16- or 35mm film camera, where he shoots two frames of the image. He then returns to the drawing and amends it through additional drawing, smudging, and erasure, before shooting two more frames. The process of creation continues like this for a period of months and results in a film that—even after editing and transfer to video or DVD for projection on a gallery wall—preserves layers of residual charcoal dust, concatenates palimpsestic images, and thus bears traces of the artist's bodily implication in his medium. In these palimpsests, traces of previous drawings remain on celluloid and in the final film, even as the drawings themselves that make up each frame disappear forever (except for the final image in each sequence, which is often displayed in exhibitions alongside the films).

Kentridge makes virtuosic use of the technique when he depicts, as he frequently does, newspapers fluttering through the air. The passage of the newspaper leaves a trail and thus supplements the ephemeral with the trace of persistence. If, as Anderson famously argues, the newspaper has served as a medium of national consciousness—figuring forth a simultaneity that would link citizens in an "imagined community" across the territory of the nation—in Kentridge's hands the newspaper becomes a figure of flux and temporal drag. Such scenes may thus be understood as intervening in the homogeneous, empty time of the nation. Using the same palimpsestic technique, Kentridge also directly reveals the human consequences of such temporal drag, which stands in opposition to the disencumbered time of progress—notably, the burden suffered, in differential fashion, by the nation's citizens and denizens, as in scenes from many of the films in which, recalling *Arc/Procession*, we follow the traces of a worker carrying a heavy load across a scarred landscape.

This technique of drawing/smudging/erasing, which makes possible the palimpsest with its layered persistence, also allows a form of morphing that highlights disappearance. The stakes of Kentridge's work emerge at the intersection of these two tendencies. *Felix in Exile*, made shortly before the first democratic elections in 1994, registers the violence of the interregnum and the problem of land distribution (a problem that even today remains largely unaddressed). Here we find Felix in a Paris hotel room as he reflects longingly on his homeland, but with an acute sense of the losses that are accumulating in his absence. Alternating "European" and "African" music evokes the layered experience of exile. While the setting in exile emphasizes the problematic of distant suffering for a white spectator, Felix simultaneously receives messages about the continued political violence back home through the drawings of a black surveyor, Nandi, which spill out of Felix's suitcase and flutter to the walls. Indeed, as Nandi appears opposite Felix in his mirror, Kentridge's alter ego seems closer to black life in South Africa than he has when at home.

An object of desire and nostalgia, Nandi maps the landscape of the dead. In her drawings, palimpsest and the newspaper are associated with death. But the drawing/erasing technique also produces a supplementary narrative that uses morphing to correlate death with disappearance and forgetting, as Nandi herself becomes a victim of violence. In a rapid sequence, Nandi is shot by unseen assailants and forensic crime scene lines appear to cordon off her bleeding body; her corpse then morphs quickly into the landscape and loses recognizability, before finally giving way fully to Kentridge's signature depiction of the postindustrial East Rand, a landscape dotted with disused mine pits and mine dumps.[29] As Nandi disappears, the landscape preserves the marks of violation in the guise of ecological devastation—even as it obscures the evidence of murder. As Kentridge has written in a discussion of this film, "The landscape hides its history. . . . There is a similarity between a painting or drawing—which is oblivious to its position in history—and the terrain itself, which also hides its history."[30] Nevertheless, by creating "imperfect" works filled with smudged images and traces of what has been erased, Kentridge's films and drawings seek to counter precisely this "hiding" or absorption of history by the landscape. Like Kincaid in her depiction of the polluted ocean, Kentridge both marks oblivion and replaces it with awareness of an ecological implication that links humans and the environment.[31]

In making time visible through a sculpting of drawn space, while working with a technique that simultaneously ensures disappearance and preservation, Kentridge brings together memory, mourning, and oblivion in an original, medium-specific chronotope whose production has ethical implications.[32] The depiction of Nandi's death indicates that the potential for trauma lies not only in political violence, but also in the erasure of that violence from human consciousness. Confronted with such a displacement, Kentridge avoids the perils of Santner's narrative fetishism by narrating that very erasure and marking irrecuperable loss in a nonfetishistic way. This double movement of marking and erasure resembles what I have called "traumatic realism."³³ A counter to narrative fetishism, practices of traumatic realism index loss and the inaccessibility of what has been lost without redemptive acts of recuperation. By depicting both Nandi's murder and the disappearance of her murdered body, Kentridge shows us why loss is unredeemable: not just because of the materiality of political violence but because of the temporal structure that accompanies it. The techniques of palimpsest and morphing make temporal progression itself an "actant" in the scene, both an experience Kentridge marks and a force against which his narrative struggles.

But Kentridge's technique also has a further specificity. The simultaneity of continuity and rupture made possible by drawing/erasing calls forth not just trauma in general, but the layered temporal dynamics of political transition: the fact that a break in the historical narrative of the nation coexists with persistent violence and the persistent traces of past violence. Kentridge's attention in *Felix* and other films to the obsolescent mine, together with his frequent representation of older technologies of all sorts—Bakelite phones, adding machines, and so on—counters what he calls "disremembering, the naturalization of things new," a process that he associates with the rhetoric of the "new South Africa" ("Landscape" 127). Against the absorption of the problems of the interregnum and an unredeemed past into the forgetful language of novelty—into the "happy ending" of the liberal transitional narrative—Kentridge's "outmoded" drawing and filmmaking techniques reinscribe transition back into landscape and memory.

In addition to challenging the temporal progression of the liberal narrative, the Drawings for Projection also undercut its disembedded subject. When *Felix in Exile* ends with the return of its protagonist to the scarred South African landscape, where he wades into a mine pit, Kentridge also suggests that the escape of exile is not an option in the face of unavoidable, embodied implication (another echo of Kincaid's tourist). In addition, by foregrounding focalization through the presence of surveyors' tools, such as the theodolite, and through mimicry of cinema's "iris" lens, Kentridge implicates viewers in Felix's gaze and in the violence projected on the museum walls. Kentridge's innovative reinvention of the medium also furthers the sense of embodied implication. In Rosalind Krauss's terms, "Kentridge's technique constantly narrativiz[es] his own process" (*Perpetual Inventory* 53). This narrativization mimics but goes beyond the kinds of self-reflexivity made familiar by postmodern authors such as Paul Auster or Italo Calvino, who reference an authorial avatar in their fiction. As in the works of those authors, the Kentridge-like figures of Soho and Felix occupy the storyworld of the Drawings for Projection and, in works such as *Journey to the Moon* and *7 Fragments for Georges Méliès* (both from 2003), Kentridge himself appears interacting with a drawn storyworld. But Kentridge's work arguably goes a step farther: he renders the very medium of his narrative worlds—charcoal on paper captured on celluloid—as a narrative of implication: the medium itself indexes the artist's body as it traverses the studio and bears the imprint of a story of material production and technique.

In a further twist, this story of technique folds back into the narrative discourse and shifts from the story of individual production to one of mass movement. Kentridge attributes the emergence of crowds in his films to the drawing/erasing technique. Referring to the opening of the third film in the series, *Mine* (1991), in which a crowd of miners spills out of a lift, he remarks:

> [The crowd's] origin has a huge amount to do with the particular technique I use. In a film using actors one would need a huge budget, thousands of extras, helicopters, an elephantine crew and a military administration to capture the huge crowds emerging from the ground. With this charcoal technique, each person is rendered with a single mark on the paper. As more marks are added, so the crowd emerges. The crowds draw themselves. It is far easier to draw a crowd of thousands than to show a flicker of doubt passing over one person's face.[34]

In other words, technique—the marking of paper with charcoal—helps generate the actors and settings of the world Kentridge creates. It leads Kentridge toward the crowd and, finally, toward the procession. The procession represents the fulfillment of the drawing/erasing technique insofar as the movement of the crowd from the horizon (their usual point of origin in the films) involves both the additive qualities of marking through which the crowd accumulates and the subtractive qualities of erasing through which the crowd displaces itself across the sheet of paper and across the space of narration.

While Kentridge uses the example of his third film in the series, *Mine*, in fact the entry of the crowd into the Drawings for Projection takes place just after the midway point of the first film, *Johannesburg, 2nd Greatest City after Paris* (1989), created at the same time as *Arc/Procession* (see Maltz-Leca 139). As the film irises out after an erotic scene in a swimming pool depicting the affair of Felix and Mrs. Eckstein, a postindustrial landscape fades in and fills up with a terraced terrain, light and sound towers, and a Hollywood-like sign announcing that this is indeed Johannesburg (and definitely *not* Hollywood!). Once the landscape is filled in, movement begins at the horizon, at the top of the image. A series of small black marks emerges and forms itself into a procession, which then snakes along an S-shaped path toward the front and bottom of the frame. As they approach the viewer and start to take on more human form, the film cuts to an apparent intertitle, which declares: "Soho feeds the poor." However, the intertitle turns out, ironically, to be an inscription on the napkin Soho has tucked into his suit as he sits down to an enormous meal, the scraps from which he will then fling at the crowds outside his luxurious abode. This first film of the series ends with a fistfight between Soho and Felix, an event whose pettiness comes into sharp relief as the film irises out in its last seconds on a receding procession of the poor. Resonant of the forced removals of the apartheid era, the procession of the impoverished masses (which is in direct relation to *Arc/Procession*) thus occupies the narrative space between Felix's affair and Soho's greed—an indictment by editing of two versions of the implicated bourgeois subject and an indication that procession and not progression provides the key to Kentridge's vision of transition. Here and in later films, the procession casts into relief the persistence of social antagonism and racial hierarchy at the moment of transition.

Although this early film from the series seems to position the masses as passive and resigned, the series as a whole also registers the becoming active of the people through public procession—a becoming that, as Leora Maltz-Leca has shown, is historically located in the new possibilities for political movement opened up at the tail end of the formal regime of apartheid (see esp. 150–51). Later films, especially *Sobriety, Obesity and Growing Old* (1991) and *Stereoscope* (1999), use the same drawing/erasing techniques to present processions as political demonstrations and often juxtapose the stagnant private worlds of Felix and the Ecksteins with the ever-metamorphosing public sphere of the transitional era. In *Sobriety*, for instance, Felix and Mrs. Eckstein look on passively as a politically mobilized crowd bearing signs and banners literally passes them by (fig. 4). The very blankness of the banners— unreadable except for an occasional, suggestive red tint—emblematizes the gap between politics and the private sphere in which Kentridge's privileged white figures attempt to live, even in the midst of the transitional era. These juxtapositions suggest that if Kentridge's particular technique leads him to the crowd, it would be misleading to imply, as he does, that he therefore foreswears the "flicker of doubt passing over one person's face." Doubt is, in fact, a powerful marker of the implicated subject, especially the white bourgeois beneficiary of racial and class oppression faced with the self-activation of the masses in procession and transition. Indeed, the mini-narratives of the Drawings for Projection focus predominantly on the flickers of doubt experienced by Soho and Felix, but the films ultimately draw their power from a double dialectic: that between the suffering and agency of the crowd and between bourgeois individual implication and the collective occupation of space.

Mining, Implication, and Multidirectional Memory

Kentridge's Drawings for Projection mobilize an arsenal of visual narrative techniques that provide a powerful alternative to the liberal story of transitional justice. They move from progression to procession as a means of representing transition; from narrative fetishism to traumatic realism via palimpsest and morphing; from disembedded individual to implicated subject in proximity to the masses. In the works I've discussed, Kentridge presents the time and space of transition as thick and dynamic, not empty and homogeneous. He drills down into the sediment of history while also tracing movements across the surface of the earth. He innovates without fetishizing the advent of the new, and he does so at the level of narrative discourse and the aesthetic medium as well as in his approach to political change. But Kentridge's narrative of transition is not simply the opposite of the conventional liberal narrative. Indeed, his work banishes neither the importance of individual responsibility nor the hope for progress (something that is also visible in his engagement with the utopian energies of the Soviet avant-garde, as in his Metropolitan Opera production of *The Nose* [2010]). Rather, Kentridge reworks responsibility in the direction of a broader notion of implication and depicts metamorphoses (political and otherwise) from a decidedly materialist and nonanthropocentric perspective.

At the same time that he broadens his notion of implication to encompass the structural implication of bourgeois subjects in a time of political transition, Kentridge also simultaneously expands the temporal horizons of historical responsibility and excavates a particularly autobiographical dimension of implication. These different features of Kentridge's work—which

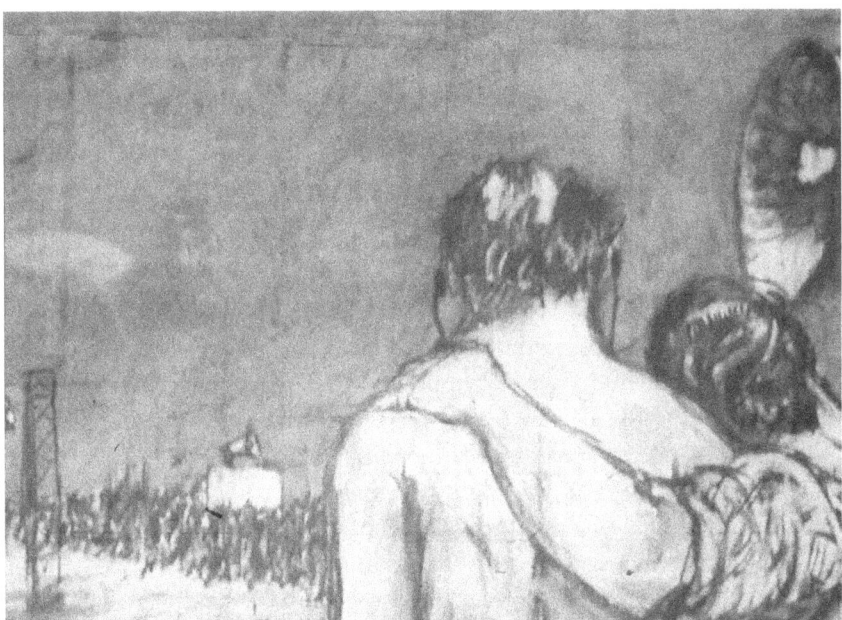

FIGURE 4. Looking on—the implicated subject. William Kentridge, video still from *Sobriety, Obesity and Growing Old*, 1991. 16mm film; video and laser disc transfer. 8 minutes, 22 seconds. Courtesy of the artist.

combine synchronic and diachronic implication—appear in especially condensed form in the 1991 film *Mine*. *Mine* was created as the third of the Drawings for Projection, but Kentridge thinks of it as the second in the series and situates it between *Johannesburg, 2nd Greatest City after Paris* and 1990's *Monument*. *Johannesburg* documents the creation of Soho's empire, including the mining town we associate with the later film, while *Monument* shows Soho as an ostensible "civic benefactor," erecting a statue in honor of the workers. *Mine*, in contrast, reveals the underside of Soho's empire in no uncertain terms. In the film's title sequence we see an isolated head that recalls both a fourteenth-century Ife bust from Nigeria and a miner with a lamp. This visual pun already suggests that the film is interested in histories that extend beyond the nation-state. As the sounds of Dvořák's Cello Concerto in B minor build, resonant of the European Romantic tradition, the word "MINE" rapidly approaches the viewer through a darkened mine shaft. Soon we will realize that this title constitutes another pun, this time verbal, which refers not only to the source of Soho's wealth but also to his proprietary relationship with the human and natural worlds (yet another level of meaning will emerge later). The brief title sequence thus begins to establish colonialist capitalism as its target while also deploying a dynamic aesthetic of juxtaposition and layered meaning that bears resemblance to an internationalist avant-garde.

The film proper opens with a scene of metamorphosis in which an explosion in a mine disrupts the landscape and transforms the land into an image of Soho sleeping. (This is the scene that Kentridge describes as the origin of the crowd in his work.) The following sequence deploys montage to crosscut scenes of miners beginning their day with the mine owner Soho. Lying in bed, the smoke from Soho's cigar becomes a bell with which to call his unseen household help, after which the cigar morphs into a coffee cup; later the pillows of the bed rotate around Soho and become a desk holding the tools of his trade, in particular the adding machine that spits out paper and then commodities, including the workers who produce his wealth and a set of Ife busts. The film moves between Soho's domestic and work spaces—shown, through Kentridge's drawing/erasing technique, to be variations on the same space—and the miners' underground work and living spaces, which similarly bleed into each other, as if to demonstrate the workers' complete subordination to the biopolitical regime of modern capitalism. This sequence bears some resemblance to Eisenstein's *Strike* (1925), which begins with alternating shots of a laughing, corpulent industrialist and laborers at work in the factory. The signature use of charcoal drawing allows Kentridge to unite the spaces of capital and labor and thus to reveal simultaneously their dependent and radically unequal nature, as does Eisenstein's editing. But *Mine* also reveals the magical metamorphoses made possible by Kentridge's technique to be complicit with Soho's power to control labor and nature: this is, then, also a portrait of the artist as implicated subject.[35]

Kentridge's answer to the industrialist's power to control time and space and the natural and human worlds consists not in a refusal of those powers but in their self-conscious appropriation. Kentridge makes visible what Soho "owns" but refuses to see. This rendering visible takes place most dramatically in a sequence that begins with Soho's coffee pot—a cafetiere, as Kentridge calls it, or a French press, as we say in the US. When Soho presses down on the coffee plunger, it does not stop at the bottom of the pot, but continues its downward movement through Soho's bed and into the mines below (fig. 5). The coffee plunger creates a miniature mine shaft that cuts into the living and work spaces of the miners, through their barracks and showers and into the cavernous mines themselves—the plunger even passes through the body of one worker, which starts a flow of blood that continues downwards. Once again, Kentridge reveals that his technique partakes of the violence it depicts, an implicit comment on the complicity of the artist in a world of structural oppression. The plunger becomes a kind of drill (and is associated with drilling performed by the miners as well as with the artist's pencil), and as the drill cuts into the rock, a strange image emerges soon recognizable as the cross section of a slave ship (fig. 6). This first association is then overlaid with the growing sense that the iconography of the mine also resembles a Nazi camp. Indeed, the image of the mine workers' compound seems to be modeled directly on a famous photograph from the liberation of Dachau (one that features a young Elie Wiesel), although Kentridge claims not to have had the Holocaust in mind at all (fig. 7). Regardless of the artist's intentions, however, recognition of this modeling also casts a dark shadow over the images of miners in the shower, which can now be seen as punning on the habitual reference to the gas chambers as "the showers."

Consistent with the entire series of Drawings for Projection, the film contains no clear narrative line or voice-over to guide interpretation of these multidirectional visual associations. If these are memories that are excavated

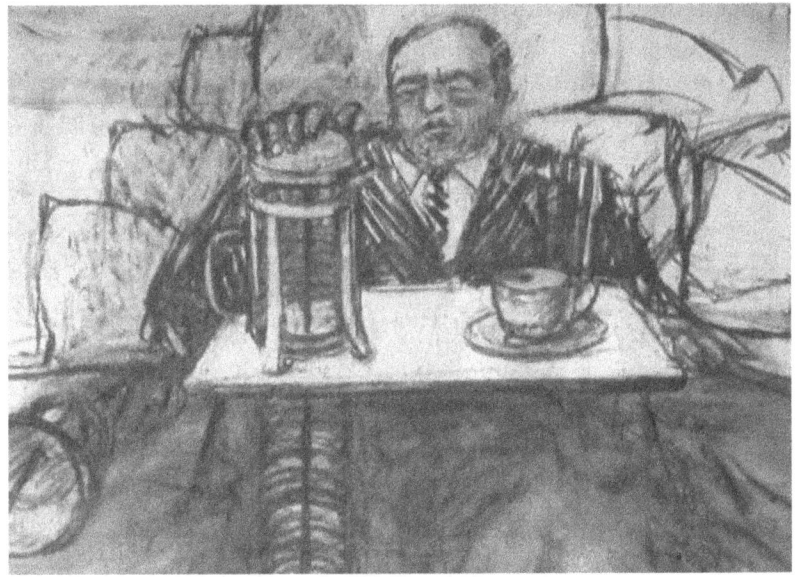

FIGURE 5. The coffee plunger. William Kentridge, video still from *Mine*, 1991. 16mm film transferred to video. 5 minutes, 49 seconds. Courtesy of the artist.

from the formations of the mine, it is not clear whose memories they are. Out of this uncertainty at least two ways to read the sequence emerge, which correspond in turn to the two ways that multidirectionality arises in it: the unmistakable allusion to the slave ship emblematizes a collective memory of the larger historical transfers and correspondences between different forms of imperial violence connecting Europe and Africa (and theorized by the likes of Aimé Césaire and Hannah Arendt, among others), while the unconscious and ghostly presence of the Nazi camp suggests the peculiar psychology of domination and complicity of white and—perhaps more pointedly—white Jewish South Africans.

Regardless of whether the mine compounds actually resemble sites of slavery and totalitarian control, Kentridge's work registers the layers of meaning that both popular and scholarly discourses ascribed to the mines during the apartheid period. As geographer Jonathan Crush has shown, the notion of "the African miner [as] a slave" living in "medieval conditions" characterized African Mine Workers' Union discourse in the 1940s and reappeared in the 1980s in the rhetoric of the National Union of Mineworkers. In addition, Kentridge draws on a historical association of the word "mine": the fact that

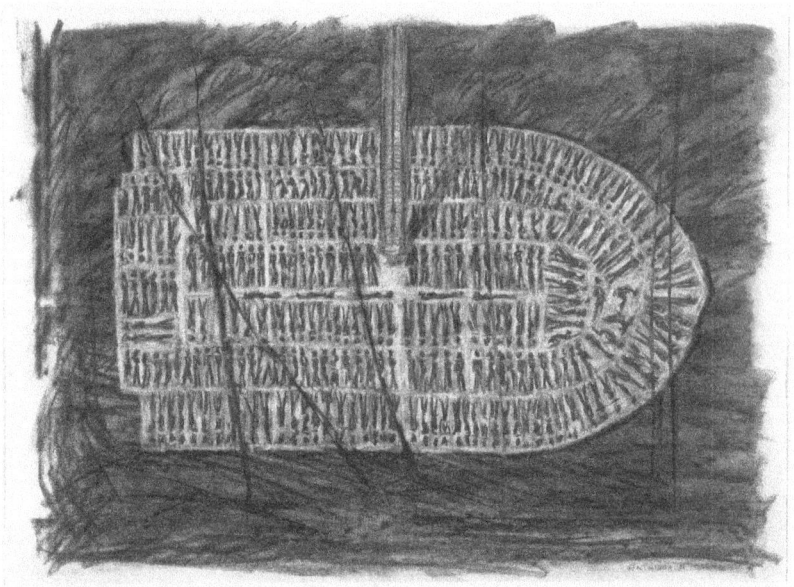

FIGURE 6. The slave ship. William Kentridge, video still from *Mine*, 1991. 16mm film transferred to video. 5 minutes, 49 seconds. Courtesy of the artist.

one of the largest slave forts on the coast of Africa was located in Elmina, "the Mine." Yet, the historicizing discourse of mining as "medieval" enslavement coexisted with—and was ultimately displaced by—Marxist and social historical accounts of the "modernity" of the mine that, in language resonating with the Nazi's concentrationary universe, depicted the compound as a "total institution" and its manager as a "supreme dictator."[36]

In delving into the mines, Kentridge certainly evinces a strong interest in the forms of domination that the mine materializes and that various discourses have attempted to describe through historical analogies; the figure of Soho clearly stands as a metonym for those forces throughout the Drawings for Projection. But, as already noted, Kentridge's approach to politics is never primarily—or simply—a matter of represented content. The nonexplicit—perhaps even unconscious—form of the Holocaust reference in *Mine* suggests that it must also represent something other than an explicit analogy between different forms of violence. Rather, to construct an alternative interpretation, we might begin by noting that the Holocaust's ghostly presence in the film seems to reference the medium itself, the palimpsestic form of Kentridge's work. Such a resonance between form and history suggests that the Holocaust

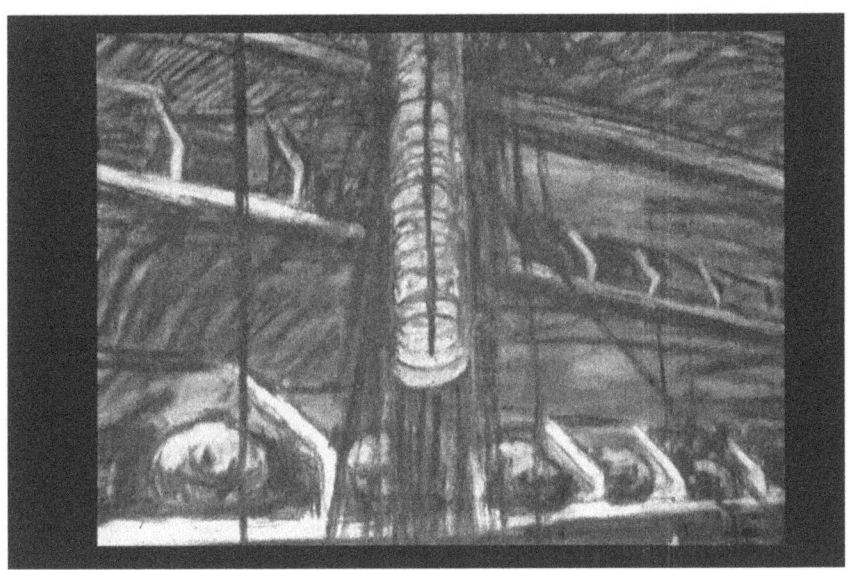

FIGURE 7. The barracks. William Kentridge, video still from *Mine*, 1991. 16mm film transferred to video. 5 minutes, 49 seconds. Courtesy of the artist.

reference involves a new level of self-reflexivity, just as earlier we observed that Kentridge's metamorphic technique shares with capitalism itself the power to shape and exchange all manner of beings and objects.

If we take Soho's name, Eckstein, and the modeling of his image on the artist's grandfather as indications that he is of Jewish descent—indications that themselves remain indirect—a new message starts to emerge that strikes at the heart of what I call complex implication. The ghosting of the Holocaust may reference the similarity between German and South African racist regimes as well as the presence of the virulent antisemitism that accompanied Afrikaner nationalism, especially during the Nazi period in Europe. But it also draws attention to the vast distance of South African Jews from the Holocaust: despite possessing a broad ethno-religious or directly genealogical link to victims of the Holocaust, Jews who immigrated to South Africa either found immediate refuge from genocide or benefited from historical good fortune in escaping ahead of time from Europe (the case for Kentridge's family, which immigrated to South Africa long before the Holocaust). To complicate matters further, the figure of Soho recalls the Jewish financiers who in the late nineteenth century fostered the growth of the mining industry. In the words of critic Claudia Braude, "The history of the Johannesburg Jewish community . . . is intimately intertwined with the history of the early mining town."[37] Soho's creation of the mine thus becomes a kind of historical allegory for one strand of Jewish South African history, but the allegory is many-sided.

Given the associations created by the film *Mine*, Soho's iconic pin-striped suit also becomes an ironic reminder of concentration camp uniforms—precisely what Soho never had to wear. The irony that, despite its racism and antisemitism, South Africa served as a refuge for Jews during World War II is noted by the South African–British writer Dan Jacobson in his memoir *Heshel's Kingdom*, where he writes of his grandmother and her children, "In leaving Lithuania for South Africa, they had exchanged an anonymous death at the hands of murderers for life itself" (Jacobson 68). Even if, in Jacobson's words, the Jews' "prominence in the development of the diamond and gold fields had done nothing to make them popular among either Britons or Boers" (90), a vast distance still separates South Africa's Jews from the fate of both their European relatives and the black populations among whom they now found themselves. Indeed, as Braude details, the post-Holocaust history of Jews in South Africa saw many in the community finding accommodation with the apartheid system and the ruling National Party—an accommodation that required what she calls "a profound suppression of memory," the memory of antisemitism and Nazi influence in South Africa (Braude xliv).

Kentridge's palimpsestic narratives of transition—along with the multidirectional legacies they evoke—thus register several things simultaneously. They uncover the specific dynamics of South Africa's political interregnum, but they also demonstrate how the larger forces of capitalism, colonialism, and genocide have framed South African history over the *longue durée*. They draw attention to the specific transitional position of the country's Jewish minority, yet also anticipate a more general return of suppressed memories that would accompany the end of apartheid. In other words, what the movement of the coffee plunger reveals is not simply a historical analogy between different sites of violence or Soho's (or Kentridge's) individual unconscious, but rather a complex, connective history of trauma, implication, complicity, and forgetting that defines a social group—South African Jews—caught in what Kentridge once wryly described as "an interesting position" between accommodation and marginalization.[38] How can an artist address problems of injustice in such a historical context marked by divergent genealogies and ongoing structural inequalities? For Kentridge, at least, it involves shuttling between the claims of the past and the present and excavating evidence of individual and collective implication from sites layered with multidirectional memory. That project continues to this day.

Still Embedded: The Return of the Procession

A decade after *Arc/Procession* and after most of the Drawings for Projection series (thus far) had been completed, Kentridge's interest in the procession exploded. In this new phase, he begins to multiply the media of his experiments. Processions emerge cast in bronze (e.g., *Procession*, 1999–2000) and printed onto the pages of atlases and encyclopedias (e.g., *Portage*, 2000). A 1999 film, *Shadow Procession*, uses ripped paper, pins, and light projected on a screen to evoke the same kind of burdened procession found in *Arc/Procession* and many of the Drawings for Projection. In 2016, Kentridge created an enormous frieze on the banks of the Tiber in Rome called *Triumphs and Laments* that, like *Arc/Procession*, refers to the Roman triumphal procession and, in Benjaminian fashion, links the glories of civilization with the "shamefulness" of violence.[39]

But among the recent pieces, it is perhaps most suggestively in a 2015 work, *More Sweetly Play the Dance*, that the issues raised in this chapter coalesce: the form of the procession and allusions to mining merge with the ambiguous multidirectionality of memory we find especially in *Mine*.[40] A large-scale eight-screen video installation that runs in a fifteen-minute loop with sound coming from four megaphones, *More Sweetly Play the Dance* uses some images that could come straight from the Drawings for Projection: the familiar East Rand mining landscape serves as the backdrop for an extended procession. Yet, in contradistinction to the animated films, *Dance* uses live actors as well as cut-out paper forms that recall *Shadow Procession* and other recent works. A combination of back and side lighting during the filming creates processions in which the figures traversing the screens approximate silhouettes but also have a greater depth and range of color than mere shadows would offer.[41]

While the installation opens with a dancer twirling from right to left across the eight screens, the remainder of the work consists of a procession from left to right involving priest-like figures, a parade of "saints," a marching band—the African Immanuel Essemblies Brass Band—that provides the sometimes mournful, sometimes exuberant music for the piece, and the usual assortment of dispossessed and afflicted people (including Ebola victims with IV drips) and hybrid human/nonhuman figures that we find in Kentridge's works dating back at least to *Arc/Procession*. The pace of the procession shifts along with the music from the slow, labored movements of figures dragging bodies or carrying heavy loads on their heads to the more frenetic pace of dancing derived from South African church ceremonies (Kentridge, *More Sweetly* 30). The fifteen-minute projection ends with the dancer and choreographer Dada Masilo—who also collaborated with Kentridge on *The Refusal of Time* (2012) and *Refuse the Hour* (2012)—twirling and striding across the screens; she first carries a spade and then, *en pointe*, a rifle that she holds above her head before she disappears into the interstices between two of the screens. The spade represents another reference to mining, since "spade dances from Johannesburg [are used] to induct young miners into the process of mining underground," while the rifle dance emerged from another project on the Chinese Cultural Revolution (Kentridge, *More Sweetly* 35, 47). The gaps between the screens ensure that the procession in *Dance* is discontinuous: the figures who pass by do not simply progress at a continuous pace over those gaps from one screen to the next, but rather disappear for variable amounts of time, often returning, but not always (the case for Masilo).[42] In its foregrounding of discontinuity and asynchronicity,

Dance continues the interruption of homogeneous, empty time we find throughout Kentridge's processions. Created two decades after the birth of the "new" South Africa, the work—seen in dialogue with the Drawings for Projection—suggests, among other things, that the transition to an egalitarian society remains unfulfilled.

Like so much of Kentridge's work, *More Sweetly Play the Dance* concatenates histories both local and temporally and spatially distant. As most commentators have observed, the procession recalls the medieval *danse macabre*—in particular, procession-like representations of it such as Bernt Notke's fifteenth-century *Lübecker Totentanz*—as well as the contemporary flight of refugees and migrants, whether in South Africa, Europe, or elsewhere.[43] Like the *danse macabre*—and, indeed, like today's mass migration—Kentridge's procession unites diverse classes of people and brings death and life, fatality and resilience, into proximity. *Dance* works with and from very local scenes and materials, but it also alludes to a far-flung set of cultural, historical, and geographical contexts. In Kentridge's words, "The piece starts with ideas of the German Dance of Death, with ideas from [Berg's opera] *Lulu* and Büchner. But in the musicians, in the actors, in the landscapes, in the figures they are enacting, it is rooted in the city of Johannesburg" (*More Sweetly* 42). The intertextual references gathered in this work could be unraveled almost indefinitely, yet there is one other important layer of meaning mobilized here that rhymes suggestively with our previous discussion: Kentridge has drawn his title from Paul Celan's famous poem of the Holocaust, "Todesfuge" ("Death Fugue").

In "Todesfuge," Celan creates a fugue-like poetic structure that recounts a scene in a Nazi camp: a commandant brutally directs his workers to dig graves and orders a group of musicians to "strike up for the dance" (*er befiehlt uns spielt auf nun zum Tanz*), while alternately writing home to his beloved in Germany.[44] Narrated from the perspective of the Jews in the camp, who famously drink the "black milk of daybreak," the poem also ventriloquizes the commandant, thus creating a fugal counterpoint between the two perspectives. As it happens, Kentridge has taken his title from a famous line in which the commandant speaks through the mediation of Celan's collective narrators. The poem's "we" recounts: "He calls out more sweetly play death death is a master from Germany" (*Er ruft spielt süßer den Tod der Tod ist ein Meister aus Deutschland*). Kentridge thus cites directly the formal word order of Michael Hamburger's translation of "Todesfugue," but also substitutes the word "dance"—transposed from earlier in the poem—for "death."

Dance does not represent the first time Celan's poem has been evoked by a South African artist: in *Country of My Skull*, poet and journalist Antjie Krog's account of the Truth and Reconciliation Commission, Krog cites several lines from Celan in German and translates one of them into English and into the South African context: "Death is a master from Africa."[45] Krog's citation takes place at the beginning of an imaginary dialogue that brings together the problem of representing the Holocaust with that of responding to apartheid (and also references Ariel Dorfman's engagement with the dictatorship in Chile).[46] Kentridge, in contrast—and in keeping with all of his work—proceeds much less directly. Yet, the Celan reference may ultimately function similarly in both works.

Dance includes no explicit comparison between the Nazi genocide and the procession it depicts, though knowledgeable viewers might be reminded of the death marches from the camps that the Nazis ordered in the waning months of their reign. Writing about the work, Kentridge himself situates the procession form in a long and heterogeneous genealogy: "The image of a procession goes back to Goya and his paintings of processions. It goes back more recently to photographs of refugees fleeing Rwanda. . . . All the movement that still exists across the continent of Africa. Further back to the images of the processions of people from the Balkans. The huge population movements of people at the end of the Second World War" (*More Sweetly* 25). More salient than this expansive, multidirectional vision, however, is the proximity of music, dance, and death in both Celan's poem and Kentridge's installation—a proximity that links multidirectionality to the problem of implication.

Despite being appropriated for educational and commemorative purposes—a normalization of his work that led Celan to disavow the poem in later years—"Todesfuge" represents a radical interrogation of the limits of aesthetics in the face of death: the function of music and poetry is put into question by the historically documented "instrumentalization" of music in the camps Celan evokes as well as by his allusions to German high culture in the title, structure, and text. (Celan references not only Bach's fugues but also Goethe's iconic love object Margarete.) Inspired by Celan, I suggest, Kentridge joins Krog in probing the relationship between representation and suffering. In other words, rather than primarily serving as a comparative reference to the Holocaust as historical event, the Celan allusion adds a self-reflexive dimension to Kentridge's installation that involves the status of the artist and the audience.

As in the Drawings for Projection, Kentridge implicates himself in his role as artist by alluding to the complicity between the creation of beauty and the fact of suffering. The self-reflexivity signaled by the allusion to Celan suggests a different ethical position in the work from that identified by Homi Bhabha in his nuanced reading of *Dance*. Bhabha builds on a fragment from Kentridge's *Six Drawing Lessons* to argue for an ethical dimension in *Dance* inspired by the French Jewish philosopher Emmanuel Levinas. In the midst of a reflection on how to represent an historical and aesthetic "cacophony of excess" (what I would call multidirectionality), Kentridge constructs a list of subject titles that he wants to find a way to "put together." In the list is the title that Bhabha extracts: "KEEPING ON YOUR FEET (THE ETHICAL DEMAND OF THE FACE OF THE OTHER)" (52). Bhabha sees here the conjunction of Kentridge's processional form ("keeping on your feet") and Levinas's dictum that the face of the other represents an infinite ethical demand connected to the biblical injunction "Thou shalt not kill." As Bhabha writes of the "anonymous load bearers of the world's weight and its weariness" found in *Dance*, "the ethical demand of foot power, like the Levinasian appeal to the face, requires us to walk alongside, to identify with the 'extreme precariousness of the other'" (236 [citing Levinas]). Bhabha recognizes the risks involved in "relations of proximity" to the dispossessed, and he does not facilely insert himself into the procession and submit to "an ahistorical, sentimental humanism" (236). Yet, it seems to me, in understanding Kentridge's ethics as one of "walking alongside," Bhabha overlooks the structure of spectatorship created in this procession and thus the problem of implication. The precariousness of the other is not in fact one with which we can identify (even though we sometimes share it!); rather, precariousness always stands in relation to the capacity to wound that defines implicated subjects, as I also argue in the next chapter, Chapter 4, on Israel/Palestine. It is that relationship between the capacity for violation and actually existing precariousness that Kentridge stages.

In *More Sweetly Play the Dance*, as in *Arc/Procession* and many of Kentridge's other processional works, we viewers are not in a position to join the procession or even to walk alongside it; rather, we are situated, along with the artist, *perpendicular* to the procession that unfolds across the screens in front of us and outside its spaces of exile, mourning, or resistance. Although the spatial relations in Drawings for Projection function somewhat differently from those in the multiscreen *Dance* installation, we have already seen how Kentridge positions his alter egos, Felix and Soho, along with the viewer, outside the procession: in *Johannesburg*, Soho confronts the procession of the dispossessed workers with cruelty and condescension; in *Sobriety*, Felix and Mrs. Eckstein stand mutely and passively outside the political demonstration that signals the political transition under way. The point of such positioning is not, however, that the figures in the animated films and the viewers who look over their shoulders are utterly disengaged from the scenes in front of them, but, to the contrary, that they are ethically implicated in them, which is to say, participating in their very distance. This is obvious in the case of the industrialist Soho, but the suggestion is just as strong for Felix, whose apparent political passivity offers no resistance to the racial and class structures he observes. Like the Drawings, *Dance* also uses the procession to raise self-reflexive questions about art's perpendicular relation to suffering and violence. In this recent work, it is primarily the invocation of Celan—in particular, the incorporation of the voice of the German "master"—that signals the self-reflexivity of the work: its questioning of what it means to depict mass migration and the suffering of refugees "more sweetly."

One significant shift that has taken place in the movement from *Arc/Procession* and the Drawings for Projection to *More Sweetly Play the Dance* and other recent works such as *Triumphs and Laments*, however, is an expansion of scale and scope. While Kentridge has long participated in collaborative work—for example, with the Handspring Puppet Company—and has long worked with composers such as Philip Miller, the new work emerges necessarily out of a large-scale studio and involves multiple collaborators. The depiction of a highly personalized mode of implication that we find in the Drawings via the presence of Kentridge's two alter egos (as allegorical as those alter egos surely are) thus opens out to a more collective vision here. The nature of the Holocaust references in *Mine* and *Dance* echo this shift in scope: from a commentary that seems to involve Kentridge's individual and communal—genealogical—relation to the Holocaust in the earlier film to a larger statement about the structural role of art in relation to local and global suffering in the recent installation.

The recent work also expands the historical archive of implication even further. In the chapter of *Six Drawing Lessons* from which Bhabha takes the Levinasian slogan, Kentridge links this shift to the conditions of the studio. In that chapter, dedicated to "A Brief History of Colonial Revolts," Kentridge describes the early twentieth-century genocide of the Herero as a history in which "we still are embedded": "The Herero genocide is part of a continuing set of questions and actions, questions of seeing, understanding, and the use of violence, a set of questions reaching from Plato's cave to where we are here, and the studio becomes an emblematic space for working with these questions" (39). Kentridge's vision of implication—of being "embedded" in histories "where we are here"—is no fixed and homogeneous vision; rather, as he writes, it is "a continuing set of questions" that he explores in the collective and collaborative context of the studio. Those with whom he collaborates are themselves a heterogeneous group, not all situated in the same way that he is to the histories this work evokes. Framing his project in terms of embeddedness—what I call implication—functions productively: the framework of implication enables the questions of seeing, understanding, and violence that Kentridge mentions and links them to perennial philosophical concerns such as those raised by Plato.

By exploring implication—and not only guilt, perpetration, and victimization—Kentridge opens up an uneven but shared space of creation and spectatorship for interrogating forms of historical and political responsibility. He is not one to provide easy answers, but then, there are no easy answers in these realms. Situated at the intersection of complex genealogies and overbearing structures of violence, he helps shift our modes of perception in order to rework what Jacques Rancière calls the "distribution of the sensible" (*le partage du sensible*)—the nexus of aesthetics and politics.[47] Such a reworking is an equally urgent agenda item in the next context we will explore: that of diasporic responses to the politics of Israel/Palestine.

4

From Gaza to Warsaw

Multidirectional Memory and the Perpetuator

Modes of Implication and Memory Conflict

In an October 2015 opinion piece for the *Washington Post*, two Jewish American scholars—and self-declared "lifelong Zionists"—published a stinging critique of Israel.[1] The authors, Steven Levitsky of Harvard and Glen Weyl of the University of Chicago, survey the state of play in the Middle East and assert, "Israel has embarked on a path that threatens its very existence." With the occupation of the West Bank having become permanent, Israel will find itself more isolated and less secure, they argue, and will imperil its claims to being a democratic state. Levitsky and Weyl thus "reluctantly but resolutely" declare their support for what has become known as "BDS"—the movement to boycott, divest from, and sanction Israel. In embracing BDS, Levitsky and Weyl do not abandon their Zionism; instead, they present their shift in attitude toward a rejection of Israeli policies as emerging *from* their Zionism: "For years, we supported Israeli governments—even those we strongly disagreed with—in the belief that a secure Israel would act to defend its own long-term interests. That strategy has failed. Israel's defenders have become its enablers." The authors then counter—by embracing—one of the most familiar critiques of the BDS movement: that it holds Israel to a higher standard than other states. They write, "Israel, of course, is hardly the world's worst human rights violator. Doesn't boycotting Israel but not other rights-violating states constitute a double standard? It does. We love Israel, and we are deeply concerned for its survival. We do not feel equally invested in the fate of other states." Distinguishing their embrace of BDS from that of some other Israel critics, they continue: "We recognize that some boycott advocates are driven by opposition to (and even hatred of) Israel. Our motivation is precisely the opposite: love for Israel and a desire to save it."

Levitsky and Weyl's column illustrates how relevant, but also multivalent, the concept of implication can be in the struggle over Israel/Palestine. At least two forms of implication can be found in their essay. First, their change of heart emerges from a growing recognition that their own earlier attitudes and actions had not countered but rather enabled the political deadlock in the region: by defending Israel without exception, they became enablers and what I call "perpetuators" of an untenable position and thus implicated in the production of further injustice. We might call this "ideological" implication. In addition, they outline a version of "affective" implication, one in which strong feelings—here, of love—connect subjects to an apparently distant political scene.[2] Levitsky and Weyl seek to break with the first form of implication while embracing the second. Although especially charged in the case of Israel/Palestine, these forms of ideological and affective implication are not unique to this case; indeed, they are common to various diaspora groups and to the forms of long-distance nationalism they often express.[3]

In the case of Levitsky and Weyl, an embrace of implication becomes the opportunity for a critical political intervention, but it also preserves an affective and ideological tie to the object of the critique: the State of Israel. In that sense, it reproduces one of the mechanisms whereby the state solicits implicated subjects for its simultaneously ideological and affective project: through its interpellation of "the Jewish people." Starting with the 1950 Law of Return—which allows all Jews anywhere to immigrate to Israel at any time—the State of Israel has positioned itself as the representative not primarily of its citizens but of an ethnically and religiously defined people worldwide.[4] The Israeli Supreme Court made this view explicit in 1972 when it stated, "There is no Israeli nation separate from the Jewish People. The Jewish People is composed not only of those residing in Israel but also of Diaspora Jewry."[5] In Saree Makdisi's terms, "As a result, not only Jewish citizens of the state but indeed all Jews everywhere are classified by the organs of the state, on the basis of their racial identity, as having 'Jewish nationality.' Whereas non-Jews, although they may be citizens of the state, are explicitly not members of the 'nation,' that is to say, Jews all over the world (whether they want to be affiliated with Israel or not), whose state Israel claims to be."[6] The break between citizenship and nationality in the Israeli context constitutes a defining feature of the state and one of the most significant sources of the ongoing dispossession of Palestinians both within the pre-1967 borders of Israel and in the occupied territories. The 2018 Nation-State Bill (Israel's fourteenth "Basic Law") only further solidifies the status quo. Palestinians can be citizens of Israel, but they can never have Jewish nationality and thus do not possess numerous privileges (especially concerning immigration, residence, and landownership) that almost any Jew anywhere does possess. This concept of nationality, which underlies the state, also provides the legal and institutional infrastructure for the affective implication that Levitsky and Weil embrace.

Israel's nationality/citizenship split—instantiated in the Law of Return and other laws and political institutions—creates a paradoxical situation of implication for diaspora Jews who may, like Levitsky and Weyl, want to stake out a critical position vis-à-vis Israeli policy: either they do so as Jews and thus risk reproducing the affective bonds to Israel that one finds in the *Post* column; or they put aside Jewishness in criticizing the state and thus risk granting the state a monopoly on the meanings of Jewishness. As "lifelong Zionists," Levitsky and Weyl do not hesitate to embrace a Jewish identity affiliated with Israel (even as they embrace BDS, a radical opposition strategy that has since been deemed illegal by Israel). Other, more radical Jewish critics mobilize implication but do so without seeking to maintain such ties of love to the state—or they do so by actively seeking to break those ties.[7] Levitsky and Weyl's column demonstrates that no singular politics follows from recognition of one's own implication in injustice. But it also reveals that Israel/Palestine represents a rich, if often depressing, terrain for exploring the political tendencies that accompany a grasp of one's own entanglement in seemingly distant relations of power. One of the primary reasons Israel/Palestine represents such a terrain is the paradoxical situation of implication that Israeli citizenship and nationality law creates for Jews.

There are few political struggles more protracted and painful than the one that frequently appears under the name "Israeli/Palestinian conflict." In Bashir Bashir and Amos Goldberg's terms, the mainstream narratives of both Palestinians and Zionists "are narratives based on binary opposition. . . . Each side is convinced that it is history's ultimate victim, while denying or downplaying the suffering of the other side in order to validate its own claim."[8] As my approach to Levitsky and Weyl's column seeks to illustrate, the question of Israel/Palestine is also one in which multiple forms of implication coexist—and where the category of the implicated subject might offer a position from which to rethink the politics of the region beyond the binaries Bashir and Goldberg identify, especially but not uniquely for those who find themselves at a distance from the events on the ground. The struggle over Palestine certainly has identifiable victims and perpetrators (even if consensus about who those victims and perpetrators are might be hard to reach across lines). Yet, as Levitsky and Weyl's column—and the recent debates about the BDS movement that it references—indicates, the conflict also involves a panoply of subjects beyond the most immediate participants. In the case of BDS, many of the disputes have involved academic boycotts considered by professional organizations such as the American Studies Association (where the boycott movement was successful) and the Modern Language Association (where it has not yet been). Proponents of the BDS movement might be seen as arguing that academics—both within and beyond Israel—are implicated subjects who significantly participate in the conflict despite their seeming remove from it. In response, opponents of BDS deny the kinds of links between the academy and the occupation that would entail implication or responsibility-at-a-distance. Yet, those critics—especially American (and other non-Israeli) supporters of Israel—also act out of a sense of implication in the situation in the Middle East. Like Levitsky and Weyl, but less surprisingly, these anti-BDS forces see their actions conditioned by "love" of Israel; they simply draw opposite conclusions about the meaning of that kind of affective implication than do the *Post* columnists. If an approach based on implication and implicated subjects does not provide simple or direct answers, it can nevertheless help illuminate the stakes and background assumptions of the BDS debate and the larger political crisis out of which it arises.

As if the situation were not already charged enough, there is a further feature of the politics of Israel and Palestine that cannot be avoided: the politics of memory. The contemporary conflict always unfolds against the backdrop of powerful memories of death and dispossession, namely memories of the Holocaust and memories of the Nakba and ongoing occupation.[9] In such a context, the memories at stake are often conflictual, contested, and competitive. In *Multidirectional Memory* I put forward a framework for thinking about memory in situations of violence and struggle that seeks to avoid the framework of the zero-sum game: the belief that the public presence of one collective memory necessarily displaces or minimizes that of another.[10] The dynamics of memory—I sought to illustrate through attention to intersecting memories of genocide, colonialism, and slavery—do not obey a zero-sum logic, but are instead generative: the conflict of memories produces more, not less, memory.

Yet, if public memory is structurally multidirectional—that is, always marked by transcultural borrowing, exchange, and adaptation—this does not mean that the politics of multidirectional memory come with any guarantees. Indeed, as the Israeli/Palestinian context illustrates, the articulation of almost any political position may come in multidirectional form. In response to the high stakes of proliferating memory discourses in situations such as this one, it becomes imperative to develop an ethics of comparison that can distinguish politically productive forms of memory from those that lead to competition, appropriation, or trivialization.[11] In the case at hand, such a multidirectional ethics of comparison can also help us think through what I called in my discussion of Kentridge complex implication: the demands that are made by distinct but intertwined histories that position subjects in relation to both victimization and perpetration simultaneously (without necessarily making them either victims or perpetrators). Just as the previous chapter sought to bring together Holocaust memory with apartheid and the postapartheid condition, so this chapter also seeks to work through what it means to simultaneously belong to the postmemory generation—the second generation after the Holocaust—and be a structurally implicated contemporary of Israel's ongoing dispossession of Palestinians. Although this is not the only route to understanding the affective implication of diaspora Jews like Levitsky and Weyl, the individual and collective "genealogical" memory of the Holocaust plays an indisputable role in connecting Jews around the world to the Israeli state project.

In the remainder of this chapter, I reflect on diasporic critique of Israel at the intersection of memory politics and complex implication. I take as the occasion for my discussion the barrage of mnemonic conflict that accompanied Israel's December 2008–January 2009 offensive against Gaza, an assault that in three weeks killed 1,400 Palestinians, many of them civilians, and destroyed vast amounts of public infrastructure in a Gaza Strip already weakened by blockade. Thirteen Israelis were also killed during the conflict, ten soldiers (four as the result of friendly fire) and three civilians from southern Israeli towns that came under Palestinian rocket fire. The UN Human Rights Commission Fact Finding Mission that studied the conflict—headed by the respected Jewish South African jurist Richard Goldstone—found that violations of international humanitarian law had been committed by both sides, but the mission's 575-page report made it abundantly clear how asymmetrical those crimes were in their human impact.[12]

My particular focus here will be a controversy that arose when a radical American sociology professor sent an email to his undergraduate students in which he declared that "Gaza is Israel's Warsaw" and forwarded a photo essay with "parallel images of Nazis and Israelis," several of which depict the Warsaw Ghetto. Because this controversy is by no means an isolated case, as the simultaneous controversy about Caryl Churchill's *Seven Jewish Children: A Play for Gaza* (2009) indicates, it calls for a critical genealogy of memory discourses.[13] Such a genealogy reveals that the reference in recent controversies to Holocaust-era Warsaw is not arbitrary. Indeed, as I will demonstrate, the Warsaw Ghetto has proven to be an enduring focus of multidirectional acts of memory that engage with the transnational legacies of colonial and racial violence. I thus begin by situating the recent controversy within a larger discursive field of Warsaw memory before returning to the specific dynamics of the Israeli/Palestinian question.

While that endemic conflict plays a significant role in my analysis, my aim is a more general mapping of the range of forms that public memory can take in politically charged situations in which complex forms of implication are at play. The bulk of the chapter consists of the mapping of this discursive field, after which I turn more explicitly to the conceptual resources offered by the theory of the implicated subject. Through mnemonic mapping, I arrive at a four-part distinction in which multidirectional memories are located at the intersection of an axis of comparison (defined by a continuum stretching from equation to differentiation) and an axis of political affect (defined by a continuum stretching from solidarity to competition—two nonsimple, composite affects) (fig. 8). Although schematic, such a map can provide orientation for an exploration of political imaginaries in an age of transcultural memory. More specifically, it leads me to propose that a radically democratic politics of memory needs to include a differentiated empirical history, moral solidarity with victims of diverse injustices, and an ethics of comparison that coordinates the asymmetrical claims of those victims. This conception of the politics of memory suggests in turn that memory discourses expressing a differentiated solidarity offer a greater political potential than those, frequent in the Israeli/Palestinian case, that subsume different histories under a logic of equation or set victims against each other in an antagonistic logic of competition.

As will be clear, my focus is not on indigenous Palestinian discourse, which would require a different set of interpretive tools. Rather, I aim at a sympathetic critique of transnational discourses of solidarity with Palestinians

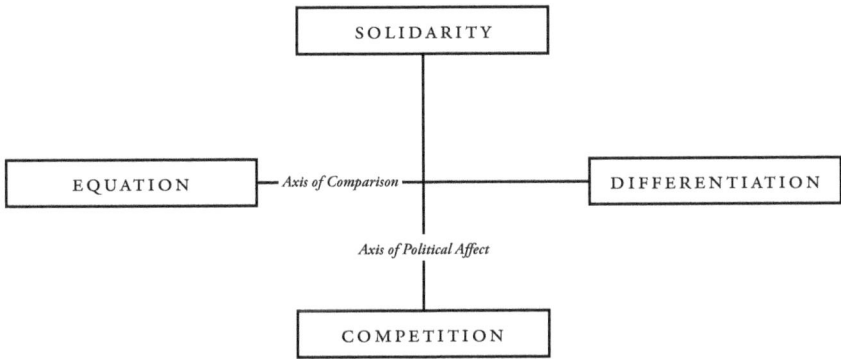

FIGURE 8. Mapping multidirectional memory. Figure created by the author.

produced by implicated subjects—in this case Jewish intellectuals and artists of the diaspora. In a concluding section, I turn to two prominent Jewish critics of Israeli policy to argue that thinking through implication—rather than either foregrounding vulnerability or embracing the position of the perpetrator—represents the most productive avenue for solidarity. With the practice of occupation and blockade continuing apace, such solidarity is as urgent as ever, but the forms solidarity takes still demand reflection. The concept of implication, I argue, offers an opportunity to confront our role as perpetuators of injustice.

On the Ruins of Warsaw

The Warsaw Ghetto has always been a resonant symbol in public discourse and a multivalenced knot of memory. Established and then quickly sealed by the Nazis in the fall of 1940, the Warsaw Ghetto held approximately 400,000 Jews in a 1.3-square-mile area.[14] Three features of the ghetto have shaped its memorial legacy: it was at once a place of almost absolute segregation and constriction where many thousands died; a way station from which hundreds of thousands of Jews were sent to extermination camps (primarily Treblinka); and a staging ground in 1943 for one of the twentieth century's most heroic, if suicidal, resistance struggles. References to Warsaw draw selectively or inclusively on all of these characteristics of the ghetto and have anchored collective memories of many persuasions—liberal, communist, Zionist, and increasingly anti-Zionist, at the very least. In the poetry of Czesław Miłosz in particular "Campo Fiori" and "A Poor Christian Looks at the Ghetto," both written in the shadow of the ghetto in 1943—we even get the perspective of a Polish implicated subject.[15] In order to set the stage for the confrontation with the multidirectional remembrance of Warsaw and Palestine and its relation to the problem of implication, I focus here selectively on only one, albeit longstanding, strand of Warsaw memory—one that puts the ghetto into dialogue with problems of race and colonization.

I begin by offering two Warsaw examples taken from *Multidirectional Memory* that can provide a starting point for the mapping I have called for. In 1949, the African American scholar and activist W. E. B. Du Bois visited Warsaw, where he saw the ruins of the ghetto the Nazis had established there and then completely destroyed after suppressing the uprising. Three years later Du Bois wrote a short article recounting his trip called "The Negro and the Warsaw Ghetto." At a moment when there was as yet no single English word to refer to what we today call the Holocaust, Du Bois reflected on the significance of the Jewish experience during World War II for the global problem of race. The result of his visit, he wrote, "and particularly of my view of the Warsaw ghetto" and of Nathan Rapoport's sculpture *Warsaw Ghetto Uprising*,

> was not so much clearer understanding of the Jewish problem in the world as it was a real and more complete understanding of the Negro problem. In the first place, the problem of slavery, emancipation, and caste in the United States was no longer in my mind a separate and unique thing as I had so long conceived it. It was not even solely a matter of color and physical and racial characteristics, which was particularly a hard thing for me to learn, since for a lifetime the color line had been a real and efficient cause of misery. . . . The race problem in which I was interested cut across lines of color and physique and belief and status and was a matter of cultural patterns, perverted teaching and human hate and prejudice, which reached all sorts of people and caused endless evil to all men.[16]

What is notable in Du Bois's short piece is both the solidarity he expresses with Jewish history and his very prescient grasp of the relationality of different histories of racial violence. Moving beyond a conception of his own experience as "a separate and unique thing," Du Bois comes to an understanding of race that is instead multidirectional. He draws on the material traces of the Nazi genocide in order to rethink his understanding of the African American past and present. Du Bois's interpretation of the larger significance of the Warsaw Ghetto derives in turn from the very experience and memory of racism that he is reconceptualizing in this article. As he continues, "I have seen something of human upheaval in this world: the scream and shots of a race riot in Atlanta; the marching of the Ku Klux Klan; the threat of courts and police; the neglect and destruction of human habitation; but nothing in my wildest imagination was equal to what I saw in Warsaw in 1949" (14). It is important to emphasize that the asymmetrical understanding arrived at by Du Bois in 1952 revises his own earlier articulation of these issues, including his often-cited 1947 claim in *The World and Africa* that "there was no Nazi atrocity . . . which the Christian civilization of Europe had not long been practicing against colored folk in all parts of the world."[17] In contrast, Du Bois's post-Warsaw vision brings black and Jewish histories into relation without erasing their differences or fetishizing their uniqueness. Proximate pasts are neither "separate and unique" nor "equal"; rather, a form of modified "double consciousness" arises capable of conjoining them in an open-ended assemblage.

About a decade after Du Bois published "The Negro and the Warsaw Ghetto," the French writer Marguerite Duras also took inspiration from the ghetto to put forward a vision of solidarity against the backdrop of difference. In "Les deux ghettos" (The two ghettos), an interview-based article for the New Left newsweekly *France-Observateur*, published in 1961 in the wake of the October 17 massacre of peacefully demonstrating Algerians in Paris, Duras brought together a survivor of Warsaw and a pair of Algerian workers.[18] While the title of the piece seems to suggest an equation between the ghettos that held Jews during World War II and those holding Algerians at a late stage of colonialism—an impression reinforced by the "parallel images" that accompany the article of an Algerian worker and a Jew bearing a yellow star—the actual answers provided by Duras's interviewees suggest as many asymmetries as similarities. Like "The Negro and the Warsaw Ghetto," Duras's text demonstrates a multidirectional sensibility—a tendency to see history as relational and as woven from similar but not identical fabrics.

The examples of Du Bois and Duras, which come from two moments when the meanings of the Nazis' Jewish policies had not yet solidified into the current, widely held understanding of the Holocaust as "a separate and unique thing," help us begin mapping the field of multidirectional memory. While Duras's article and many of the other invocations of the Holocaust in the context of the Algerian War look at first like forms of solidarity based on an equation of histories, they frequently join Du Bois in a vision of solidarity constructed through differentiated similitude. These examples provide us with the opportunity to observe a now almost-forgotten understanding of the Shoah in which its specificity was grasped at the same time that its potential links to other histories of racism were also in view. In moving to the present—and the Middle East conflict—it is important to recall both the multidirectional dynamic these acts of memory illustrate and the distance Holocaust memory has come since the 1950s and early 1960s.

"Gaza Is Israel's Warsaw"

In early 2009 a controversy erupted at the University of California, Santa Barbara, when a sociology professor found himself threatened with disciplinary action because of an email he sent to his undergraduate class on the sociology of globalization. At the tail end of Israel's bombing of Gaza—and on Martin Luther King Day—Professor William Robinson sent his students an email with the subject heading "parallel images of Nazis and Israelis." In the body of the email he asserted, among other things, that "Gaza is Israel's Warsaw," and he forwarded a photo essay, taken from the website of political scientist Norman Finkelstein, that juxtaposes images from the Nazi persecution of European Jews during World War II and images of Israeli oppression of Palestinians. Among the Holocaust-era photographs are several taken from the so-called Stroop Report, a Nazi-produced document that "celebrates" the destruction of the Warsaw Ghetto.[19] After receiving this email, two Jewish students dropped Robinson's class. A few weeks later, after an intervention by the Anti-Defamation League and other pro-Israel groups, a university investigation of Robinson began.

There are many ways of approaching this case, which was subsequently dropped by the university but whose implications remain. That the case against Robinson was a deliberate attempt to restrict academic freedom is crucial to state up front, especially because it brings to mind too many other recent American cases in which scholars critical of Israel have been the target of campaigns orchestrated on distinctly nonscholarly grounds.[20] Yet my approach brackets the urgent question of academic freedom as it does the issue of politically engaged pedagogy, an issue that is also one of the ultimate horizons of discussion. Instead, I read the Robinson case through its participation in the tradition of multidirectional Warsaw memory in order to continue mapping the politics of memory.

Warsaw has always figured conspicuously in the circulation of Holocaust memory in proximity to Palestine/Israel. In the period just before statehood as well as in the pre–Eichmann trial years, commemoration of the Warsaw Ghetto uprising in Israel condensed Zionist ambivalence toward the Holocaust. Zionist ideology celebrated the Warsaw "martyrs" while distancing itself from alleged diasporic passivity. As Idith Zertal demonstrates, the meaning of Warsaw was also integrated into the conflict with Palestinians and other Arabs in the region and instrumentalized as a form of Zionist legitimation.[21] This was true from the earliest days, when Zionist settlers read the uprising as an imitation of their own struggles with the indigenous population (Zertal 25), up through the consequential period of the beginning of the occupation, when a kibbutz leader "argued that Israel's 1967 Six-Day war was a continuation of the ghetto uprisings."[22] Already during the unfolding of the Nazi genocide, Gaza and Warsaw were implicitly associated. In 1943, the left-wing organization Hashomer Hatzair established a kibbutz within a few miles of what would become the border of the Gaza Strip; they named it Yad Mordechai, after the martyred leader of the Warsaw Ghetto Uprising, Mordechai Anielewicz, and later installed Nathan Rapoport's sculpture of Anielewicz on the kibbutz, which today stands facing Gaza.

Of course, the centrality of the Holocaust and the Warsaw Ghetto to legitimation of the state has led critics of Israeli policy to appropriate the same tropes and reverse their charge. Thus, for instance, in June 2003, Oona King, a British Labour MP, traveled to Israel and the occupied Palestinian territories and then wrote an account of her trip for *The Guardian*. In the article by King, who like Robinson is Jewish, but also has an African American father, one sentence in particular ignited controversy. Reflecting on her first day in the Gaza Strip, a day in which an Israeli helicopter attack killed a woman and child and injured dozens of civilians, King wrote: "The original founders of the Jewish state could surely not imagine the irony facing Israel today: in escaping the ashes of the Holocaust, they have incarcerated another people in a hell similar in its nature—though not its extent—to the Warsaw ghetto."[23] Two years after her visit to Gaza, King faced an irony of her own—her support of the US-led war in Iraq contributed to the loss of her seat to RESPECT Party candidate George Galloway, who later regularly deployed a similar Gaza/Warsaw analogy during the January 2009 assault.[24]

In declaring "Gaza is Israel's Warsaw," William Robinson thus certainly joins a well-established analogical tradition. Robinson's rhetoric mobilizes both verbal and visual means—it deploys a logic of linguistic equation and analogy, while supplementing that logic with the images of the photo essay. What drives this rhetorical strategy, which has proven so widespread? Perhaps most crucially, Robinson's references to Warsaw and the Holocaust—both verbal and visual—engage in the political struggle Judith Butler describes in *Frames of War* over which lives are perceived as human and thus recognized as "grievable": "It is only on the condition of certain embedded evaluative structures that a life becomes perceivable at all. . . . [I]t is only by challenging the dominant media that certain kinds of lives may become visible or knowable in their precariousness" (51). Robinson's invocation of the Holocaust in the context of the Israeli/Palestinian conflict confirms Butler's argument and suggests that a need exists to counter what Jacques Rancière would call the dominant "distribution of the sensible" (*le partage du sensible*) in order to render Palestinian lives visible and thus grievable.[25] Like so many others outraged not only by Israeli aggression but also by the conditions of perception in the centers of global power, Robinson calls upon an established repertoire of images in order to render Palestinian suffering commensurable with the epistemological and affective frames that dominate media narratives. It is surely true, at least in the US, that a great inequity in the distribution of grievability exists whereby Palestinians are routinely rendered as less than fully valued human lives. But questions about this strategy remain.

The photo essay and brief accompanying texts Robinson also forwarded obey a logic similar to Robinson's Gaza/Warsaw analogy and seem to literalize the desire to render Palestinian suffering visible. The essay begins with the title "Deutschland Uber Alles" and the explanatory subheading (all in capital letters) "The Grandchildren of Holocaust Survivors from World War II Are Doing to the Palestinians Exactly What Was Done to Them by Nazi Germany." A vertical strip of images follows, with black-and-white photographs depicting Nazis and Jews on the left side of the page and color images of Israelis and Palestinians on the right. The images range from scenes of the construction of fences, walls, and camps to depictions of prisoners behind barbed wire, confrontations of soldiers and civilians, and gruesome images of corpses. While a similar use of parallel images accompanies Duras's article "Les deux ghettos," Duras's text, as I have suggested, works against equation and symmetry, and even the images of the Algerian worker and presumed Warsaw ghetto inmate are separated by a very thin white border—a form of framing absent from the photo essay, where the images in each of the six sections abut each other without any gap. The lack of space in the photo essay between either the vertical or horizontal axes creates a continuous strip of images and suggests that the histories at stake blur into each other without remainder.

The images in the photo essay are artfully chosen to display various forms of visual matching (through the arrangement of figures, repeated gestures, etc.). The photo essay thus works to create identity out of difference and in doing so translates the work of comparison into the assertion of equation. This strategy of bringing Palestinians into view via stock images of the Holocaust points to limits in the struggle for recognition, since, as Butler points out, the categories opposite to invisibility and ungrievability are notions of visibility and grievability that are often themselves compromised. Even when recognition becomes possible for previously occluded subjects, "the very features that are 'recognizable' [may] prove to rely on a failure of recognition" (141). In much the way Butler's analysis anticipates, the Robinson email and the photo essay draw Palestinian suffering into a form of recognition based on the thoroughly familiar features provided by a stereotypical rhetoric and iconography of the Holocaust. They thus suggest the likelihood that the forms of recognition they promote will also entail a failure of recognition—in this case, a failure to recognize the specificities of both the Palestinian plight and that of Holocaust victims. To give one of the most disturbing examples, in the section of the photo essay on "check points," an image of an Israeli-established checkpoint at Huwara, near Nablus, is juxtaposed with a photograph from the ramp at Auschwitz-Birkenau.[26] The latter image is not, of course, a checkpoint at all, but rather a depiction of a selection at which prisoners are about to be assigned to two groups—one that will remain in the camp and one that will be sent immediately to death in the gas chambers. We also need to recall the provenance of such images: almost without exception, photographs of the unfolding of the Holocaust are perpetrator images taken by the Nazis themselves, while journalists, international activists, and Palestinians themselves have produced a substantial visual archive of the Israeli occupation.[27] Superficial visual similarity—and even more substantial similarities involving the regulation of space and dominated subjects—should not lead to the overlooking of such profound distinctions. Both a checkpoint and a selection point are "evils"—to adopt the language of the radical Israeli philosopher Adi Ophir—because they distribute unnecessary, "superfluous" damage and suffering through a socially instituted order. Such distributions are open to comparison, as Ophir demonstrates in his massive study *The Order of Evils*. But when careful comparison gives way to equation between the technologies of genocide and those of occupation, significant moral and political errors occur.[28]

The stakes of such error become especially clear when we look more closely at Robinson's text. Despite the understandable desire to introduce Palestinians into a US public sphere that persistently denies and denigrates their suffering, Robinson's rhetoric leaves the frameworks of the dominant political order intact and even mimics its reifying tendencies by eliding different forms of domination. While Robinson's email might be seen as subscribing to Du Bois's precept that no suffering should be considered "separate and unique," it forgoes the important corollary specifying that different legacies of suffering are not therefore "equal"—which is not a moral judgment but a historical one with ethical and political consequences. A deep logic of equation runs through Robinson's email, as can be seen when he writes: "Gaza is Israel's Warsaw—a vast concentration camp that confined and blockaded Palestinians, subjecting them to the slow death of malnutrition, disease and despair, nearly two years before their subjection to the quick death of Israeli bombs" (email of January 19, 2009).[29] At issue here is not the description of Palestinian suffering, which is well within the bounds of reasonable discourse, but rather the elision of the Warsaw Ghetto with a "concentration camp," a confusion of forms of incarceration that is typical both of heated political rhetoric and our own theoretical moment when the camp has been termed the "nomos" of modernity—but the confusion is no less damaging for that.[30] Part of the problem lies in the uncertain referentiality of the concentration camp itself, a site of political detention that is sometimes confused with extermination camps—places, like Treblinka, only established for the purpose of genocidal killing. The Warsaw Ghetto was neither a concentration camp nor an extermination camp, but rather, as I've stated, both a place of mass death and a way station for people slated to die in extermination camps.[31]

I offer these brief attempts at distinction not out of pedantry, but because they matter morally and politically. Several opportunities are lost in discourses that equate the Warsaw Ghetto with Gaza and the Israeli occupation. Besides obfuscating the fate of certain victims of the Holocaust—a moral wrong and an illustration of how easily forgetting accompanies apparent acts of memory—the reference to Warsaw obscures the conditions of Palestinian life and death in significant ways. For instance, the discourse of equation in Gaza/Warsaw analogies imports a dangerous model of victimization into Palestinian politics. As a key element of a genocidal machine, the Warsaw Ghetto ultimately offered no exit except the suicidal struggle that the resistance fighters waged in 1943. The situation in Gaza is dire, but still allows forms of politics beyond suicide. As historian Mark LeVine writes, "if Gaza is today's Warsaw, then Palestinians have no hope."[32] In addition, while the Holocaust framework taps into a ready channel of public discourse, its evocation discourages thinking through the novel forms of domination being developed in the occupation and blockade that are distinct from industrialized genocide. The situation in Gaza is the result of forms of Israeli control not even feasible during the Nazi genocide as well as overlapping and clashing modes of sovereignty that encompass intra-Palestinian conflicts, local powers Israel and Egypt, and the global structures of empire underwritten by the US.[33] Foregrounding those dispersed modes of power and sovereignty has the advantage of alerting us to the participation of a large number of implicated subjects—for instance, those of us in the US whose government and tax dollars prop up and perpetuate the occupation.

While the logic of equation in Robinson's rhetoric is clear, also important is its competitive tonality. The equation at work in the text and images is not intended to create solidarity between two communities of suffering. Rather, the Gaza/Warsaw equation enacts an appropriative transfer of affect from past to present; the legitimate solidarity it seeks to create with oppressed Palestinians emerges at the expense of those whose lives supply the analogous affective charge—past victims who, the analogy insinuates, are either now victimizers or have had their victim status canceled by the later actions of others acting in their name. It is true that victimization of Palestinians has often, perversely, taken place in the name of "honoring" the memory of the Holocaust, but Robinson's analogy maintains that perverse logic of moral property, citing the State of Israel as a kind of possessive individual when it speaks of "Israel's Warsaw." In the photo essay in particular, which emphasizes the "familial" link between Holocaust victims and Israeli perpetrators, equation becomes a form of competitive aggression at the same time that it represents a clear case of mimetic desire for another's history of suffering. The possibility of recognizing the asymmetrical complexity of implication—which Kentridge accomplishes in bringing together apartheid, Holocaust, and slavery—goes missing in the symmetries of this discourse.

Recognizing the conjunction of equation and competition allows us to situate Robinson's rhetoric on our map of multidirectional memory. It also puts him in surprising company. The same conjunction characterizes the Israeli right-wing "second Holocaust" discourse, which sees any move toward peace as setting the scene for another, more horrific genocide.[34] Even more precisely, Robinson's discourse recalls those Jewish Gaza settlers who, during Israel's "disengagement" from the territory in 2005, sent their children out to confront Israeli soldiers in poses imitating the iconic Warsaw Ghetto boy. For them, too, Gaza was Israel's Warsaw, and the suffering of the Holocaust was appropriated for contemporary political ends.[35] Such a mapping of equation and competition also prompts us to plot an inverse but analogous position that Robinson no doubt intends to contest: that mixture of extreme differentiation and competitiveness that emerges in some sacralized and instrumentalized assertions of the Holocaust's uniqueness. Here the affective transfer runs in the opposite direction: the potential affect of empathy is drained from all non-Holocaust victims and claimed as the unique property of a particular group whose suffering originated in the past.

Solidarity: From Equation to Differentiation

The two axes of our map—comparison and affect—are at least semi-autonomous; hence, equation cannot be limited to the competitive affect produced in Robinson's analogy or the settlers' provocation. To the contrary, the combination of equation and solidarity is a frequent permutation in the map I am sketching. While the mix of equation and competition concatenates desire and envy into a resistance politics rife with the potential for *ressentiment*, the combination of equation and solidarity produces a form of liberal universalism with multicultural accents. Such a combination can be found, for instance, in André Schwarz-Bart's novels of Jewish and black diasporas, where a litany of shared suffering produces a strong form of empathetic identification. His novel *A Woman Named Solitude* actually articulates that identification by juxtaposing the ruins of the Warsaw Ghetto with those of a Caribbean slave revolt.[36] Even in the highly charged Israeli/Palestinian context, such forms are frequent—and sometimes build on the very same materials deployed by Robinson.

Two of the images that appear in the photo essay distributed by Robinson reappear to different effect, for instance, in the Israeli-British artist Alan Schechner's *The Legacy of Abused Children: From Poland to Palestine*, a 2003 digitally altered photograph and DVD projection. The photo essay concludes by juxtaposing the frequently reproduced photograph of a boy in the Warsaw Ghetto with his hands up—perhaps the most famous image from the Holocaust—with two photographs of Palestinian boys confronted by Israeli soldiers.[37] In Schechner's work, these photographs are no longer simply juxtaposed but set in motion. In the DVD projection, the camera zooms in on the Warsaw photograph to reveal that the boy, whose hands are empty in the Stroop Report image, is holding a photograph (fig. 9). As the camera gets closer, it becomes clear that this is a photograph of a Palestinian boy, who has apparently wet his pants in fear, being carried away by soldiers. As the camera zooms in on this image, we see that the Palestinian boy is himself now holding a photograph: none other than the photo of the Warsaw boy (fig. 10).

In folding the two images into each other, Schechner could easily be described as using a strategy of equation. In his own account of the piece, he confirms this reading but also adds nuance to this discourse by suggesting that it is not an equation of events that interests him, but rather the psychological condition of victimhood. As he writes, "Whilst I have no interest in comparing the two events (The Holocaust and the Intifada) to see which was the most horrific . . . I am interested in exploring the very real links between them. . . . In this project I am using the theory that abused children, unless treated, often become abusers themselves. By applying this to the current situation in Israel/Palestine where both Israelis and Palestinians are victims who replicate and repeat the abuse they have suffered[,] the possibility for constructing solutions to this terrible conflict become[s] more real."[38] While

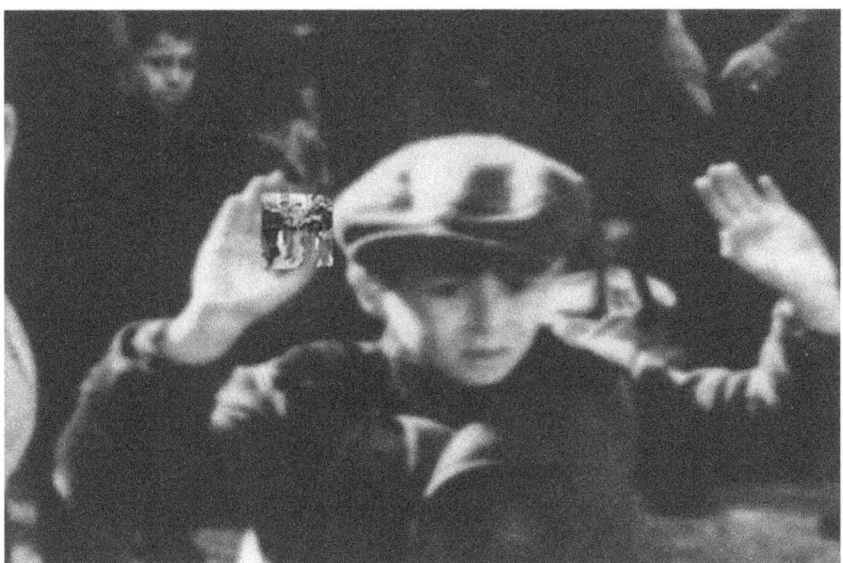

FIGURE 9. Still image from *The Legacy of Abused Children: From Poland to Palestine*, a looped projection by Alan Schechner. Courtesy of the artist.

offering, like the photo essay, a genealogical explanation for the current conflict—that is, one based on a sense that today's horrors are built on yesterday's victimization and passed on from generation to generation—Schechner reverses the affective charge from antagonistic competitiveness to empathy. That is, the photo essay turns past victims into the ancestors of today's perpetrators and tends to blur the distinction between those past victims and today's perpetrators: "The grandchildren of Holocaust survivors . . . are doing to the Palestinians *exactly* what was done to *them*" (my emphasis). Notice not just the blatantly ahistorical "exactly," but also the ambiguous pronoun "them," which erases the distinction between the generations. Schechner, in contrast, might be seen to transfer the Holocaust suffering of the past onto both Israelis and Palestinians, who are portrayed in his comments equally as victims. If that were the case, then the work would seem to imply that solidarity requires a logic of equation, a requirement that stands in tension with the work's obvious desire to reach across differences. While preferable to competitive discourses, this vision would also risk downplaying historical heterogeneity, with uncertain effects for political mobilization and moral vision. In Iris Marion Young's terms, its promotion of "symmetrical reciprocity"

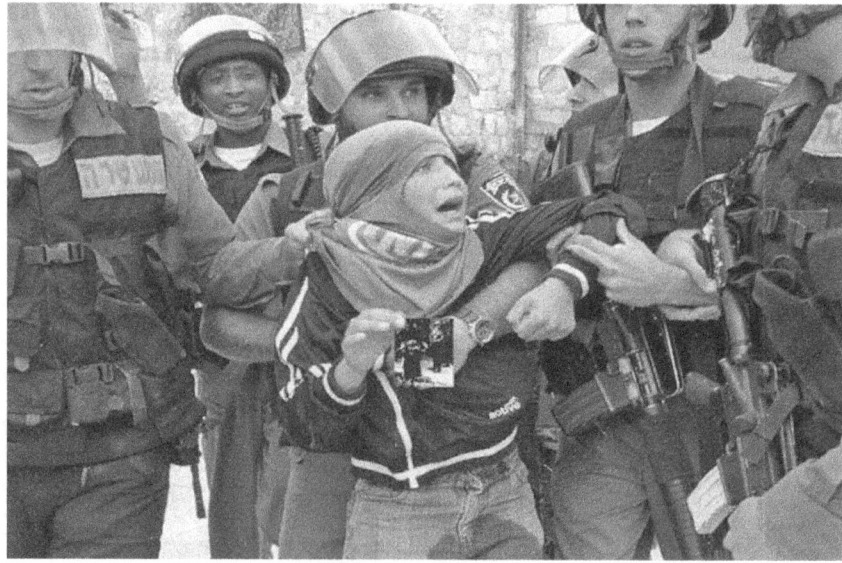

FIGURE 10. Still image from *The Legacy of Abused Children: From Poland to Palestine*, a looped projection by Alan Schechner. Courtesy of the artist.

would project too simplistic a vision of the world that reproduces the failure of recognition it sets out to oppose.[39]

However, if one reading of *The Legacy of Abused Children* places it securely in the equation/solidarity quadrant of the map of memory, a re-reading of the work also suggests another possibility. Through its self-consciously manipulated form, *Legacy* undermines deterministic genealogical explanations that present an endless cycle of reciprocal violence and reproduce notions of two victim peoples. The digitally manipulated photographs ironize "realist" accounts of causality. Hence, even as the endless loop of the video suggests the circular nature of violence, it also subverts all claims to the morally justified originary position of the victim that frequently justifies violence—and certainly does so in the Israeli case, where Holocaust memory has been mobilized for just this purpose.[40] The particular nature of the photographic manipulation is also crucial and leads us back to the question of implication: in placing a photograph in each boy's hand, Schechner transforms an image of absolute innocence and abject powerlessness into one of solidarity, defiance, and constrained agency.[41] Indeed, one might say that Schechner transforms the children from pure victims into victims who can also conceive themselves as implicated subjects. Their suffering is not canceled by being placed in relation to the suffering of the other, but rather recontextualized. If Robinson deploys an appropriative logic, this rereading of *The Legacy of Abused Children* suggests that analogy need not function in this way. By deconstructing the claims to origin that underlie much of the rhetoric of the Israeli/Palestinian conflict (in terms of land claims and suffering), the artwork offers the possibility that analogy can become part of a depropriative and transformative work of memory in which the juxtaposition of different histories reorganizes understanding of both. Ultimately, of course, the implicated subjects—and potential subjects of solidarity—at issue here are not the boys in the images, but the artist himself and many of the artwork's viewers. Indeed, Schechner challenges viewers to consider their own implicated relation to the histories of violence depicted in the piece—and by analogy to other histories of victimized children.

In opening up a potentially differentiated solidarity along the lines illuminated by Du Bois, Schechner's work begins to imagine the outlines of a new conception of justice—one in which transcultural comparison does not simply produce commensurability out of difference, but reconfigures the elements it brings together. Cultural memory and discourses on the past do not themselves constitute institutionalized agencies capable of redressing injustices. However, they can create arenas where injustices are recognized and new frameworks are imagined that are necessary if not sufficient for their redress.

Nancy Fraser, whose work helped us rethink redress for slavery in the previous chapter, characterizes the production of such new frameworks of justice as a two-step process: first, she argues, we need to recognize how many conflicts arise from situations of "abnormal justice," situations similar to what Lyotard calls the "differend," where no common language for articulating wrongs exists; but second, and contrary to Lyotard, we need to attempt to move beyond abnormality to a conception of "reflexive justice." Reflexive justice involves in turn a dual commitment, writes Fraser: "entertaining urgent claims on behalf of the disadvantaged, while also parsing the meta-disagreements that are interlaced with them" (73).

Those who wield the Gaza/Warsaw analogy exemplify the first commitment to hear the urgent claims of the dispossessed, but too often they lack the flexibility of the second commitment to a reflexive parsing of meta-disagreements about what Fraser calls the "who," "what," and "how" of justice. Rather, Robinson and many others on both sides of the Israeli/Palestinian conflict who invoke the Holocaust attempt to reestablish a *known* frame in order to stake a claim in resolving the dispute or obtaining justice. The Nazi genocide is conventionally thought to exceed all "normal" conceptions of justice and to estrange familiar categories such as "guilt," "punishment," and even "the human." Yet, invocations of the genocide in the context of the Israeli/Palestinian conflict tend to reference the Holocaust as the bearer of shared norms of human rights and clear-cut moral distinctions. In scenarios of equation, not only is the past anachronistically rewritten from the vantage point of a very different present (a rewriting that characterizes many acts of memory), but as a result, the present loses its potential as a locus of novelty. While the discourse activates a universalizing framework of recognition through which underrecognized subjects become visible as victims, this framework works not so much to acknowledge difference as to translate difference back into a reduced vision of sameness. That is, regardless of the complexities of the Nazi genocide as a historical phenomenon, the images of the genocide that circulate in the present reduce it—as well as the contemporary cases to which it is analogized—to a stereotypical scenario of good and evil, innocence and absolute power. A discourse based on clear-cut visions of victims and perpetrators or of innocence and guilt evacuates the political sphere of complexity and reduces it to a morality tale. Even in the case of genocide, a seemingly exceptional situation of polarized innocence and guilt, the most thoughtful responses have been forced to reflect on uncomfortable questions of complicity and ambivalence in "the gray zone" first described by Primo Levi. As Susannah Radstone has argued in relation to the photo of the Warsaw Ghetto boy, we need strategies of rereading the image that "wor[k] against the grain of identifications with 'pure' victimhood . . . by undercutting the sense of an absolute distinction between 'good' and 'evil' and by proffering, or even foregrounding potential identifications with perpetration as well as with victimhood."[42] I agree with Radstone's call to go beyond good and evil, but suggest a different route to accomplish that. If a discourse that turns on absolutes of innocence and guilt can only anchor an absolutist, perhaps even apocalyptic politics, then acknowledging implication—as opposed to identifying with either victims or perpetrators—can put the conflict on another footing more amenable to transformation.

Ultimately, the goal of a radical democratic politics of multidirectional memory today is not only to move beyond discourses of equation or hierarchy, but also to displace the reductive, absolutist understanding of the Holocaust as a code for "good and evil" from the center of global memory politics. This task is time- and place-specific and demands a vision of reflexive justice: critical intervention today is necessarily different from what it was, say, in Du Bois's time, when Holocaust memory was not yet as central to moral discourses. Today, even critical invocations of the Holocaust under the sign of equation keep in place Israel's most potent legitimating symbol: a narrative genealogy of ultimate victimization coupled with absolute innocence. The displacement called for today does not entail a removal of Holocaust memory from the public sphere, but rather a decentering of its abstract and reified form. Resources for such a decentering can be found in the archive of multidirectional memory, including not just the work of Kentridge and Schechner but also the example of Marceline Loridan-Ivens, which is the focus of the next chapter. Decentering, in turn, does not mean relativization of the historical facts of the Nazi genocide. The persistence of Holocaust denial suggests that in certain arenas memory of the Holocaust can still play a progressive role. But working through the implications and particularities of genocides needs to be separated from a discursive sacralization of the Holocaust that legitimates a politics of absolutism. Such a sacralization has become so powerful and simultaneously so empty of meaning that it seems to exert a magnetic force even on those who seek to oppose the politics it legitimates.

There is no singular way of approaching the desacralization and decentering with the care and nuance that are necessary, but Schechner's work—along with Kentridge's—suggests that a focus on implication and the implicated subject can offer new avenues for thinking about reflexive justice and nonabsolutist morality. To be sure, Schechner's depiction of the two boys as equally implicated in each other's suffering is, once again, too symmetrical if read literally: the chronological and geographical distances that separate them make a "realist" notion of implication untenable, even at the "metaphysical" level of guilt posited by Jaspers. Yet, we can also consider that this depiction is meant as an expression of the artist's solidarity with both histories offered from a position of complex implication. Schechner is, after all, a Jewish artist who earlier in his life emigrated to Israel and joined the Israeli army. His ongoing—often provocative—engagement with Jewish suffering in the Holocaust derives from his disenchantment with Holocaust memory's role in legitimating Israeli domination.[43] *The Legacy of Abused Children* responds to Schechner's own implicated role in that history of domination as a member of the Israeli army, but it does not simply ironize Holocaust memory, as some of his other works do. Instead, it builds a case for differentiated solidarity from a position of complex, mutual implication. The artist, through his digitally manipulated avatars, seeks in this work to "hold" both histories together: simultaneously to recognize the legitimate claims to recognition that victims of the Holocaust and the Nakba make and to expose the manipulation of Holocaust memory that has been used to justify (or, as in the photo essay discussed above, critique) the oppression of the Palestinians. The reflexivity that we find in both Schechner and Kentridge—the ways that they place themselves figuratively and literally in the frame—reaches out toward the mode of justice theorized by Fraser: one in which incommensurability and complexity are acknowledged without sacrificing the need for forthright critique of injustice.

Conclusion: Perpetration, Vulnerability, Perpetuation

The famous picture of the Warsaw Ghetto boy has often functioned to provide a sentimental identification with the child, the absolute figure of victimization and vulnerability. As Radstone points out, however, the original image from the Stroop Report also offers another position for identification: that of the Nazi perpetrator, who faces the camera and is easily visible in Schechner's video loop. Prominent critical Jewish voices on Israel/Palestine have in recent times used both positions—the position of vulnerability and that of perpetration—to offer counternarratives to the ongoing dispossession of Palestinians. While Schechner's work does not rule out such strategies, I have suggested that its staging of complex implication provides a third avenue for critique consonant with the perspective I lay out in this book. In the remainder of this chapter, I put aside the question of multidirectional memory as it manifest itself in artistic projects like those of Schechner and Kentridge and return to the problem of implication in order to rethink the approaches of two influential theorists working on Israel/Palestine.

In confronting "the transformation of Palestine into Israel," the Israeli theorist and curator Ariella Azoulay—now based in the US—takes up the challenge offered by Radstone to grapple with the position of the perpetrator. She describes the foundation of the State of Israel as a scenario in which "dispossession and the creation of new subjects of oppression were accompanied by the shaping of other subjects as perpetrators."[44] Azoulay writes incisively of the need to think perpetration and victimization together and to undo the history of dispossession by "[exercising] the right not to be perpetrators": "The formation of a class of victims went with the formation of a class of perpetrators. . . . Isolating victims and their vulnerability is therefore problematic, not because it is the history of others that we are not allowed to narrate so as to give a voice to the oppressed but because the oppressed do not have a history apart from our own—apart from my own" (n.p.). This desire to work through the co-creation of victims and perpetrators is crucial, but Azoulay's argument loses its sharpness when she turns to the legacies of those founding dispossessions: "In this history, we citizens—and I—are perpetrators, descendants and heirs of perpetrators; in this history, we—and I—were made perpetrators, inherited, naturalized, and transmitted modes of perpetration" (n.p.). In Azoulay's discussion, "perpetrators" and "descendants and heirs of perpetrators" are identical, and they are opposed in binary fashion to victims. In making this move, we could say that Azoulay collapses Jaspers's notions of "criminal guilt" (which refers uniquely to active, individual perpetrators) and "political guilt" (which encompasses all citizens). This slippage between perpetrators and their descendants is clearly deliberate—an admirable attempt to take on the burden of responsibility for the foundational and ongoing crimes of one's polity. In the case of Israel, which has near-universal conscription, it is also the case that a large number of citizens will have taken part in quite direct forms of perpetration against civilians or have participated in the everyday work of occupation.

But is the translation of citizens into perpetrators—a new iteration of the collective guilt thesis that Jaspers, Arendt, and others set themselves against in the post–National Socialist period—the best way to think about the legacies of nation-state formation in a settler colonial context? Even if the occupation and the denial of the right to return to Palestinians carry forward the trauma of the Nakba—the ongoing Palestinian catastrophe out of which Israel was born—conceptualizing citizens as perpetrators strikes me as the wrong way to diagnose the situation; it turns a political question into a legal case and implies the need for prosecution instead of transformation.[45] I would argue, in contrast, that the descendants of perpetrators are not perpetrators—at least, not of the same deeds as their ancestors—but rather implicated subjects who bear a real, although different, responsibility distinct from that of those who came before them. In the case of Israel and other settler colonial societies, the better term may be "beneficiaries," but "beneficiary" does not capture equally well all the subjects of societies that have perpetrated extreme violence—hence the need for a more capacious notion of implication that extends beyond the material realm into that of cultural and symbolic politics and calls for various forms of working through the past.[46] The responsibility of such heirs may be, precisely, to stop perpetuating and instead undo the deeds of their ancestors, but the need for such an undoing—decolonization, considered broadly—implies neither that the implicated subjects are guilty of the original crimes, nor, inversely, that their acts of decolonization could ever exonerate the perpetrators who committed the original deeds (an additional risk, it seems to me, of collapsing the generations). The deeds of perpetrators and those who come after them cannot be considered according to the same criteria of judgment or made subject to the same forms of remediation; they derive from overlapping but relatively autonomous scenarios. Confusing perpetrators with their descendants—beneficiaries and perpetuators of the system, or even perpetrators of new deeds, though they may be—muddies the boundaries between the legal, moral, and political realms. Perpetrators should be held responsible—in whatever fashion—for their deeds;

implicated descendants, as Iris Marion Young might say, have a future-oriented responsibility to repair and remake the world their ancestors created and from which they (may) continue to benefit (see Young's *Responsibility for Justice*).

This distinction between perpetrators and implicated subjects becomes even more pronounced, of course, when we consider the diasporic Jewish subjects who are my primary concern in this chapter. In that case, the position of perpetrator loses the plausibility and critical edge it still retains in Azoulay's discussion of Israel proper and thus obscures more than it illuminates. Yet, many diasporic subjects are surely perpetuators in both material and ideological ways that deserve interrogation and critique.

The shift from perpetrators toward implicated subjects understood as perpetuators is also illuminating when we start from the other side: from the question of vulnerability. The most prominent theorist working through the category of vulnerability in recent years has been Judith Butler. In a series of texts over the last decade, Butler—whose work has helped frame my approach to the Gaza/Warsaw analogy—has sought to "reimagin[e] the possibility of community on the basis of vulnerability and loss."[47] "Each of us," she writes, "is constituted politically by virtue of the social vulnerability of our bodies. . . . Loss and vulnerability seem to follow from our being socially constituted bodies, attached to others, at risk of losing those attachments, exposed to others, at risk of violence by virtue of that exposure" (*Precarious Life* 20). Theorizing from the site of loss, as Butler does, makes vulnerability and precariousness the bases for a critique of violence and the construction of solidarity—a strategy she uses in her frequent interventions into the question of Palestine. But what if our relation to others is characterized by excess in addition to loss? By a capacity to wound as well as a fundamental vulnerability? Might this starting point provide an alternative perspective on the uneven distribution of precarity that concerns Butler and ought to concern us all?

In recent writings and public appearances, Butler has been one of the most visible Jewish-American critics of Israel as well as an unofficial spokesperson for BDS in the US.[48] Her engagement with the question of Palestine from a diasporic position strikes me, however, as better explained through the concepts of implication and perpetuation than through the concepts of vulnerability and precariousness that she has been elaborating in recent writings. For instance, in *Parting Ways*, Butler's most significant scholarly contribution to the debate about Israel/Palestine, she writes that if we are "to depart from [the] communitarian moorings" that undergird the project of political Zionism, we also need "to depart from a concern only with the vulnerability and fate of the Jewish people" (27). Butler's formulation implies the need to recognize the vulnerability of Palestinians (and others) alongside that of Jews—certainly a necessary project and one that resonates with Schechner's multidirectional artwork. But it can also be read against the grain as a call to explore Zionism from the perspective of indirect responsibility and implication rather than vulnerability. Indeed, given the extent to which support for Israel among Jews worldwide is often premised on fears for the state's presumed vulnerability, taking precarity as a starting point strikes me as at risk of reinforcing Zionist ideology.

Although she does not use the term, it seems to me that Butler does in fact approach the conflict as an implicated subject, and to my mind, this is one of the most important features of her approach: rather than mobilizing a critique uniquely on universal, "objective" grounds, she also attempts to work through her subjective formation as a Jew in order to break with those aspects of Jewishness that might support an ethnically absolutist ideology. She draws on the resources of Jewish (as well as Palestinian and other) philosophy, art, and political theory in order to de-link Jewishness and Zionism—the project that Levitzky and Weyl do not manage to accomplish in the *Post* op-ed with which I opened this chapter. In contrast to those "lifelong Zionists" who act out of love for the state, Butler seeks to foster a non-Zionist, diasporic Jewishness that is inseparable from the conditions of Palestinian life and death and that opens onto a binational, post-Zionist future. Butler's point is not that a critique of political Zionism must come from an attempt to work through the formation of Jewish subjects or can only come from such an attempt, but the fact that she pursues her critique via this path demonstrates a recognition of the philosopher and activist as implicated subject. In her writings on Israel/Palestine, it seems to me, her wager has been that working from and through implication carries moral weight and opens up political possibilities.

Bruce Robbins's film *Some of My Best Friends Are Zionists* (2013) offers similar insights.[49] *Some of My Best Friends* consists of interviews by the prominent critic and theorist Robbins with Jewish-American intellectuals (including Butler) about how they came to change their minds about Israel and play a more critical role in the American Jewish community. The film's interviews make palpable both the production of implication—in the stories of how Jewish Americans are inculcated into unquestioning support for Israel—and the recognition that such implication produces, in turn, long-distance responsibility.[50] Not all the interviewees in Robbins's film have the visibility of Butler or of the playwright Tony Kushner, who is also featured, but they have all decided to confront their uncomfortable implication as diaspora subjects in a state project of occupation that interpellates them as Jews and that they have come to see as unjust.

The attention to one's own position as implicated subject fostered by Butler and Robbins can provoke more robust and politically efficacious forms of self-reflection than a sole focus on vulnerability and perpetration, which—at least in the case of Israel/Palestine—can feed the dynamics of violent conflict. Such attention serves to caution us against self-righteousness and encourage us to acknowledge how we are caught up in the very policies we oppose. For Butler and Robbins, as for me, our implication as Jewish diaspora subjects needs to be thought alongside our equally consequential position as citizens of the US. We are implicated not just because Israeli law and propaganda claim to speak for us as Jews, but also because our own country helps perpetuate the occupation through billions of dollars of military aid and other forms of material and ideological support to which we inevitably contribute. We are perpetuators: citizens and taxpayers who bear political responsibility for our nation's foreign policy—and not just in the case of Israel. Implication is, in that sense, multidirectional: it does not remain limited to one set of entanglements but encompasses a range of powers and interests that frame our actions. Recognizing one's position as an unwilling perpetuator of injustice does not necessarily result in a radical critique of that injustice—as the example of Levitzky and Weyl suggests. Yet such recognition represents a necessary, if not sufficient, condition for a disengagement from implication and the construction of solidarity with those who suffer directly from our indirect entanglements. The two chapters of the next section focus especially on the nature of solidarity in transnational contexts marked by crosscutting histories and responsibilities.

PART III

Long-Distance Solidarity

5

Under the Sign of Suitcases
The Holocaust Internationalism of Marceline Loridan-Ivens

Solidarity from Afar: *Loin du Vietnam*

In 1967, SLON, a collective of prominent Paris-based filmmakers led by the enigmatic Chris Marker, released *Loin du Vietnam* (*Far from Vietnam*), an omnibus indictment of the American war in Vietnam and a declaration of support for the people of that former French colony.[1] The film opens with a sequence of three brief scenes: we watch as soldiers on an American aircraft carrier prepare bombers for deployment; then we see Vietnamese soldiers advance stealthily through tall grass; and, finally, Fidel Castro and his comrades walk calmly across hilly terrain in Cuba. Over this sequence of shots we hear the voice of Maurice Garrel describe the stakes of the war in terms that echo and reinforce the images—a war of the rich against the poor, a war to prove the viability of world revolution. Finally, just as Castro walks out of the frame, the voice-over concludes and the credit sequence begins. In place of the image of Castro, a long list of names, including Alain Resnais, Agnès Varda, Joris Ivens, Claude Lelouch, Jean-Luc Godard, and—a little further down—Marceline Loridan, appears in simple white lettering on a black background, followed by a series of intertitles. The intertitles state that the filmmakers "made this film during the course of 1967 / to affirm, by the exercise of their profession, their solidarity with the Vietnamese people in their struggle against aggression." The remainder of the two-hour-long film consists, primarily, of documentary footage taken by collective members in Europe, North America, and Indochina, but it also mixes in newsreel footage and staged fictional scenes.

As the film's preamble suggests, the filmmakers intend the concept of solidarity to hold together the heterogeneous materials out of which they have fashioned *Loin du Vietnam*.[2] Yet, the question of solidarity in *Loin du Vietnam* is not an easy one, for as the title indicates, this is also a film about distance.[3] The filmmakers were well aware of the complexities of making a solidarity film about a war that remained, for most of them, far away. As the disappearing image of Castro in the opening moments might suggest, their work as filmmakers took place outside the "frame" of the revolutionary struggles in Vietnam (but also Cuba and elsewhere) that they sought to depict.[4] One of the most memorable sequences of the film, a monologue by Jean-Luc Godard, emphasizes the problem of distance and addresses it through a characteristic self-reflexivity. Declaring that, since he could not obtain a visa, he decided to stay in Paris, Godard turns the camera on himself. His somewhat rambling monologue, which evokes both the distance of Vietnam and his desire to let "Vietnam invade us," is accompanied, for the most part, with shots of him operating his large American Marshall film camera, although these are also intercut with shots of a Vietnamese soldier and strikes in France, as well as with excerpts from Godard's own *La Chinoise* (also from 1967).[5]

An hour later, as the film's final sequence turns outward, it seeks to produce a similar self-reflexivity in its hoped-for European audience. The concluding voice-over monologue addresses spectators directly: "In a few minutes this film is going to end. You will leave this room and many of you will go out into a world without war. It is also our world and we know how easy it is to forget certain realities. We are far from Vietnam, and the Vietnam of our emotions and our indignation is sometimes as far from the true Vietnam as indifference would be. We live in a society that has gone far in the art of hiding its own goals . . . and especially its own violence." Accompanying these words are images of a burning Vietnamese village and marching Vietnamese soldiers wearing branches and leaves as camouflage that alternate with peaceful urban street scenes from France and the US. At the level of both words and images—as well as between words and images—the film dialectically juxtaposes "here" and "there," imperialist violence and bourgeois everyday life, in order to provoke its audience into a realization about the invisible but material interconnections between a real war and a phony peace that constitute that audience's implication in a far-off war. To declare oneself "far from Vietnam" in this sense is to approximate the form of implicated nonidentification that motivates the statement "We are not Trayvon Martin."

The question of solidarity and distance was already articulated during the film's production. Although some of the filmmakers remained, like Godard, at home, others did venture to the site of the war. Marker sent two of the filmmakers to Hanoi to request permission to film in North Vietnam. The note they brought with them already thematized the audacity of the project as a problem of solidarity at a distance:

> Words of friendship and solidarity, however sincere they may be, are only words. . . . Saying "solidarity" from afar and without risk, may also be a convenient way of easing one's conscience. Our solidarity occurs in towns that no one bombs, in lives that no one menaces. What does this mean? . . . Where is our place? To answer these questions, we have undertaken to make a film. It is a response that is neither praiseworthy nor heroic, but which has the sole motive of being tangible, within our means and within our limitations. It is with our work, it is within the context of our profession, that we want to bring a little life to this word "solidarity."[6]

In asking "Where is our place?" and attempting to answer through the creation of a film dedicated to solidarity at a distance, the filmmakers both reflect on the problem of their own implication in the war and seek to turn that problem, via a collective project, into an occasion for intervention. Instead of trying to speak *for* the Vietnamese, they seek to speak *with* those Europeans who share their world and who think they occupy a "world without war," but in whose name wars of counterinsurgency are being waged. Solidarity here does not mean simple identity of position or cause; it refers instead to attempts to incite change in and from a place that is not immediately connected to the site of conflict, but rather is connected to it through real social and political mediations. The film offers a version of what I called differentiated solidarity in the previous chapter, but it does so primarily through the thematization of difference as distance: the distance between metropolitan and (anti)colonial locations.

A product—and catalyst—of the cultural-political ferment of the 1960s, *Loin du Vietnam* remains a touchstone of engaged cinema that helps focus questions about the possibility of solidarity in the face of the paradoxical need to acknowledge both implication (i.e., political-economic connection) and distance. Linking the metropolitan centers to scenes of anti-imperialist struggle, the film uses the visual and verbal means of cinema to reveal to citizens of the global center how they are "socially connected," to use Iris Marion

Young's term, to events far from Paris and New York. In doing so, it raises the central dilemmas of this section of the book: whether and how recognition of implication, complicity, and privilege can be transformed into active forms of resistance to structures of violence and exploitation. In other words, can implicated subjects become political subjects? The answer the filmmakers provide allies them with a significant current of twentieth-century political activity: internationalism. As the note to the North Vietnamese regime makes clear, the filmmakers do not simply employ the language of solidarity, but a language of internationalist solidarity that recognizes distance and difference but seeks to minimize their potentially deleterious effects.[7] Inspired by overlapping socialist and anti-imperialist internationalisms, *Loin du Vietnam* (along with the other works of the SLON collective) constitutes a material instance of—and as we will see in the next chapter, has become an intertextual reference point for—solidarity crafted from a position of implication, a position marked by both distance and proximity.

In the two chapters that make up this part of the book, I explore a pair of very different politically engaged filmmakers whose work intersects with *Loin du Vietnam* and twentieth-century histories of internationalism: Marceline Loridan-Ivens and Hito Steyerl. Indeed, it was Loridan-Ivens, the subject of this chapter, who—together with her partner Joris Ivens, a well-known Dutch communist documentarian—carried the SLON collective's note to the North Vietnamese leadership and shot much of the Vietnam footage included in the film; Loridan-Ivens also testified at the Russell International War Crimes Tribunal about what she had witnessed in Vietnam.[8] Loridan-Ivens, who died in 2018 at the age of 90, was a French Jewish survivor of Auschwitz who went on to experience firsthand both the emancipatory and destructive possibilities of the moment of revolutionary struggle when she took up anticolonial and Third World causes. Steyerl, the subject of the next chapter, is a German artist and theorist born in 1966. Also attuned to histories of colonial and genocidal violence and in dialogue with the avant-garde aesthetics of *Loin du Vietnam*, Steyerl picks up the history of internationalism where Loridan-Ivens leaves off: while Loridan-Ivens worked in some of the sites of revolutionary ferment in the 1960s and 1970s, Steyerl starts from the conviction that we live in a postrevolutionary age in which "the myth of the leftist hero [has] come crumbling down."[9] The artistic practices of Loridan-Ivens and Steyerl do not offer us a "pure" internationalism cleansed of its contradictions and less attractive legacies; rather, they teach us about the possibilities and problems created by implicated subjects who seek to become political actors. Despite their radically different biographies and aesthetic projects, they provide us with examples and lessons that enable us to think about what internationalism can be in a moment defined by both intensified globalization and resurgent nationalism.

In the work of Loridan-Ivens and Steyerl, we find different degrees of what I will call "affirmative" and "critical" internationalisms. Like *Loin du Vietnam*, affirmative internationalism seeks to construct lines of solidarity across national borders in order to combat transnational capital and state-sponsored imperial projects. Critical internationalism engages with transnational configurations of power without retreating into nationalist or localist frameworks, but also without committing to particular internationalist projects. In a rough sense, Loridan-Ivens's work in the 1960s and 1970s adheres to the affirmative model of socialist and anti-imperialist internationalism, while Steyerl's work in the first decade of the twenty-first century consists of a postrevolutionary, critical internationalism. Yet, experiences of loss and betrayal complicate the aesthetic-political projects of both filmmakers. Loridan-Ivens's affirmative approach is tempered and rendered more complex and critical by the personal experience of trauma, the recognition of political error, and the changing political landscape during her lifetime. Inversely, Steyerl's critical engagement with cross-border politics derives from the mourning of and fidelity to a close friend who gave her life in a late version of "affirmative" socialist internationalism; this fidelity transforms Steyerl into a new kind of internationalist subject who today finds herself in turn occupying a transformed political conjuncture. Exploring the way affirmative and critical internationalisms jostle with each other in the work of these two figures provides purchase on the movement from recognition of implication to the construction of solidarity and the development of new models of political subjectivity.

In the present chapter, I begin by briefly exploring varieties of internationalism and focus in particular on the versions relevant to both Loridan-Ivens and Steyerl: socialist and anti-imperialist internationalism and the discourse of human rights. As a Holocaust survivor who was active in anticolonial causes, Loridan-Ivens's trajectory cuts across these very different models of cross-border solidarity. In the 1960s, when Loridan-Ivens first bore witness publicly to her deportation to Auschwitz and moved in the circles that led her to support Algerian and Vietnamese independence struggles, the dominant progressive discourse was that of the socialist and anti-imperialist internationalism we have seen exemplified in *Loin du Vietnam*.[10] In the wake of the 1960s, however, these movements entered into crisis, even if, as we will see especially in the next chapter, committed adherents remain. As anti-imperialist internationalism declined, recent decades witnessed the dramatic rise of discourses and practices of human rights. In addition, the promulgation of international human rights norms has paralleled, and become closely allied with, the globalization of Holocaust memory, as scholars such as Daniel Levy and Natan Sznaider argue.[11]

While the human rights imperative is not irrelevant to Loridan-Ivens's story, my focus here is especially on the moment just before its rise to hegemony, when other forms of internationalism offered nation-transcending progressive visions. A look at the period before the globalization of Holocaust consciousness in the 1990s suggests a conception of transnational memory that looks quite different from the cosmopolitan memory oriented around human rights described by Levy and Sznaider. Indeed, the testimony of Loridan-Ivens in Jean Rouch and Edgar Morin's 1961 film *Chronique d'un été* (*Chronicle of a Summer*) served in my previous book as the inspiration for the concept of multidirectional memory, which was meant as an alternative to Levy and Sznaider's account.[12] Here I follow Loridan-Ivens's trajectory beyond Rouch and Morin's film as she becomes a filmmaker and later memoirist in her own right. Leaving behind—without fully abandoning—the position of victim of genocide, Loridan-Ivens takes on new identities as internationalist and implicated witness. Considered holistically, her story reveals an unexpected constellation of trauma and long-distance solidarity that remains singular, but is also suggestive for thinking responsibility in light of the successes and failures of movements for decolonization and human rights. Her story continues to speak to the present.

Internationalisms: Socialism, Anti-Imperialism, Human Rights

Although Jeremy Bentham coined the term "international" in 1780, the concept of "internationalism" started to take off in the mid-nineteenth century as material conditions—in economics, technology, and communications—created an increasingly interconnected world.[13] Since then, diverse internationalisms have offered competing political visions of the political space opened up by the new term and the conditions to which it referred. Initially—and still predominantly—a concept used in the North Atlantic world, alternative internationalisms derived from the colonized world and the Global South have also circulated.[14] In the "minimal and neutral" definition offered by Perry Anderson in a useful historical survey, the term "internationalism" "may be applied to any outlook, or practice, that tends to transcend the nation towards a wider community, of which nations continue to form the principal units."[15] Because the imagined community of the nation often constitutes a break on recognition of broader allegiances and responsibilities, a political outlook or practice that transcends the nation's borders while still recognizing their continuing force often aligns with a critique of implication. Although such a critique also concerns injustices that remain domestic, political responsibility in the modern world quickly overruns the borders of the nation; thus, some form of internationalism is intrinsic to the self-conscious politicization of implicated subjects. Indeed, in the twentieth century, internationalism was one of the dominant modes of solidarity that sought to transform implication into its opposite: resistance to accommodation with power.

Although internationalism in Anderson's definition encompasses a broad range of movements, two strands are most relevant to the discussion in this chapter and the next. The form of internationalism at stake in *Loin du Vietnam*—as well as in the case that will make up the focus of this chapter—grows out of socialist internationalism, progressive internationalism's best-known and most contested variant. Since the establishment of the First International in the mid-nineteenth century, various forms of socialist internationalism have offered visions of solidarity linked to revolutionary struggles against imperialism and globalized capitalism. Such internationalism arose from the perception of shared interests among workers of all nations faced with exploitation by an internationally active capitalist system. If capital tended toward globalization, resistance to its regime required a similar reach. Yet, as Anderson argues, the institutionalization of internationalism in the Soviet Union and the triumph of Stalinism ironically entailed that "the activities of the Third International were utterly subordinated to the interests of the Soviet state, as Stalin interpreted them": "With its mixture of heroism and cynicism, selfless solidarity and murderous terror, this was internationalism perfected and perverted as never before" (15). The capture of internationalism by the Stalinist state meant that long before the Soviet Union's collapse and the end of actually existing socialism in most of the world, that tradition had lost much of its traction, even as the problems it confronted continued to exist. Still, despite the "deformed" and "perverted" form of internationalism associated with the Soviet Union, internationalist visions have continued to inspire many people around the world to join in struggles for justice.

For the collective that produced *Loin du Vietnam*, socialist internationalism was inseparable from anti-imperialist internationalism. As Kristin Ross points out, SLON originally screened *Loin du Vietnam* at the Rhodiaceta factory, site of a strike that Marker had also been involved in filming. Footage from the strike is even incorporated into the Vietnam film in the Godard sequence. At the same time that they highlighted their distance from Vietnam, the filmmakers—and other elements of the French left at the time—also imagined a seamless overlap between far-flung struggles, what Ross describes as "a passage from 'Vietnamese fighter' directly to 'French worker'" (89). Despite the difficulties of sustaining belief in such a direct link today, anti-imperialist movements constitute one of the key sites where internationalist visions have persisted, even after the high-water mark of the era of decolonization in the 1960s.

Another, very different internationalism began its rise just as the anti-imperialist project of decolonization lost its luster in the 1970s: international human rights. Although already announced decades earlier with the Universal Declaration of 1948, the vision of international human rights only became an effective, widespread movement during the course of the 1970s, as Samuel Moyn has argued in his influential and controversial book *The Last Utopia: Human Rights in History*. In order to buttress this periodization, Moyn draws a clear line between earlier anti-imperialist internationalism and the new culture of human rights. He argues that decolonization struggles focused on "collective liberation, not human rights": "Insofar as anticolonialism gazed beyond the state, it was in the name of alternative internationalisms, in a spirit very different from that of contemporary human rights."[16] Conversely, the "contemporary reinvention [of the doctrine of rights] as 'human rights' is best understood as following from its survival in a difficult struggle against internationalist rivals old and new" (14). In other words, it is the "collapse of other, prior utopias"—such as socialist and anti-imperialist internationalisms—that offers the "best general explanation for the origins" of the social movement for human rights (8). Even if one contests Moyn's argument about the very recent origins of human rights, as many have, two convincing aspects of his argument remain relevant here: that a significant difference exists between decolonization and international human rights (with the first focused on national liberation and the second dedicated to relativizing nation-state sovereignty); and that the human rights regime experiences a dramatic takeoff beginning in the 1970s.[17]

Human rights discourse has two features that are particularly salient for an exploration of the implicated subject: the way it incorporates the importance of memory into its theory and practice, and the way it provides a framework for thinking about solidarity across social and geographical borders. In *Human Rights and Memory*, the sociologists Daniel Levy and Natan Sznaider address both of these dimensions of the current discourse and argue for the crucial role that mediations of the past play in the contemporary rise of internationalist sentiment. For Levy and Sznaider, historical memories—which they define as "shared understandings and responsibilities for the significance the past has for the present concerns of a community"—provide an "analytic prism" for examining the link between human rights and sovereignty.[18] They argue that "the global proliferation of human rights norms is driven by the public and frequently ritualistic attention to memories of their persistent violations." Levy and Sznaider do not argue that nation-states have become irrelevant because of these transformations, but they suggest that the legitimacy of national sovereignty claims now necessarily passes through reference to a "global cultural 'memory imperative'" framed by human rights (4). Remembrance of suffering becomes a vehicle for the articulation of new political norms that elevate human rights while confronting national sovereignty with "a 'universalistic minimum' involving a number of substantive norms that must be upheld at all costs" (7).

For the two sociologists, the globalization of a "cosmopolitan" Holocaust memory plays a particularly significant role in the instantiation of human rights norms.[19] In earlier work, they argued that in the twenty-first century "memories of the Holocaust facilitate the formation of transnational memory cultures, which in turn, have the potential to become the cultural foundation for human rights politics."[20] The link between Holocaust memory, cosmopolitanism, and human rights has "normative and institutional" consequences and has been facilitated by the "decontextualization" of the Nazi genocide and its reconfiguration as an "abstract" symbol of "good and evil" ("Memory Unbound" 93, 102). Part of the work of this chapter will be to explore what a transnational—or internationalist—Holocaust memory looked like before the normative, institutional form of human rights became dominant.

As the example of the globalization of Holocaust memory illustrates, human rights discourse—while founded on a connection to events historically distant—forges in turn relations between geographically separated subjects. In breaking the hegemony of the nation, Levy and Sznaider argue, "the language of human rights provides us with a framework to begin to understand why pictures of strangers being beaten and tortured by other strangers concern us": it facilitates "identification with distant others" (*Human Rights* 2, 9). These new, more global forms of identification are not completely different from those prevalent in the age of nationalism, but national identity and human rights consciousness do differ in at least two significant ways, according to Levy and Sznaider's account. In the age of nationalism, a collective that imagined itself as homogeneous looked back at its ancestors' heroic deeds in order to produce and stabilize its identity. In the age of international human rights, in contrast, a cross-border identification with the suffering of others and a self-critical relation to one's own nation helps usher in a new cosmopolitan image of society (*Human Rights* 23).

The self-critical moral and ethical stance of human rights discourse clearly contributes to the possibility of thinking implication and conceptualizing the implicated subject. Yet the framework of human rights and memory identified by Levy and Sznaider also risks depoliticizing—and thus reproducing—the relations of power that produce human rights violations in the first place. The turn from anticolonial movements (which were not always invested in theory or practice in individual rights) to a human rights consensus entails both gains and losses: the respect for individual lives promoted by international human rights regimes has come at the cost of the more radical, structurally transformative visions of the anti-imperialist struggles of the 1960s. And, as Moyn has also argued, the takeoff of the human rights framework has coexisted with skyrocketing economic inequality and a deprioritization of social rights.[21] Bruce Robbins would add that the human rights framework described by Levy and Sznaider relies largely on the figure of the "disinterested spectator" and avoids confronting causal relations with distant others such as those made available by the "discourse of the beneficiary"—or indeed the concept of implication.[22]

One item on the agenda of a politicized understanding of implication would then be the need to work through these socialist, anti-imperialist, and human rights visions of internationalist solidarity and action: to assess their strengths and weaknesses, the conceptual and practical resources they offer, and the reasons for their ascent and decline in order to create new visions of cross-border politics. The figures who interest me in this section—Loridan-Ivens and Steyerl—emerge out of this history of shifting internationalist allegiances. But my interest in them is not primarily historical. Rather, I want to explore how the trajectories of their work and lives reveal the impasses of internationalisms past and make visible the outlines of new internationalisms.

Rethinking the "Era of the Witness"

Born Marceline Rozenberg in France in 1928 to Polish-Jewish immigrant parents, Marceline Loridan-Ivens (also known as Marceline Loridan or simply Marceline) was deported to the Nazi camps as a teenager along with her father.[23] After returning home alone, she entered the "era of the witness" in 1961—an epochal year for Holocaust memory and testimony—when she told her story in public for the first time on film.[24] In the fifty years since then she has been a globe-traversing, politically engaged documentarian, a septuagenarian autobiographical feature filmmaker, a memoirist, and a talking-head representative of what "being Jewish in France" means. Loridan-Ivens's life and work exemplify what the feminist philosopher María Lugones calls "'world'-travelling": "Through travelling to other people's 'worlds' we discover that there are 'worlds' in which those who are the victims of arrogant perception are really subjects, lively beings, resistors, constructors of visions, even though in the mainstream construction they are animated only by the arrogant perceiver and are pliable, foldable, file-awayable, classifiable."[25] Characterized by an "openness to surprise" and set against forms of domination that rely on the separation of worlds or on imperial conquest, Lugones's notion of "world"-traveling resonates with Loridan-Ivens's testimonial project, which encompasses both her experiences as a survivor of Auschwitz and the decolonizing contexts of Algeria and Vietnam in which she went on to produce films.[26]

Following the trajectory of Loridan-Ivens's life and work helps us recalibrate our understanding of the relation between the past and present of Holocaust memory and prompts us to think differently about the ethics and politics of remembrance at a moment of generational transition. The multifarious testimonies of Marceline Loridan-Ivens produce what I call a "Holocaust internationalism" that has rarely been glimpsed, much less taken seriously, by scholars of the genocide. Inflected by both anticolonial and communist internationalism, and sensitive to the ongoing legacies of trauma, the "world"-traveling Holocaust internationalism of Loridan-Ivens offers an untimely, politicized form of remembrance that represents an alternative to both the sacralization and sentimentalization of the Holocaust's uniqueness and the liberal cosmopolitanism of human rights that have dominated memory culture in recent decades.

Loridan-Ivens's story was also at the origins of my concept of multidirectional memory. While in the midst of thinking about the comparative and transnational movements of memory, I discovered her testimony in the 1961 cinema verité experiment *Chronique d'un été* (*Chronicle of a Summer*), an important work in film history and a clear precursor to Claude Lanzmann's *Shoah*, but at that time little known by scholars of Holocaust testimony.[27] With the filming of *Chronicle of a Summer*, Jean Rouch and Edgar Morin set out to document everyday life in Paris in the summer of 1960 through direct interviews with a range of Parisians—students, workers, political activists, and ordinary men and women—who were asked "Are you happy?" by interviewers the filmmakers sent out into the streets. 1960 was a potentially tumultuous moment in France, as decolonization was rapidly remaking the political order. It was a time of violent transition in the Congo and a tense moment in the already six-year-old Algerian War of Independence. Although these events are briefly mentioned or hinted at in the film, fairly little of this dramatic political context actually made it into the film's final cut—quite deliberately, but also quite understandably, given the massive state censorship targeting discussion of the Algerian conflict.[28]

Instead, the surprising center of *Chronicle of a Summer* turns out to be the testimony of Marceline Loridan, as she was then known, seen early in the film as one of Rouch and Morin's street interviewers and only later revealed as a survivor of Auschwitz in a powerful scene where the camera silently tracks down to her tattooed arm. Rouch and Morin subsequently film the testimony of Marceline in two linked sequences, one in which she walks through the Place de la Concorde and another in which she enters the old market building Les Halles.[29] In these scenes she bears witness in a condensed testimony to her deportation to the camps as a young teenager along with her father, scenes of violence in the camps, and her painful return to her surviving family—without her father—after liberation.[30] Marceline's passage through the streets, her absent-minded humming of a song of the French resistance, and her clearly affected demeanor as we seem to "overhear" her story make this a powerful example of testimony's site-specific, embodied force that appears to offer itself to us in its "immediacy."

Yet, the many factors that make Marceline's testimony important and powerful all involve processes of mediation.[31] First, the testimony marks an important stage in film history, because its very recording relies on innovations in camera and sound technology that allow Rouch and Morin to capture the testimony in a public space—with the use of a lightweight and mobile camera—while also preserving the intimacy of her address, through a portable microphone and Nagra recorder that the witness carried with her while strolling through Paris. As Loridan put it in a 1961 interview, "The rhythm of my steps led me to share those memories."[32] In other words, far from "abstracting" Marceline's testimony, new possibilities of technological mediation enable a form of testimony harmonized with the movements of the body in public and in proximity to the grain of the voice.

In addition, this medium-specific event mediates and is mediated by state politics. From the perspective of the history of Holocaust memory, Marceline's testimony could not have come at a more significant time. Filmed in the year that Israeli agents arrested Adolf Eichmann and released in the year that survivor testimony at Eichmann's trial in Jerusalem would permanently change our understanding of the Nazi genocide and help usher in what Annette Wieviorka has called the "era of the witness," Marceline's presence in *Chronicle of a Summer* helps provide an alternative genealogy of Holocaust testimony and cultural memory. Instead of emerging through the carefully staged—and judicially debatable—context of Israeli state pedagogy in the Eichmann trial, Marceline's staged appearance aligns at least indirectly with a challenge to the French state in a moment of war and crisis. That is, Marceline's testimony possessed a mediated, allegorical significance in the moment of its appearance: her tale of suffering in the recent past occupies the place of those testimonies to contemporary political violence that could not be told openly in decolonizing France because of state censorship and were thus forced to pass through either underground and extralegal paths or, as in this case, indirect evocation. Marceline's testimony takes on this allegorical meaning because of the careful way Rouch and Morin situate her testimony in the wake of brief discussions among its cast of real-life characters about the Algerian War and about the ongoing processes of decolonization reported daily in the news. Although the Holocaust as historical event differs immeasurably from France's late colonial war, Holocaust testimony at that moment cannot be separated from testimony to colonial violence; rather, the two forms of testimony mediate each other. Already we can see that Loridan occupies a complex position: she is not only a surviving victim but also an embodied allegory for the broader implication of French society in ongoing violence.

But the mediation of Marceline's testimony is even more complex. First of all, it is premediated by two significant postwar films. The testimony sequence is immediately preceded by an uncomfortable scene on the roof of the Musée de l'Homme in which Rouch draws attention to Marceline's tattoo and asks two African students if they understand its significance. They admit that they do not, although one of the students then mentions having seen a film about the camps, probably *Night and Fog*. Although it is not mentioned in *Chronicle of a Summer*, *Night and Fog* had had one of its first screenings in the Musée de l'Homme, a site during World War II of resistance activity, and its director, Alain Resnais, considered the film an allegorical protest against the just-begun Algerian War.[33] But another Resnais film also figures here: as Marceline Loridan later wrote, in giving her testimony she imagined herself as Emmanuelle Riva in Resnais and Duras's New Wave classic *Hiroshima mon amour*, which had recently appeared and featured Riva meandering through the streets, much as Marceline does while giving her testimony. As we have already seen in our opening discussion of *Loin du Vietnam*, these intersections with the oeuvre of Resnais—and various sites of violence, including Japan, Europe, and Vietnam—will multiply in the following years. Through premediation, Marceline's testimony in *Chronicle* already participates in the network of associations between different scenes of violence made available by Resnais's films.

Yet, if the conditions of possibility for Marceline's testimony in *Chronicle of a Summer* lie in its premediation by a range of discourses, texts, and technologies, the multiple remediations of her testimony subsequently established it as a publicly meaningful and politically vital act. In the urgent struggle over Algeria, the testimonial form and staged dialogue established by Rouch and Morin's film reappeared frequently. *Chronicle* opened in Paris in the fall of 1961 in the midst of one of the major crises of the late colonial state: the October 17 massacre of dozens—and roundup of thousands—of peacefully demonstrating Algerians in the streets of the French capital. In the weeks immediately following the massacre, the anticolonial New Left newsweekly *France-Observateur* published two interview-based pieces that, like *Chronicle*, linked the Holocaust with the violence of decolonization. Previously we saw how Marguerite Duras's "Les deux ghettos" took part in a work of differentiated solidarity by participating in a tradition of thinking the Warsaw Ghetto alongside other histories of racial violence. Now we can see that Duras, whose *Hiroshima, mon amour* premediated Marceline's testimony, also remediates *Chronicle*: she uses the documentary's interview form to juxtapose discussions with two Algerians and a survivor of the Warsaw Ghetto, whom Duras dubs "M" (a possible echo of Marceline).[34] Two years later, strikingly similar connections are also made in another text that seems to remediate *Chronicle*, African American writer William Gardner Smith's novel *The Stone Face* (1963), the first novel to treat the Paris massacre, which also features at its center a female Holocaust survivor whose name begins with "M"—not to mention an African American protagonist who finds himself complexly implicated as a "privileged" foreigner in France's late colonial war.[35] In Duras's and Smith's works, as in Rouch and Morin's film, the encounter between a female Holocaust survivor and colonized men of color serves as a gendered and racialized trope of intersecting memories, complex implication, and a tension-filled solidarity across difference.

Such intersecting solidarities from the era of decolonization exhibit neither the process of abstraction nor the polarization of good and evil that Levy and Sznaider find in the later moment of Holocaust-inflected human rights; rather, they involve embodied encounters, complex and ambivalent affective translations, and emerging awareness of problems of implication. Occupying the place of the victim, as Marceline certainly does, does not exclude her from participating in the racial hierarchies of postwar France, which are also on display in some of the exchanges in *Chronicle of a Summer*. The experience of historical trauma does not inoculate subjects against implication in other regimes of power. Even as it stages an unprecedented Holocaust testimony and provides an attenuated critique of late colonialism, Rouch and Morin's film also suggests—whether intentionally or not—the gray zones of race and nation that implicate all subjects of an imperial state.

Toward a Holocaust Internationalism

But Loridan did not simply remain the object of representation and remediation. By becoming a filmmaker and later a memoirist, Loridan herself very deliberately began to remediate the testimonial impulse, sometimes at great personal risk and often as an expression of internationalist solidarity. For the last half century, she has sought to craft for herself what Fiona Ross calls "a voice with a signature," but she has also put that voice into service for projects that move beyond the reproduction of her own past and extend into a future defined by an encompassing vision of collective liberation.[36] Already in the year after *Chronicle*'s appearance, Loridan went from being in front of the camera to being behind it—where she remained for the next half century. She traveled to the newly independent Algerian state and made a forty-minute documentary with Jean-Pierre Sergent, who also appears in Rouch and Morin's film. *Algeria, Year Zero* (1962), like *Chronicle*, seeks to assess the state of life in a moment of historical transition. Because of its politics, it was banned in France for more than forty years, an indication of how seriously state power takes the force of circulation.

Loridan continued the process of remediating her own testimony in a series of films she went on to make with her companion Joris Ivens, the important Dutch communist documentarian she met through her role in Rouch and Morin's film. "I could marry that woman," Ivens reportedly said after seeing *Chronicle*—and he did. Together Ivens and Loridan (later Loridan-Ivens) made documentaries such as *How Yukong Moved the Mountains* (1976), a twelve-part, twelve-hour series about everyday life in China in the wake of the Cultural Revolution, described by one contemporary critic as "témoignage direct" (direct testimony) about China, even as the film was also criticized for its clearly partial portrait of the country.[37] After Ivens's death and now in her mid-seventies, Loridan-Ivens made her first feature film, *La petite prairie aux bouleaux* (*The Birch-Tree Meadow*, i.e., Birkenau [2003]), a fictionalized autobiographical account of an Auschwitz survivor who returns to Poland for the first time decades after the war.

Reflecting back on her life with Ivens some years after his death, Loridan-Ivens described their relationship as one defined by mediation and international solidarity: "Our first encounter was through the screen: he had seen me acting in the film *A Summer's Chronicle* [sic]. He was 62 then and four years later we went to the 17th parallel, the area in Vietnam that been bombed most intensively, to show the world what it means to fight for your country against B-52 bombers" ("Wind of Tides" 4). The film Loridan-Ivens evokes here, *Le 17e parallèle: La guerre du peuple* (*The Seventeenth Parallel: The People's War* [1968]), provides a powerful example of how testimony and mediation continued to intersect in the Holocaust internationalism that Loridan-Ivens fostered since first giving public testimony about her deportation and return.[38] Filmed by Ivens and Loridan beneath those falling American bombs on the front lines in Vietnam in 1967 (the same year that they contributed to *Loin du Vietnam*), *The Seventeenth Parallel* follows *Algeria, Year Zero* in transforming the testimonial impulse beyond the autobiographical subject into a collective militant practice: instead of dramatizing their own process of bearing witness to decolonization (à la Godard), the filmmakers provide a forum for ordinary Vietnamese to testify to their experience of war and the struggle for national liberation.[39] Part war documentary, part exploration of daily life in extreme circumstances, part revolutionary propaganda, *The Seventeenth Parallel* uses a collective voice-over narration in French—attributed to a woman from the Vihn Lihn region where the film was made—together with direct and indirect address to the camera in Vietnamese by peasants and local party members. The film documents the peasants' attempts to continue tending their rice paddies, to construct elaborate underground shelters, and to contribute to the war effort against "the enemy," the Americans. Using terms associated with the Holocaust, they testify that they will "never forget" the crimes of the Americans (fig. 11). One of the predominant (perhaps self-reflexive) motifs of the film is the ingenuity of the villagers in transforming—we might say remediating—the weapons of war: parts from downed American planes and rockets are turned into bicycles and a printing press, while bomb craters become fishponds. Such resistant bricolage also shows up in some of the footage Ivens and Loridan sent back to Marker for *Loin du Vietnam*; there we see the citizens of Hanoi constructing individual bomb shelters with humble materials.

Through their collaboration, the filmmakers themselves also remediate the war, turning it into an "aural" testimony. The nature of the collaboration that lies behind *The Seventeenth Parallel* between the older, established male documentarian Ivens and the younger, lesser-known female Loridan is a complex one, but one that bears on the questions of mediation and testimony. In early accounts, Loridan is often referred to merely as an assistant on Ivens's films, but more recently her contributions have been granted

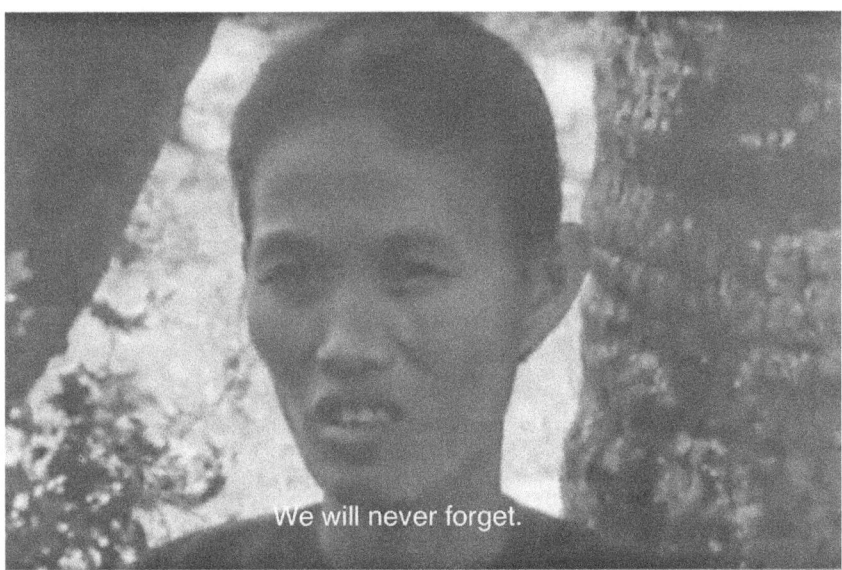

FIGURE 11. "We will never forget." Still image from Joris Ivens and Marceline Loridan, *The Seventeenth Parallel: The People's War* (1968). Author's collection.

co-director status (e.g., on the new DVD edition of Ivens's films).[40] However one resolves the issue of authorship and addresses the gender asymmetries that lie behind it, Loridan's contribution in *The Seventeenth Parallel* is both clear and clearly indebted to her earlier experience with what was then considered "new media" in *Chronicle of a Summer* (a film that also emerged from collaboration): the lightweight camera and recording technology used to elicit her testimony in Rouch and Morin's film.[41] In Loridan-Ivens's words, "We were a perfect team. Joris, a child of the age of the silent cinema, a master of the image, and I, formed by the Sixties, the age of the new synchronized sound and the Nouvelle Vague.... We were like a two-headed Hydra and we made twenty films together" ("Wind of Tides" 4). Jean-Pierre Sergent confirms that it was through Loridan that Ivens discovered "direct sound," a technique still relatively new and crucial for the testimonial effect produced by *The Seventeenth Parallel*.[42] Direct sound—and direct cinema, a genre related to cinema verité—involves the simultaneous recording of sound and image in "real-world" settings, a process that we now take for granted, but that was technically complicated until the early 1960s. Indeed, synchronous sound may be the most powerful form testimony takes in *The Seventeenth Parallel*: the persistent roar of American jets and the explosions of American bombs throughout the film (as well as the clatter of Vietnamese antiaircraft weapons) take the place of a musical soundtrack and bear aural or sonic witness to the risks involved in the filming and the seemingly impossible conditions in which the villagers were living and resisting their fate. As Loridan said shortly after completing filming, "We never went for five minutes without hearing an explosion near us or in the distance, and at night we were unable to sleep because of the hundreds of airplanes flying overhead."[43]

Aural testimony is also linked to a recoding of trauma. In the book accompanying the film, Loridan describes situating herself in a hole fifty meters from the village where they are staying in order to capture the sounds of an American air attack; she uses a Nagra recorder, precisely the kind she carried while Rouch filmed her testimony in the summer of 1960.[44] Yet the recordings Loridan makes do not simply reproduce the traumatic testimony at the center of *Chronicle of a Summer*. For one, Loridan's subject position has shifted from first-person to third-person witness and from surviving victim to implicated subject offering solidarity. With this shift in position, the "sound" of testimony also shifts. Returning to the village after the end of the attack, the filmmakers visit a school where a fourteen-year-old girl had died a few days earlier in a previous American shelling. While they are in the underground school, the alarm rings for yet another attack, and, Loridan reports, "without panic, very orderly, the children arrange their things carefully: pen, ink, books, notebooks are their weapons. And they descend into the shelter joyously, as during recreation. The tape that I recorded mixes strangely the whistle of airplanes and their laughter."[45] If Loridan's presence with a Nagra recorder suggests that Rouch's cinema verité technique has premediated *The Seventeenth Parallel*, the latter film also remediates the earlier scene of testimony. *Chronicle* had staged a highly mediated Holocaust testimony that itself became the occasion for the articulation of other traumatic histories, as I have shown. Now Loridan as sound recorder has herself become the medium for an address from and to a new set of others. But not only the channels of mediation have changed; the message has shifted as well: from an articulation of personal traumatization to the laughter of collective resilience in the face of overwhelming violence. This affirmative account of the Vietnamese anticolonial struggle brings with it in turn a more aggressive political message than we find in Rouch and Morin's film or in discourses of human rights. On the classroom wall above where the young victim of American bombing used to sit a sign now hangs: "We must work even harder to avenge the memory of our little sister Xuan."[46] In the spirit of militant documentary, Ivens and Loridan's Vietnam film recodes trauma as the occasion for a new, antagonistic politics of memory.

In recoding trauma and memory, Loridan also commits to a new politics of testimony. Both the politics and the form of this commitment deserve critical discussion; certainly neither is unproblematic, especially when viewed with the clear vision of hindsight. In the views of both Ivens and Loridan there is, for instance, the evident risk of a romanticization of "Third World" resistance and the imposition of too homogeneous a view of collectivity.[47] In retrospect, Loridan-Ivens would concur and has described her commitments of the time as "false, naïve, and simplistic."[48] Even more serious is the obscuring or forgetting of crimes committed in the name of the communist internationalism that motivated them. Such a serious political error, especially relevant to the case of their post–Cultural Revolution China film, *How Yukong Moved the Mountains*, ended up weighing heavily on the filmmakers. Loridan-Ivens describes a deep "inner depression" whose "cause was the Paradox we discovered: we believed what the Chinese in front of the camera said that they believed, but it all turned out to be a bitter illusion. This crisis, a political, artistic, philosophical and ideological crisis, would last a few years" ("Wind of Tides" 4).[49] The failures of the massive film about China suggest, among other things, the risks of forgetting the lessons of solidarity from afar that had been one of the core insights of *Loin du Vietnam*: a plunge into immediacy ignores the uneasy coexistence of proximity and distance necessary to internationalist projects. Seeking to confront the prejudices of the capitalist West, Ivens and Loridan ended up implicated in another kind of state violence.

In the wake of that crisis, Loridan-Ivens turned in new directions—and turned back to the original trauma that defined her life: Auschwitz. After Ivens died in 1989, Loridan-Ivens writes, "I was left behind with my grief . . . and with the next film that I would have to make without him. About Auschwitz. Joris encouraged me to tackle it. And now that he has passed away, I have the space to return to my own origin, to my Jewish background. And I have the courage to return to the stench of corpses, the dull colors, the moaning in the hell of Auschwitz" ("Wind of Tides" 5). The film that emerged from this return, *The Birch-Tree Meadow*, is decidedly more autobiographical and less multidirectional and internationalist than the works of the 1960s.[50]

My reason for evoking this internationalist era of Loridan's productivity has not been to celebrate it as a model that can be applied "immediately" to the present, but rather to make a point about the history of memory and the future of testimony: the turn to militant cinema that Loridan takes in collaboration with Ivens is both inscribed in the experimental genesis and political context of Loridan's first public testimony in *Chronicle of a Summer* and is yet an outcome that could never have been foreseen in any deterministic account. There is no straight path from Auschwitz via a Holocaust testimony during the Algerian War to the filming of testimony under falling bombs in Vietnam. Yet this itinerary suggests a Holocaust internationalism shared by others that offered an actually existing alternative to the canonization of the Holocaust's uniqueness taking place at the same time.[51] It also continues to offer an alternative narrative of the globalization of Holocaust memory centered on collective political struggle instead of cosmopolitanization in the age of liberal human rights.[52]

The Seventeenth Parallel is not a Holocaust testimony, and yet it emerges from the unexpected testimonial project of a Holocaust survivor who, enabled by processes of mediation that were anything but abstract, found herself engaged with and implicated—bodily and politically—in a history allegedly far from her own. She took this responsibility seriously, not simply spending months living underground in a war zone, but also continuing to speak out about the atrocities she witnessed. In November 1967, a few months after finishing *The Seventeenth Parallel*, Loridan testified before the Russell International War Crimes Tribunal in Copenhagen and screened parts of the film.[53] For Loridan—and I suspect for many other survivors of traumatic events—testimony is not the culmination of an experience, but an essential step in the fashioning of a future that helps her to move: a "departure," in Cathy Caruth's terms.[54] Of course, movement into the future is not absolute freedom: the witness takes her baggage with her.

Under the Sign of Suitcases

In 2008, Loridan-Ivens produced another iteration of her testimonial project: the memoir *Ma vie balagan*. In that text, whose multilingual title draws on the Hebrew/Yiddish word for chaos, Loridan-Ivens sums up her life with a pithy epigram: "Je vis sous le signe des valises" (I live under the sign of suitcases).[55] With this phrase, Loridan-Ivens activates a polyvalent figure for the work of memory and testimony. Most obviously, given her history, the suitcase calls up one of the icons of concentrationary memory. In Loridan-Ivens's words, these are the suitcases "we had to abandon on arrival in the camp, the ones that accumulated at Auschwitz, with their labels and their names" (173).[56] In a further turn, the suitcases come to figure memory and repression simultaneously: "And then there are the 'container' suitcases. . . . Full of diverse souvenirs that you would prefer not to see again. Sometimes you open the suitcase, you see the too burdensome past, and you close it up again" (173). Here we find echoes of what Charlotte Delbo has called "deep memory."[57]

But if the suitcase is a potent symbol of dispossession as well as a kind of crypt containing "deep" memories too traumatic to handle directly, it also has yet other, potentially more affirmative associations. It marks the life of a "world"-traveler and suggests the compulsion she shared with Joris to "go elsewhere, [into] exile" (173). The valise might also be the bag Marceline carries (holding the Nagra recorder) as she gives her testimony in *Chronicle of a Summer*, an act linking personal experience and public space in a manner that at the time was practically unprecedented. Or it might recall the schoolbag young Marceline carried before deportation—a scene captured in a photo displayed at the Mémorial de la Shoah in Paris that uncannily prefigures her appearance in *Chronicle*.[58] Finally, it certainly signals active solidarity: Loridan-Ivens calls this chapter of her memoir "La porteuse de valises" (The carrier of suitcases), an explicit reference to her activities as one of a small number of French women (and men) who "carried suitcases" for the underground Algerian independence movement.[59] Indeed, those suitcases of money for the FLN were sometimes stored in Loridan-Ivens's apartment—at great personal risk—as Jean-Pierre Sergent reports.[60]

For Loridan-Ivens, the suitcase is simultaneously the form, medium, and content of testimony—at once the depth of the past, the burden of suffering, and the means for making the past public and moving with it into futures not yet written. The rhetoric of suitcases thus suggests the proximity for Loridan-Ivens of history, trauma, travel, mediation, and anticolonial, internationalist politics. Although not necessarily a harmonious mix, the very heterogeneity of these associations may provide the grounds for a synthesis of the best features of socialist, anticolonial, and human rights internationalism.

Besides being a powerful figure for Loridan-Ivens's complex life trajectory and for the ethics and politics of Holocaust memory more generally, "the sign of suitcases" is also a suggestive figure for implication. The suitcase is a medium that assists a human agent in an act of transportation, but can also become a burden, a weight that must be borne. The sign of suitcases references testimony as a medium for speech and action that take place when one leaves home and circulates in the public realm; when one becomes implicated in the world—consciously or unconsciously—and creates bodily and verbal connections between diverse sites of history, memory, and trauma. For those of us concerned with multidirectional Holocaust memory and the problem of implication, the example of Loridan-Ivens offers additional messages: an ethical future for memory demands that we cultivate what Lugones calls an "openness to surprise" as well as a self-reflexivity about the surprising ways we are entangled in and weighed down by histories that at first seem to take place far from home. The lesson that we are inevitably entangled in distant conflicts also haunts the subject of the next chapter, Hito Steyerl, whose artistic trajectory moves through different versions of internationalism as she grapples with personal and political implication.

6

"Germany Is in Kurdistan"
Hito Steyerl's Images of Implication

Remembering Ronahî

In October 1998, a battle took place near Van in eastern Anatolia between the Turkish Army and elements of the PKK (the Kurdistan Workers' Party). In many ways this was an "ordinary" battle in an area some consider northwestern Kurdistan. Over the course of the 1990s, the Turkish state waged a brutal war of counterinsurgency against Kurdish militants that killed tens of thousands of fighters and civilians, destroyed thousands of villages, and displaced as many as a million people, all while denying the substantial minority of Kurds in Turkey basic human rights to language, culture, and political representation.[1] The PKK, considered a terrorist organization by the European Union, the US, and Turkey, has fought for decades in the name of Kurdish independence and autonomy. A certain liberalization and de-escalation of the crisis within Turkey occurred in the first decade of the twenty-first century and was then followed by further setbacks in the years since. Meanwhile, the reputation of the PKK has undergone significant change.[2] All in all, the Kurdish question remains an unresolved flashpoint in Turkey and the region. During the course of the writing of this chapter, ongoing developments near the Turkish border in Syria and Iraq, including the highly visible resistance in Kobanê and the cross-border assault on Kurdish-controlled Afrin, have brought the Kurdish question back into the news, as did the reigniting of the Turkish state's war against Kurds within its own borders in winter 2015–16.

The battle in October 1998 ended as many did, with the army capturing and, it seems, summarily executing a number of the Kurdish fighters.

Among those fighters was one who would become an icon of the Kurdish cause: Sehît Ronahî—Martyr Ronahî—from the YAJK, the women's brigade of the PKK.[3] While the iconography of Kurdish martyrs is extensive—and includes many women who have fought with this secular, revolutionary movement—Martyr Ronahî represents an unusual case. Ronahî was born in Munich in 1965 and was known by her birth name, Andrea Wolf, before she joined the PKK in the mid-1990s. Previous to enlisting in the women's brigade, Wolf had been involved in radical left politics in Germany, had served time in jail, and may have been affiliated with the Red Army Faction (RAF). Her experience in the radical left—and possibly the threat of returning to prison—eventually moved her to align herself with the Kurdish cause, as did a couple dozen other Germans in this period.[4]

Various groups claiming allegiance to Andrea Wolf's legacy have commemorated her death in multiple sites by constructing what Astrid Erll would call a "plurimedial" constellation of memory.[5] Indeed, it would not be an exaggeration to say that, in the years since her murder, Wolf has been transformed into a *lieu de mémoire* of internationalism that condenses an array of not entirely compatible currents. Wolf has simultaneously become a martyr for Kurdish national liberation, a symbol of socialist internationalism, and an object of human rights campaigns by Turkish, German, and European organizations. In 1999, at the PKK's yearly convention, the party voted unanimously to make Wolf a symbol of internationalist struggle, and her memory remains central to the Kurdish cause.[6] As a PKK guerilla commander who witnessed Wolf's death explained, "It was her internationalist view that made Ronahî join the ranks of [the] PKK."[7] In 2013, two years after a Turkish human rights organization discovered a mass grave holding Wolf's remains along with those of forty other militants, a massive tomb in the region near Van where she died was named in her memory. Speaking at the tomb's dedication ceremony in Çatak, a Kurdish guerilla evoked Wolf as "a manifestation of the diversity and internationality of the Kurdish movement" ("Monumental Tomb"). Shortly after the tomb's unveiling, the ruling AK Party ordered its demolition, as it has in the case of other Kurdish gravesites.[8]

At the same time that commemoration of Wolf has taken place in the transnational Kurdish region, her memory has also remained present in Germany and Europe. There her story and image have been memorialized and remediated in books, posters, exhibitions, ceremonies, street demonstrations, and videos—most of them produced or organized by coalitions of radical

German leftists and diasporic Kurdish activists.[9] In 2010, a case brought by Wolf's mother to the European Court of Human Rights ended with Turkey being convicted of obstructing investigation into Wolf's disappearance, a violation of Article 2 of the European Convention on Human Rights.[10] Her memory remains alive in the mainstream press as well; a 2014 report in the Berlin newspaper *Tagesspiegel* evoked Wolf while discussing the suddenly fashionable topic of Kurdish women fighters in Kobanê.[11] In the same context of renewed interest in the Kurdish cause during the fight with ISIS, a news report on "Medya," another German woman who joined the PKK twenty years ago and works as a doctor in the Kurdish region, noted that "Wolf's portrait [is] prominently displayed" in the doctor's consultation room.[12] Even before her death, Wolf had already constituted herself as a kind of living memory site when she took her nom de guerre from that of a young Kurdish woman in Germany who had set herself on fire in 1994 in an act of protest.[13] The story of Andrea Wolf thus takes place at the contentious site where the politics of memory intersects with the memory of politics.

Against the backdrop of the modes of memorialization that have followed Wolf's death, I reflect in this chapter on a long-term artistic project undertaken by the internationally prominent German artist and theorist Hito Steyerl, a childhood friend of Wolf. With the twenty-five-minute video *November*, from 2004, and subsequent videos, performances, and essays that constitute a still-unfolding oeuvre, Steyerl both joins the acts of memorialization by Wolf/Ronahî's radical comrades and seeks to create a countermemory of Wolf by interrogating the processes of remediation and heroization that have followed her death. Steyerl examines these processes through an optic that is pertinent both to the politics of martyrdom and to her own ongoing reflections on the relation between aesthetics and politics: she focuses on Wolf's posthumous circulation as an image, which eventually leads to a self-critical reflection on what it means for the artist to be implicated in such a circulation of images.[14] Although Steyerl evokes all the incompatible elements that have coalesced in Wolf's commemoration—including the internationalist paradigms of socialism, human rights, and terrorism—her work ultimately produces an alternate conception of internationalism by linking it to the politics of images and the problem of implication.

In the hands of Steyerl, at least, Wolf's story—a story of trauma and violence, to be sure—complicates all the features of what I have called the victim/perpetrator imaginary and opens up the question of the implicated subject. If Steyerl addresses what looks at first like an exceptional, singular story of violence, she quickly resituates it instead in a broad, transnational context of cultural, economic, political, and military power. Additionally, in contrast to the dominant discourse of victimization, she leaves us in a morally ambiguous, impure zone. While Wolf's comrades celebrate her as a martyr and internationalist hero and the dominant media have typically labeled Wolf a terrorist, Steyerl comes to a more complex and ambivalent verdict about her friend and her commitments. As she says at one point, "Not even in fiction are the heroes innocent" (*November*). Finally, in refusing binary simplifications and, especially, in highlighting how the complexities of Wolf's story intersect with her own story, Steyerl's project helps us interrogate the implicated subject as a figure of historical responsibility and internationalist solidarity in a time of globalization.[15]

In particular, the life and death of "Andrea" serve in Steyerl's work as an opportunity to address questions of implication in an age defined by what the artist calls "traveling images." The traveling image of Andrea prompts us to ask whether and how a new transnational political subject can emerge from a recognition of implication. Although Steyerl's work engages intensively with the forces of capitalist globalization, it emerges out of a conviction that we live in a postrevolutionary age in which internationalism has lost its luster and "the myth of the leftist hero [has] come crumbling down."[16] In the face of this postrevolutionary, postheroic moment, Steyerl's theoretical writings propose a shift from the subject to the object and from emancipation to participation. By highlighting the way subjects become entangled with the circulation of objects and images, these shifts make possible a grasp of implication, but they also evacuate the position of the subject from which a new politics might emerge. Against the grain of Steyerl's own writings, I find the unresolved question of the subject at the center of her work and at the core of the political possibilities it alternately forecloses and opens up. I argue that the subject—and especially the implicated subject—remains central to Steyerl's investigations, and that she remains closer to an internationalist vision—albeit a critical one—than her explicit statements suggest.

Recent events, including the events in Rojava, also necessitate a critical rereading of internationalist subjectivity. The emblematic and instantly commemorated death on October 5, 2014, of Suphi Nejat Ağırnaslı, a young Turkish/German leftist militant who was fighting with the Kurds in Kobanê, suggests that the internationalist impulse may not be as dated as it appeared to Steyerl in the early years of the new millennium.[17] At the same time, that impulse remains politically ambivalent. In addition to the relatively small-scale internationalist mobilization that has accompanied Kurdish resistance, those who fought against the Kurds in Kobanê under the banner of the Islamic State are also configured as a nonnational force and have been highly successful in recruiting from an international pool of Muslim-identified youth. Against the backdrop of these clashing forces, internationalism is again on the agenda as an urgent political impulse demanding explanation.[18] I want to illustrate, via Steyerl's Wolf project, how a self-reflexive grasp of one's implication in apparently distant contexts of violence can be the start of a politicized process of internationalist subject creation. In Steyerl's work, critique and self-critique function as a subject-making fidelity to the memory of politics.

From Loridan-Ivens to Steyerl: Mediation, Multidirectionality, and the Implicated Subject

In considering the "sign of the suitcase" in the work of Marceline Loridan-Ivens, we have been able to trace how acts of remembrance are premediated by prior image repertoires and then subsequently remediated in ways that both confirm their place in the canons of cultural memory and reroute them on new and unexpected itineraries. Loridan-Ivens's autobiographical and cinematic itineraries produce multidirectional memories—creating new links between seemingly unconnected histories of trauma and resistance in Algeria, Europe, and Vietnam—and embed those memories in histories of implication and empire.

The connection between mediation, multidirectionality, and the implicated subject also defines the work of Hito Steyerl. Steyerl's films and videos as well as her writings and lecture-performances explore some similar ground to what we have seen in our chapter on Loridan-Ivens: for instance, the intersection of the Holocaust and its legacies with others forms of imperial violence. Yet Steyerl—born in 1966 and active as an artist since the 1990s—comes to these questions with a very different sensibility. She takes a distance from the internationalism that characterizes Loridan-Ivens's trajectory during the 1960s and 1970s (as Loridan-Ivens later would as well). In contrast to the tendency of *Algeria Year Zero*, *The Seventeenth Parallel*, and *How Yukong Moved the Mountains*—filmed within ongoing revolutions—Steyerl begins from the belated perspective that Loridan-Ivens only comes to later: she narrates history from an explicitly postrevolutionary moment. Yet, the oeuvres of Steyerl and Loridan-Ivens also converge around the problem of long-distance solidarity—a convergence signaled, in part, by the return of *Loin du Vietnam* in the work of the younger artist.

Steyerl first came to prominence with her sixty-two-minute-long essay film *Die leere Mitte* (*The Empty Center*; 1998), a multidirectional archaeology of Berlin's Potsdamer Platz that uncovers layers of colonial, National Socialist, and Cold War history and tracks contemporary forms of migration. The film's multidirectionality is not simply a matter of historical content; Steyerl also develops formal means to embody the film's historical and mnemonic intersections. As in all of her work, she mixes materials of distinct provenance in *Die leere Mitte*: footage she has shot and interviews she has recorded occupy the same cinematic space as archival images and footage from feature films and newsreels. If *Die leere Mitte* focuses predominantly on stories of victimization defined by race and religion, it also implicitly complicates a victim/perpetrator framework by suggesting the ways that exploited and persecuted people also participate in the reproduction of racial hierarchies. Implicated subjects appear in the interstices of the film's overarching narrative about the construction and reconstruction of borders.[19] Although characterized by sophisticated forms of montage and juxtaposition, the film differs from Steyerl's later video and performance work in ways that ultimately limit its exploration of implicated subject positions, however. In *Die leere Mitte*, implication is primarily the problem of others, and—in contrast to Steyerl's later work—the filmmaker herself remains outside the frame and the image and sound tracks.[20] That is, while the film documents the implication of exploited subjects in the oppression of other exploited subjects, the filmmaker herself seems to remain at a distance from the problem of implication. That distance will be greatly reduced—and rendered productively problematic—in the videos and performances that make up Steyerl's Wolf project in the first decades of the twenty-first century.

Displacements, or How a German Friend Becomes a "Kurdish Terrorist"

Steyerl's artistic investigation of Andrea Wolf begins with the 2004 video *November*. The tale Steyerl tells there does not allow for easy paraphrase, but a capsule summary would note that the film opens by recounting how Steyerl and Wolf made a feminist martial arts film together as teenagers (fig. 12). It continues by reflecting on how, years later, Wolf reappears as a "real" warrior fighting with the PKK. The video—which has been widely screened in galleries, museums, and festivals and is also available on the web—consists almost entirely of repurposed footage. *November* incorporates images taken from Steyerl and Wolf's early film, from newsreel footage of Wolf as a guerilla, and from avant-garde and popular feature films; its soundtrack includes found film dialogue and music along with voice-over by Steyerl and interviews made specifically for *November*. Going beyond Wolf's story, the video also contains a postscript about German militants who took inspiration from a Costa Gavras feature film about South American guerillas, with mixed, comic results.

November opens with the sound of helicopter blades as the camera slowly zooms in on a picture of a young woman's face. The image of the woman, who looks down and to the left, is a blurry, faded, and creased black-and-white

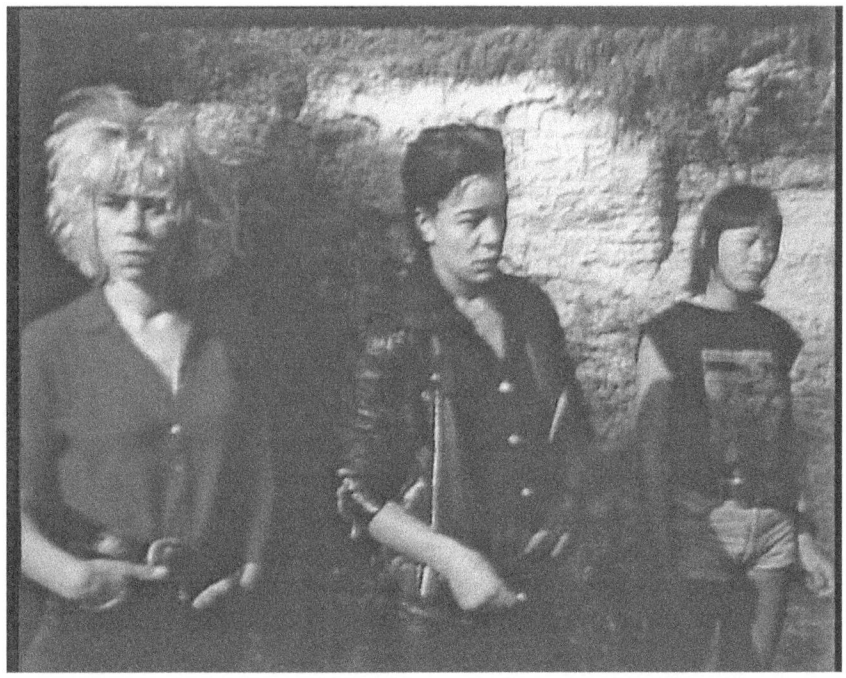

FIGURE 12. An image incorporated into *November* of Andrea Wolf (*center*), Hito Steyerl (*right*), and an unnamed collaborator in Hito Steyerl's early martial arts film. Hito Steyerl, *November*, 2004. DV, single channel, sound. 25 minutes. Image CC 4.0 Hito Steyerl. Image courtesy of the artist and Andrew Kreps Gallery, New York.

photograph that appears to have been reproduced multiple times. As a shadow plays across the shroud-like photograph—adding another layer between viewers and the woman depicted and suggesting the presence of an observer—we hear the filmmaker begin narrating off-screen: "My best friend when I was seventeen was a girl called Andrea Wolf." At the conclusion of this sentence, the screen fades to gray while the helicopter blades continue, and we hear the narrator again: "In 1998 she was shot as a Kurdish terrorist." All of a sudden, the whir of the helicopter ceases and a dramatic cut takes place accompanied by chords that evoke a hard-boiled detective film. An image appears depicting the same attractive, somewhat butch woman from the shoulders up, now filmed in color and wearing a leather jacket against a clear blue sky, as she turns to face the camera. Once again the screen fades to gray and is replaced by the title "November"; meanwhile, The Bostweeds' title song from Russ Meyer's camp classic *Faster, Pussycat! Kill! Kill!* plays on the soundtrack. Intercut with another title frame letting us know this is "a film by Hito Steyerl," we see the woman yet again in the same leather jacket as she gets out of a Mercedes with two other women and starts to beat up a group of men. The narrator tells us: "This is my first film." As a different young woman appears on-screen, beating a helpless man with karate moves, the narrator informs us, "This is me." Another close-up and freeze-frame on the now familiar woman in the leather jacket confirms, "This is Andrea." In this early martial arts film, the teenage Hito and Andrea were part of a girl gang bent on terrorizing any men they came across. But the story is impossible to reconstruct, Steyerl tells us, because only the fighting scenes were shot and the film stock did not even permit sound recording.

In this opening minute of *November*, we already find essential aspects of Steyerl's aesthetic practice along with tantalizing hints at the story of Andrea Wolf. In the course of a few seconds, Steyerl creates a complex montage of sound and images from multiple sources—some of which are identifiable or identified (such as the theme song from *Faster, Pussycat! Kill! Kill!* and Steyerl's own film footage), and others of which remain underdefined (the black-and-white photograph of Andrea, the sound of the helicopter). At the level of the image, the core of the opening sequence—both the photograph and the film footage—is what Steyerl has theorized as the "poor image": "The poor image is a copy in motion. Its quality is bad, its resolution substandard. As it accelerates, it deteriorates." Everywhere to be found in our globalized world of pirated, copied, shared, and downloaded files, poor images "testify to the violent dislocation, transferrals, and displacements of images—their acceleration and circulation within the vicious cycles of audiovisual capitalism."[21] In the film, as in her writings, the low resolution of the poor images Steyerl uses also constitutes a kind of visual pun evoking the "unresolved" nature of the stories she seeks to tell—something hinted at in the opening of *November* when she describes the impossibility of reconstructing the story of her first film. The low and nonresolution of the film echoes, in addition, the unresolved nature of Wolf's death, which neither Turkey nor Germany has wanted to confirm (although, as already mentioned, a grave purportedly holding her body was later discovered).

With its as yet unexplained reference to Wolf's being "shot as a Kurdish terrorist," the film evokes a mystery that the film seeks to explore, even if it cannot fully resolve it. The film becomes, in part, an essay in detection, and the mystery it addresses involves not primarily whether and how Wolf died, but rather how a young German woman from Bavaria came to die as a Kurdish terrorist. *November* thus links its exploration of "poor images" with the question of long-distance solidarity. In other words, the case of Steyerl's protagonist raises questions about what it means to be implicated in—and indeed, to stake your life in—a history seemingly far from "your own." *November* is, at one level, a search for an answer to that question. However, the film approaches its central question indirectly by tackling another dilemma: the relation between the transnational movement of images and the possibilities of a transnational politics. This dilemma ultimately implicates the artist herself in the story she is telling.

If poor images are characterized by "dislocation, transferrals, and displacements" in the realm of media, the story through which Steyerl has chosen to explore poor images emerges out of dislocation and displacement in two other realms as well: that of the hundreds of thousands of Kurds displaced by the Turkish state and that of the diasporic and internationalist solidarity movement that rose up as a direct outcome of and response to the war.[22] While many Kurds had come to Germany in the 1960s and 1970s as part of the "Turkish" guest worker migration, the conflict in Turkey created new categories of border-crossing migrants and transformed the meaning of Kurdishness in the diaspora—a transformation that in turn had consequences in the primary conflict zone. Here is a first answer to the question of how a German friend becomes a Kurdish "terrorist." The presence of a German woman in the PKK, however rare it might be, follows from these various kinds of dislocation, which brought a new wave of Kurdish refugees to Germany and made Europe into the site of a Kurdish politics that sought to intervene in the conflict "back home."

In fact, these different realms of displacement—media, refugees, and international solidarity—are conjoined. As the political scientist Bilgin Ayata has argued, the transnational dynamic linking the Kurdish conflict to Europe involved an important media component. Because of restrictions in Turkey, Europe became the site of Kurdish television with the 1995 founding of ROJ-TV, a satellite channel sometimes associated with the PKK. An example of "the transnational activities of the Kurdish diaspora [that] have boomeranged back to Turkey," ROJ-TV opened up a new front in the conflict in which the "battles shift[ed] to [the] airwaves."[23] Without explicitly commenting on this context, Steyerl's film captures the interweaving of the transnational flows of images, people, and ideology that Ayata describes and reveals how those interwoven displacements created the context in which Andrea could become Ronahî. Indeed, the film even incorporates part of an interview with Wolf on Kurdish television taken from precisely this diasporic media constellation. In moving from her earlier work in film to the use of video in *November*, Steyerl not only takes up the medium "that has come to be privileged by and definitional to [the] representational economy" of the age of globalization, as one critic has argued; she also deploys a medium that was central to the Kurdish political struggle that defines Andrea's story.[24]

Turkish state policy and Kurdish diasporic politics and media constitute a necessary but not sufficient context for understanding Andrea's story. What remains to be explained is the subjective, affective bond that brought someone like Wolf to join such a cause. The specific conditions of post–National Socialist, Cold War (West) Germany certainly shaped the internationalist impulse of the radical left of which Wolf was a part. Recent histories of the German 1960s and 1970s have uncovered a range of internationalist links connecting German radicals with postcolonial and Third World causes. The Vietnam War, which, as we will see, also figures in *November*, played a significant role in galvanizing internationalist solidarity, just as we saw it do in France with the example of Marceline Loridan-Ivens.[25] But there is also a more proximate, affectively charged history that presages Wolf's story. In a published treatment of *November*, Steyerl mentions that Wolf had been wanted in Germany for having allegedly "participated in terrorist activities, more precisely the destruction of the deportation prison in Weiterstadt," and that she was "suspected of having assisted the Red Army Faction in carrying out the attack."[26] Since the early 1970s, the RAF—to which Wolf was close if not actually a member—has had a mythical presence on the German scene. Although associated most famously with the German Autumn of 1977, the RAF only officially disbanded in 1998, the year of Wolf's death, and their mystique lives on, as a steady stream of books and films attests. In Jeremy Varon's words, "West German terrorism was a tortured form of *Vergangenheitsbewältigung*—a symptom of Germany's difficulty in confronting and working through its Nazi past."[27] A commitment to working through this form of diachronic implication certainly characterizes much of Steyerl's work, but her primary focus in tackling the question of terrorism in *November* is elsewhere.

In addressing the question of how a German friend ends up being shot as a Kurdish "terrorist," *November* "finds" Andrea in a specific history of war, migration, and extremist violence, but that specific history, Steyerl emphasizes, is not only rooted in a constellation of Turkish, Kurdish, and German conditions; it also finds its meaning in the broader and more general phenomena of mediation and internationalism—the same phenomena we have seen expressed and interrogated in *Loin du Vietnam*. Ultimately, Steyerl's approach to Andrea's story is neither historicist nor sociological, but primarily imaginative and aesthetic: her interest lies in the consequences that flow from the production and circulation of images.

Internationalism, or How a Revolutionary Becomes a Poster

November begins with the intimacy of the filmmaker's friendship with Wolf—they were once "best friends" in Bavaria, she insists. Yet the film operates by necessity in a mediated field of indirection and reconstruction because its center lies beyond Steyerl's firsthand knowledge and because, for Steyerl, the field of mediation is where politics takes place; as such, the film becomes a reflection on what it means to be an implicated but distant witness in a moment of crisis. In Steyerl's account, the crisis concerns the status of internationalism, itself a political technology for overcoming distance.

The filmmaker tells us early on in the voice-over narration that she last saw Andrea "two years before she went underground, five years before she was executed in Kurdistan." As Steyerl recites those lines, we look directly into a film projector; simultaneously, we hear both the turning of spools of film in the projector and the whir of helicopter blades we heard during the opening of the film, now punctuated by gunshots. Another voice-over—identified as "a reconstructed witness account by a female guerilla fighter"—informs us of the circumstances of Wolf/Ronahî's death. The editing then returns us to the martial arts film Steyerl made with Wolf as the narrator lays out "coincidences" that link that film with Wolf's later biography. The film, she tells us, was about fighting for justice, but in that fictional version—as we observe in the incorporated footage—Steyerl herself was shot and Andrea, in contrast, "rode off into the sunset" on a motorcycle. Switching gears yet again, Steyerl returns to the "real" Wolf. Another close-up still image comes into focus on the screen, and we now see an image of Wolf in three-quarters profile from the left and situated in front of a red star and green wreath, symbols of the PKK. The narrator comments: "Her body never came back. What came back instead was this poster." Wolf's return as a poster supplements her status as a Kurdish "terrorist" and points us toward the film's exploration of the politics of internationalism (fig. 13).

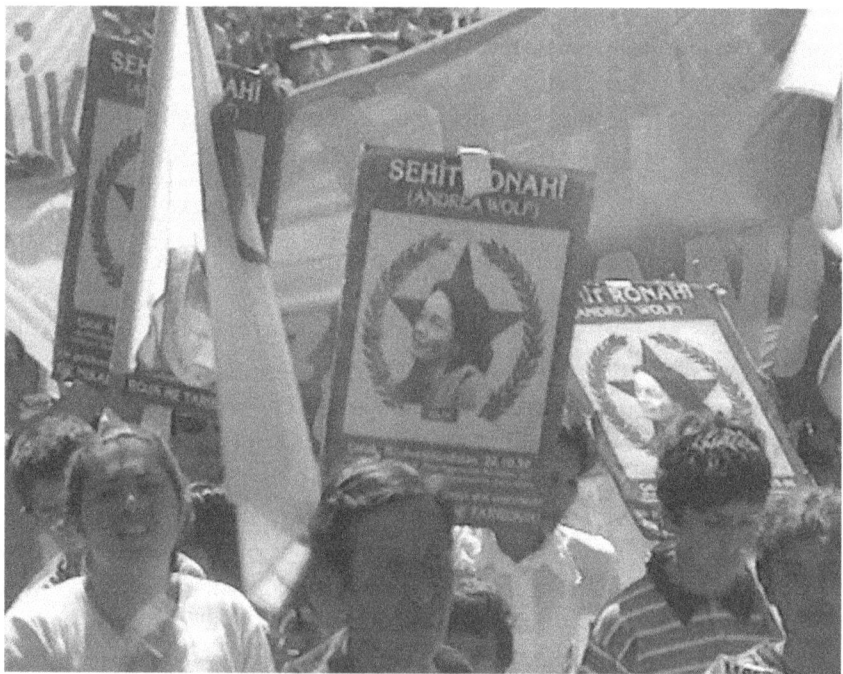

FIGURE 13. An image incorporated into *November* of Andrea Wolf as a "poster" in a Kurdish demonstration in Germany. Hito Steyerl, November, 2004. DV, single channel, sound. 25 minutes. Image CC 4.0 Hito Steyerl. Image courtesy of the artist and Andrew Kreps Gallery, New York.

In foregrounding Wolf's transmutation into a poster, Steyerl opens up questions about the transnational iconography of resistance; indeed, posters of political martyrs are part of resistance movements around the globe. As the anthropologist Lori Allen writes regarding Palestinian "martyr memorialization," such posters index "heroic activity and commitment," but they are also "semiotically complex, representing both the person killed and the martyr that person has become."[28] Doubly coded, the posters help reveal that "martyrs died because of a collective political situation affecting everyone, but they were always also mourned as someone's dear relative or friend" (115). In *November* and subsequent works, Steyerl repeatedly draws attention to the double nature of the martyr as public hero and privately mourned friend. In doing so, she evokes this doubleness as a source of tension: the distinction between the collective and the personal that Allen notes also correlates, at least in the case of Andrea, with a supplementary tension between the national and the international. The famous and still circulating poster of her friend embodies these tensions, with its juxtaposition of Wolf/Ronahî's two names, its text in two languages (German and Kurdish), and its quotation, in German, from the Black Panther Assata Shakur, who herself took on a new name and ended up far from home—in Cuban exile after escaping from prison. Because Wolf's story is not easily contained in what Allen calls the "dominant frame" of the nation (114), her story calls for interrogation of internationalism as a mediated, nonorganic form of solidarity.[29]

In emphasizing the mediated nature of our access to Wolf's story along with her afterlife as an icon, Steyerl links the question of the image with the history of radical internationalism. She explores this conjunction not only through evocation of the Kurdish struggle that attracted her friend, but also through reference to the canon of politically engaged European cinema that constitutes one of the primary contexts of her own artistic practice. These references create a direct, if complex, constellation with Loridan-Ivens and the cultural-political milieu in which she worked. First, Steyerl's self-reflexive shots of the film projector in the sequence described above recall Dziga Vertov's *Man with a Movie Camera* (1929), which, from its opening shot on, insistently depicts the technological apparatus of cinema and foregrounds the internationalist role of the camera and montage in "establishing a visual bond between the workers of the world."[30] In addition, this sequence from *November* also clearly evokes Godard's famous contribution to *Loin du Vietnam*, the 1967 internationalist portmanteau film in which Loridan-Ivens participated. Steyerl directly incorporates a different sequence of Godard's contribution into *November* a few minutes later. *Loin du Vietnam*'s vision is both internationalist (stimulating sympathy for the Vietnamese cause from afar) and multidirectional (locating Vietnam in a network of geopolitical references). Chris Marker, for instance, includes parts of Hanns Eisler's soundtrack from *Night and Fog* (an earlier collaboration between Marker and Alain Resnais) in *Loin du Vietnam*, thus "link[ing] the atrocities of the extermination camps and those taking place in Vietnam."[31] In a fictional sequence contributed by Resnais, a former member of the anti-Nazi resistance declares that "the Americans are [now] the Germans of the Vietnamese" and even laments the fact that the suffering of the Kurds receives so little attention! When Godard—who the following year would form the Dziga Vertov Group, a collective dedicated to militant cinema—was refused a visa to travel to Vietnam, he decided instead, we have seen, to film himself posed with a camera in France while offering a monologue about how "he lives in Paris and didn't go to North Vietnam." Instead of "invading Vietnam," he decides to "let Vietnam invade us" so that we "recognize the place it occupies in our everyday life." The one direct image of Vietnam that interrupts or "invades" Godard's monologue is the 360-degree shot of the Vietnamese soldier provided by Ivens and Loridan. Like Godard imagining Vietnam invading France (and different from Loridan, who actually was in Vietnam), Steyerl emphasizes both the distance between her German-based intervention and the most literal site of the film's political content—Kurdistan—and the fact that "Kurdistan was not only there, but also here" in Germany. However, despite this and other parallels, Steyerl alludes to *Loin du Vietnam* primarily in order to contrast her approach to the internationalist thrust of the Vietnam film and to reflect skeptically on the radical projects of earlier eras.

Continuing her investigation of media and transnational solidarity, Steyerl incorporates actual footage from *Loin du Vietnam* into *November* as her film transitions from a segment introduced by the intertitle "Travelling Images" to one titled "Internationalism." In this sequence, Steyerl tracks Andrea Wolf's transposition from rebellious German teen to poster child for Kurdish nationalism while integrating footage both from "low-brow" corners of film history and the avant-garde. Referring to the fact that her early film with Andrea was inspired by Russ Meyer's buxom rebels in *Faster, Pussycat!* and the "lonely wandering fighter" of Bruce Lee's globally circulating martial arts films, Steyerl comments: "First, we picked up and processed travelling images, global icons of resistance; then Andrea became herself a travelling image, wandering over the globe, an image passed on from hand to hand, copied and reproduced by printing presses, video recorders, and the internet." The intertitle "Internationalism" appears on the screen, followed by the *Loin du Vietnam* excerpts from Godard: we watch a sequence from *La Chinoise* with Jean-Pierre Léaud and Juliet Berto as we hear Godard announce, "I have decided to speak in every film about Vietnam."[32] Made in the same year as *Loin du Vietnam*, *La Chinoise* tells a story not unlike that of *November*, one in which Parisian youth make a fatal transition from revolution to terrorism.

While the excerpts from Godard roll, the narrator indicts the political vision of her predecessors—and those who glorify "Ronahî": "At the moment it seems impossible to universalize this kind of icon, as at the time of leftwing internationalism, when the icons of famous internationalists monopolized the fantasies of metropolitan youths." (One might think here, for instance, of the presence of Fidel Castro in *Loin du Vietnam* and, more broadly, of the New Left's heroization of Che Guevara.) Incorporating shots from Eisenstein's *October*, Steyerl describes how that film depicts "the Cossacks decid[ing] to join the Russian proletarians in internationalist brotherhood during the Bolshevik revolution." As we see the opening, blurry image of Andrea once again—now legible as part of a banner at a commemoration of the Bavarian Soviet Republic of 1919 that took place a few days after Wolf's death—Steyerl clarifies the intertextual resonance of her film's title: "Now we are in the period of November. In November the former heroes become madmen and die in extra-legal executions somewhere on a dirty roadside, and hardly anyone takes a closer look. November is the time after October. A time when revolution seems to be over and peripheral struggles have become particular, localist, and almost impossible to communicate. In November, a new reactionary form of terror has taken over which abruptly breaks with the tradition of October." Although Steyerl never directly condemns Andrea's decision to join the PKK, the editing in this sequence strongly associates the cult of martyrdom dedicated to her childhood friend with the transformation of heroes into madmen and terrorists, and relegates such martyrdom to an outmoded and Eurocentric ("metropolitan") political vision. Steyerl also refuses to romanticize the resistance movement her friend joined: another segment of the film recounts the crimes of the then infamously authoritarian PKK against fellow Kurds.

Here then is the crisis *November* explores. Coming to terms with Andrea Wolf's death means witnessing at a distance. Witnessing at a distance involves recognizing the unavoidability of mediation while trying to overcome separation. In the twentieth century, internationalism was the dominant political affiliation dedicated to overcoming such distance— be it based on class, ethnicity, or nation—but internationalism is now in crisis. In its moment of crisis, Steyerl asserts, internationalism regresses from revolution to terrorism and its romantic icons fade into poor images of useless martyrdom. Yet, even as she distances herself from such an internationalist politics, Steyerl remains close to the critical aesthetics of internationalism, as her citation of Godard's humorous, montage-based practice suggests (itself indebted to the early twentieth-century practice of Vertov and Eisenstein). Instead of abandoning internationalism altogether, I argue, she has replaced an affirmative internationalism with an internationalism of critique. Steyerl's critical internationalism seeks to redirect attention from the revolutionary subject to the agency of the image and object. But can the turn to the object Steyerl calls for also lead to a new political subject? If so, it will be a subject who passes through a self-reflexive attention to the problem of implication. In the following sections we will see how Steyerl's self-reflexive pursuit of Wolf's story ultimately results in a reimagined internationalist project built around the figure of the implicated subject.

Implication, or How an Artist Becomes a "Kurdish Protestor"

In the essay "A Thing Like You and Me," Steyerl announces the end of the "the myth of the leftist hero" and declares: "The hero is dead. Long live the thing."[33] While once there were possibilities for identification with revolutionary subjects, now "if identification is to go anywhere, it has to be with this material aspect of the image, with the image as thing, not as representation. And then it perhaps ceases to be an identification, and instead becomes participation" ("A Thing" 63). The move from identification to participation displaces, in turn, the centrality of emancipation as the telos of historical practice: "Emancipation was conceived as becoming a subject of history, of representation, or of politics. To become a subject carried with it the promise of autonomy, sovereignty, agency" (63). In contrast, "to participate in an image—rather than merely identify with it—could perhaps abolish" the relations of representation that have defined politics until now and could entail giving oneself over to the "potential agency" of the image (65, 69). If the object displaces the subject, what is it that comes after emancipation in the time of November?

Steyerl's emphasis on participation instead of identification suggests that the answer may be implication. As spectators, we do not simply identify with the traveling image of Ronahî, but participate in the dislocations that produce that image and circulate it across media and national borders. We come to recognize ourselves as objects implicated in the visual regimes that make possible violent ideologies and practices. In her essay "Missing People," Steyerl returns once again to the terrain of *November*: "The mass grave that is supposed to contain the remains of my friend Andrea Wolf is located in the mountains south of Van, Turkey. The gravesite is littered with rags, debris, ammunition cases, and many fragments of human bone. A charred photo roll I found on site may be the only witness to what happened" (*Wretched* 155). Here, Steyerl adopts a "flat," "object-oriented" ontology in order to describe what she understands as the "entanglement" of people and things.[34] This "forensic" approach to Andrea's remains cannot, however, adequately comprehend either Steyerl's affective connection to this story—as in the film, she refers here to "my friend Andrea Wolf"—or the "politically constructed," "epistemic violence" that Steyerl also suggests maintains Andrea's story in its unresolved state of injustice and that cannot be the result of the object's agency alone (155). The shift from the subject to the object, the image, and the thing (which seem interchangeable in her account) evacuates the grounds on which we might theorize an implicated subject in this new media environment. Yet, even as Steyerl's writings push toward the abolition of the position that would allow us to theorize a subject implicated in and complicit with the realm of the traveling image, her aesthetic practice opens up a more differentiated and dialectical perspective on the relation between subject and object.[35]

By staging her own multilayered implication as friend, citizen, and artist, *November* and Steyerl's related works reopen the question of subjectivity in the articulation of a critical internationalism. If Steyerl's project seems, at first, to be about the search for Andrea, it ultimately turns out to be a self-reflexive critique of the artist herself. Returning to the opening sequence of *November*, we already find her present in multiple modalities. Most obviously, we hear her voice as it recounts an episode from her teenage years, and we see her younger self in footage from her first film. More subtly, but more consequentially, the opening montage also hints at the filmmaker's implication in the material she is revealing to us. As the camera zooms in on the black-and-white image of Wolf, we see a shadow that may be that of the filmmaker; because the zoom is accompanied by the sounds of a helicopter, the film also implicitly connects its own technological capacity to relocate itself in a field of vision with the military technology that constitutes the proximate cause of Wolf's death (an echo of the way Kentridge draws attention to the complicity of his own techniques with those of capitalism). The film reinforces that connection between the sound of the helicopter, Wolf's death, and the affordances of cinema when the noise of the helicopter returns during the "reconstructed witness account" of Wolf's capture and execution on October 22, 1998. These opening hints at the filmmaker's own role in the story play themselves out as a significant dimension of the film's concerns over the course of the work.

Although never expressed directly, Steyerl's references on various occasions to German involvement in Turkey/Kurdistan evoke what Jaspers called "political guilt," the responsibility of the citizen for the actions of her government. In *November*, she points out the historical irony that "after the fall of the Berlin Wall, the weapons of the former National People's Army of the GDR are given to the Turkish Army," where they are used against the Kurdish people. Such weapons transfers—another form of displacement joining those of images and people—help create the "mixed territories" the film references and ensure that "Germany is in Kurdistan" as well as vice versa.[36] As this sequence on German complicity continues, we hear again from a Berlin-based director who had interviewed Wolf in the mountains and who recounts being shocked to see German munitions employed by Turkey; after all, he says, "a large number of my friends have always been Kurdish people, and of course I had a relation [*Bezug*] to this conflict." In the words of this (possibly Turkish-German) director, we find the coming together of intimate and political implication.

As Steyerl makes clear in a much-discussed sequence, her implication in Andrea's story extends beyond the general responsibility of the citizen for the deeds of her government and into the very medium through which she tells that story. While a TV news announcer intones "The war in Iraq ranges as far as Berlin," we watch footage of Steyerl carrying a candle and wearing a scarf with Kurdish colors as she marches in a demonstration. "This is me as a Kurdish protestor in a TV documentary," she tells us (fig. 14). If *November* initially explores the question of how Andrea Wolf ended up being shot "as a Kurdish terrorist" and returning to Germany as a poster, now the film

"Germany Is in Kurdistan" 189

offers us a new twist: the story of how its director went from being a German filmmaker to becoming a "Kurdish protestor." She recounts: "I went to this demonstration against the Iraq War as a camera person. Because the director knew about my film project, he suddenly took over the camera. He grabbed a flag, wrapped it around my neck, stuffed a torch in my hand, and told me, 'Now look sad and meditative. Look as if you were thinking of Andrea.'" Readily entering into the director's spontaneous script and then deliberately including this footage (which, we are told, was the only shot from the protest that was broadcast!), Steyerl foregrounds her own complicity in the commodification of resistance: "There is the pose of the militant hero, but there is another pose which is much more problematic, and this is the pose of the sensitive, contained, and understanding filmmaker, who tells a personal story. But I don't understand anything and this pose is much more hypocritical than even the crudest propaganda icon." In exposing the

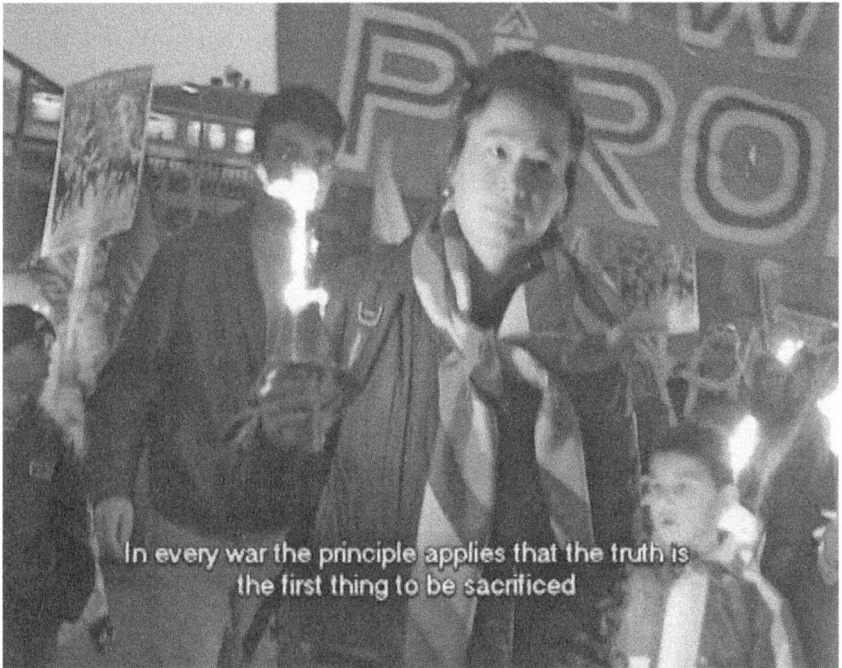

FIGURE 14. An image incorporated into *November* of the artist as a "Kurdish protestor." Hito Steyerl, November, 2004. DV, single channel, sound. 25 minutes. Image CC 4.0 Hito Steyerl. Image courtesy of the artist and Andrew Kreps Gallery, New York.

hypocrisy of the sensitive artist, Steyerl turns the critique of internationalism back on her own work and, in that sense, distinguishes her memorialization of Andrea Wolf from the affirmative commemoration of revolutionary martyrdom found among Wolf's comrades. But the scene also stages the return of the subject, even if it is a subject caught—like Andrea before her—in a material web of traveling images.

This surprising turn, in which the artist puts herself in the position of the Kurdish protestor whose trajectory we thought she was tracking, does not constitute the end of Steyerl's Wolf project but something like its beginning. Since completing *November* in 2004, she has not abandoned the search for Andrea; instead, she has followed the story's threads in ever more ambitious directions; in some ways, she has even become a "Kurdish protestor"! Like Kentridge's Felix/Soho series and his ongoing experimentation with the procession form, Steyerl's Andrea series continually shifts her approach and responds to historical transformation.

The 2012 dual-channel video *Abstract*, a further chapter in the exploration of Andrea's story, continues to pursue a notion of implication that is simultaneously personal and political. Rather than remaining merely "abstract," as its title ironically suggests, the film actually stages Steyerl's physical presence in both Turkey and Germany (fig. 15). *Abstract* includes footage from Steyerl's visit to the mass grave where Wolf's dead body was likely dumped and complements the forensic approach theorized in essays such as "A Thing like You and Me" and "Missing People." In other words, here Steyerl starts to come closer to the internationalist project of Ivens and Loridan (and to move farther from Godard's ironic distance): she journeys to the site of conflict instead of remaining in the metropole. Her version of an affirmative internationalism, however, resembles the internationalism of human rights more than the socialist internationalism that motivated Wolf, Ivens, and Loridan. It is, after all, human rights groups that have pursued the location of Wolf's grave and have attempted, through the European Court of Human Rights, to pressure Turkey into investigating Wolf's death.

Abstract also includes shots of the filmmaker herself in a Ramones t-shirt standing in front of the Brandenburg Gate on Pariser Platz in Berlin: she uses her iPhone to film the headquarters of Lockheed Martin, which describes itself as "a strategic partner of the Bundeswehr and the German aerospace and defense industry" and whose Hellfire missiles played a role in Wolf's death.[37] The shots of the filmmaker with a camera once again echo the Godard of *Loin du Vietnam*, but, in contrast to Godard,

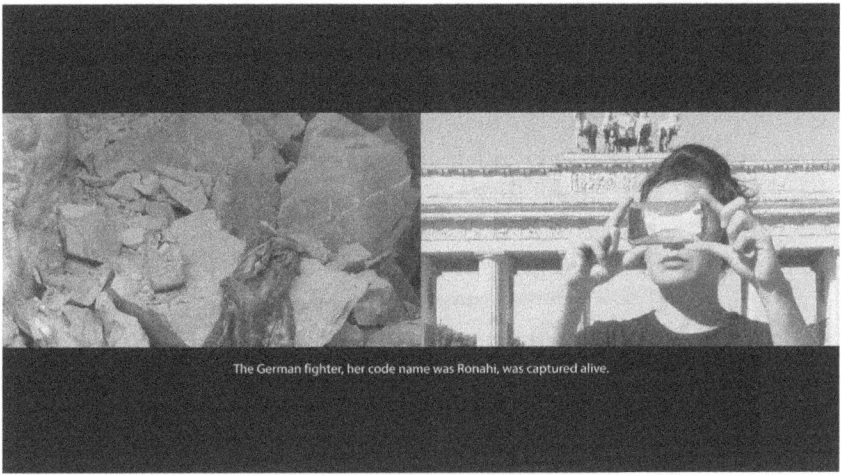

FIGURE 15. On the left, footage of the mass grave near Van, Turkey, where Andrea Wolf's remains were reportedly found. On the right, the artist with her mobile phone in front of the Brandenburg Gate in Berlin. Hito Steyerl, *Abstract*, 2012. Two-channel HD video with sound. 7 minutes, 30 seconds. Image CC 4.0 Hito Steyerl. Image courtesy of the artist and Andrew Kreps Gallery, New York.

emphasize the proximity of the violence that transnational capital produces as well as the new, intimate forms of witnessing made possible by small-scale electronics.[38] As in *November*, the forensic turn to the object makes no sense without the persistence of the investigating, implicated subject—here seen turning the personalized consumer technology of the smartphone and the rebellious iconography of punk rock against the military-industrial complex. In the words of the Art Institute of Chicago, which exhibited *Abstract* along with *November*, this seven-minute-long film "links cinematic shooting and military warfare together, implicating Germany's role in the operation" that killed Andrea.[39] Taken together, the two channels of the video thus suggest that Steyerl's exploration of Andrea's death uses aesthetic form to supplement Jaspers's political guilt and Arendt's collective responsibility—the responsibility of the citizen—with both her relation to a realm of embodied implication and the "abstract" sphere of the transnational corporation. The use of the split screen also brings together the more critical version of internationalism represented in *Loin du Vietnam* by Godard and the more affirmative version instantiated by Ivens and Loridan.

If *Abstract* presents embodied implication as a provocative indictment of the state and the corporation, this indictment also comes to encompass art itself. Not just the artist as individual subject (as in *November*), but art as institution is caught in the webs of implication Steyerl uncovers—something we witness especially in her 2013 lecture-performance "Is the Museum a Battlefield?" at the Istanbul Biennial. A genre that both draws on and parodies a scholarly art-historical lecture, with slides, notes, and lively hand gestures, the lecture-performance simultaneously exposes the artist in front of her audience and activates her aura as part of the international art world's star system.[40] "Is the Museum a Battlefield?," which incorporates footage from the film *Abstract*, exploits this double potential. Combining whimsical, associative thinking and deadly serious content, the piece serves as a reflection on art's implication in structures of violence and commodification as well as an example of such capture.

With "Is the Museum a Battlefield?," Steyerl pursues her own implication as an artist to its logical conclusion, while also commenting indirectly but provocatively on Turkish politics. In addressing the performance's eponymous question, Steyerl returns (yet again) to an actual battlefield, the site in southeastern Turkey "where my friend Andrea Wolf was supposed to have been extra-judicially executed as a member of the women's section of the so-called PKK." As scenes from *Abstract* are projected behind her in which a local guide sorts through the debris found at the site—including scraps of clothes, part of a Hellfire missile, and a 20mm bullet shell manufactured by General Dynamics—Steyerl pursues her forensic methodology. Although again evoking a human rights internationalism, she also parodies that impulse and that methodology via her playfully serious aesthetic.

Holding an imaginary shell between her fingers, she explains, "I tried to follow the few pieces of debris back to their makers . . . the places they were launched from initially." Such a procedure should allow her to identify who shot the bullet, she supposes. This time, following the itinerary of the debris leads not only to the corporate headquarters of Lockheed Martin, as in *Abstract*, but also to the headquarters of the global art world. Tracing the link between the military technology industry, the funding of art museums, and the world of "starchitecture" (high-visibility architectural projects by the likes of Frank Gehry), Steyerl reports that the shell she found at the site of Andrea's murder led her to the Art Institute of Chicago, which is "strongly supported by some members of General Dynamics' founding family." Entering the Art Institute in pursuit of the bullet that may have killed Andrea, she finds something even more surprising: "What did I find when I followed the bullet's trajectory backwards? I found a picture of myself, actually, shooting video on an iPhone with the caption 'This is a shot.' So did *I* shoot the bullet I found on the battlefield myself?" With this final twist, which is accompanied by the relevant scenes from *Abstract*, Steyerl takes the question of implication full circle. In her rendering, the works of art that grow out of an encounter with political violence find their conditions of production, circulation, and reception in the same military-industrial complex that enabled the violence in the first place and in the collapse of the art world back into that complex.

When we follow Steyerl's Andrea Wolf project to its (temporary) conclusion, then, we find an echo of the circular structure that also characterizes Alan Schechner's video loop "The Legacy of Abused Children." Now, however, the artist joins her subjects in the circularity of art and violence. Steyerl neither takes this circularity as an occasion for despair nor disavows the levels of implication that link the artist to the violent content and context of her work through the funding structures of the museum. To the contrary, she embraces implication and tries to work from within its webs of complicity: "Rather than withdraw from such spaces because of their connection with military violence and gentrification, I would on the contrary try to show this video work in every single art space connected to this battlefield." In connecting the globalized art world to a battlefield in Kurdistan, Steyerl may forgo the form of internationalism that motivated her friend Andrea, but she nevertheless incorporates some of its critical resources into another internationalist project.

Recycling images from mainstream and alternative news media as well as an international corpus of films—some of which, like *Loin du Vietnam*, employ a similar aesthetic of recycling—Steyerl's *November* both follows from and remains close to the radical political aesthetic she calls "October."[41] Might this proximity to internationalism be a source of strength rather than an indication of unwanted contamination? Is it possible to move from critical internationalism toward a new affirmative internationalism, one that would retain the self-reflexivity of Steyerl's project, but also link it with the possibility of new collective subjects who could contest the conditions that produce complicity?

Just as Steyerl's work refuses to let go of Wolf, instead returning repeatedly to her life, her death, and her afterlife as an image, Steyerl cannot fully let go of the framework of internationalism. She rejects an affirmative socialist internationalism and ironically subverts a human rights internationalism, but she simultaneously crafts a critically internationalist aesthetic that arises from a sense of implication and moves her across national borders in acts of long-distance solidarity.[42]

Most recently, this long-distance solidarity has taken Steyerl back to the Kurdish region, where she has worked with artists and refugees from Kobanê in the Turkish town of Suruç.[43] In a special issue of the journal *e-flux* dedicated to "Strange Universalism," Steyerl also helps bring visibility to the simultaneously Kurdish and internationalist struggle in Rojava. She interviews a member of the Rojava Film Commune—the Turkish filmmaker Önder Çakar—about the militant filmmaking practices in the region, and she joins the Film Commune in interviewing four women commanders from the YPJ (Women's Defense Units), who discuss their approach to revolution.[44] As the women of the YPJ state, in terms that carry an echo of the intersectional approach of the Combahee River Collective, "Through the color of women, we would like to establish equality. If women don't take part in a revolution, then that revolution is useless. Without women, our revolution would collapse just like real-existing socialism. Because women are leading, this revolution will survive" ("Color of Women" n.p.).[45] And this vision, which combines feminism, ecology, and socialism, is also decidedly internationalist: "Women from all around the world are gathered here with us. German, Iranian, American—women from all nations joined us. And together we work on the revolution" ("Color of Women" n.p.). This internationalism is shared by the Rojava Film Commune as well. As Çakar remarks to Steyerl in his interview, "The Rojava Film Commune was one of the first organizations founded in the liberated territories. There were some filmmaker friends who made a few documentaries about the Islamic State massacres in Shengal, also some other folks who came to Rojava as internationalists and had experience in filmmaking. We joined forces and founded the film commune" ("I don't have time!" n.p.). We are, in some ways, back on the terrain of the SLON collective with which we opened the previous chapter on Loridan-Ivens—albeit here organized from the periphery as a subaltern project.

Steyerl presents herself in this recent work with the Kurdish internationalist movement not as an autonomous artist or an insider to the Film Commune or the YPJ, but rather as an implicated subject building collective solidarity in a moment of urgency. As she writes in a footnote to the interview with the women: "I am just filling in here, as many of my journalist friends who would be much better equipped to do political interviews are in Turkish jails. . . . As soon as [these imprisoned journalists] are freed, I promise I will go back to writing about JPEGs or VR [virtual reality]. Please support the freedom of journalists, writers, artists, and liberal and leftist activists in Turkey, or you will have to endure more terrible journalism" ("Color of Women" n.p.). Deploying her usual mix of humor and serious political engagement, Steyerl's "terrible journalism" nevertheless signals a new phase of her work. As the dynamics of the conflict in the region have changed along with the ideology and strategy of the Kurdish struggle, so has Steyerl's own practice transformed: passing through engagement with Andrea Wolf's affirmative internationalism and moving into her own critical internationalism, Steyerl has now moved back into proximity with an actually existing internationalist politics. It is too early to know what will emerge next, either in Kurdistan or in Steyerl's work. What is clear from this case, however, is that a self-reflexive grasp of one's own implication need not lead to a paralyzing descent into melancholia; to the contrary, as Steyerl's practice makes clear: it can be enormously generative of new aesthetic forms and new forms of solidarity.

Conclusion: From Implication to Fidelity

Neither Loridan-Ivens nor Steyerl arrives at a "complete" figuration of a collective subject who would draw from the strengths of socialist, anticolonial, and human rights internationalisms while also learning from their errors and weaknesses. Perhaps the political subject who emerges from grappling with implication can (and should) never be complete. Loridan-Ivens's multidirectional career emerges from trauma, traverses anticolonial resistance and revolutionary engagement, and returns in a postrevolutionary moment to a reckoning with trauma "under the sign of the suitcase"—a multivalent sign that holds together the different stages of her life and work. Steyerl's ongoing artistic project involves coming to terms with "Andrea"—a friend who, in the artist's hands, has also become a multivalent sign that encompasses the rebelliousness of pop culture, the motivating force of socialist internationalism, the risks of terrorism, and the webs of complicity that branch out from state violence and the transnational military-industrial complex and swallow up artists and their publics. Both filmmakers leave us with postheroic figurations, but they do so in a way that moves us through the affective force field of internationalism and maps transnational political dynamics.

Perhaps the concept of "fidelity" developed by the philosopher Alain Badiou can help us understand what is at stake in these two oeuvres.[46] Fidelity entails remaining true to the rupture of an event. For Badiou, an event exposes the "void" of a given situation; that is, it draws attention to its unthought, unspoken contradictions. According to his system, events can take place in four fields: love, science, art, or politics. The examples he uses are generally "positive" events—the French Revolution, May '68, Schönberg's invention of the twelve-tone system, an amorous encounter. Yet, as Bruno Bosteels, one of the philosopher's most incisive commentators, notes about Badiou's conception of politics, "a politics starts out from that point in the social order that signals the excessive power of the state. This point is the place, or site, of the political event."[47] Acts of fidelity construct truths out of the voids of state violence; they name the event and make possible the slow, fundamental transformation of the structure of the situation.[48] Unlike everyday understandings of fidelity in which we presuppose a subject who either remains faithful or instead enacts a betrayal, Badiou proposes that the act of fidelity *produces* a new subject: "I call 'subject' the bearer [*le support*] of a fidelity, the one who bears a process of truth. The subject, therefore, in no way pre-exists the process. He is absolutely nonexistent in the situation 'before' the event. We might say that the process of truth *induces* a subject" (*Ethics* 43).

In the cases that interest us here, acts of fidelity are forced to confront a multiplicity of events; fidelity is an iterative act and, in distinction to Badiou's theory, the event shifts with each iteration. Loridan-Ivens might be said to emerge as a subject of fidelity who testifies across the decades to various experiences of rupture: of genocide, decolonization, and postrevolutionary disappointment. Steyerl becomes a subject by remaining faithful to the event of Andrea's death. However, in her iterative acts of fidelity, new understandings of the event emerge along with new configurations of the subject. In *November*, Andrea's death initially seems to testify primarily to the limits of internationalism "in the time after October." In *Abstract* and

"Is the Museum a Battlefield?," however, the event spirals out from the battlefield where Andrea died to globally dispersed centers of military, corporate, and cultural power. Ongoing events in the Kurdish region subsequently interpellate Steyerl and land her (at least at the time of this writing) in even greater proximity to the Kurdish cause. Fidelity to these reconfigured events produces an implicated, critically internationalist subject.

The process of iteration does not entail a full-scale displacement of the original event. As Badiou would insist, without holding on to the event through acts of iteration and investigation there would be no fidelity. Two things remain constant across the iterations of Steyerl's project: the repetition of an intimate affiliation ("my friend Andrea Wolf") and the return to a localized geographical site (the area near Van where Wolf was killed and, more recently, the larger Kurdish region). As Badiou argues, the universality of truths arises from singular encounters, encounters that can encompass love as well as politics. The implicated subject can become a political subject when the fact of implication becomes the occasion for a work of fidelity that creates the conditions for a new subject. Implication, in other words, defines the "pre-eventual" state of the situation; recognition of implication constitutes an event with the potential to create new figures that contest their status as implicated subjects. Steyerl's fidelity to Andrea opens up that potential, but individual fidelity is not yet political, because it is not yet collective. The affirmative internationalism of Andrea as well as Loridan-Ivens suggests the risks of the collective. What remains to be created is a collective, affirmative internationalist fidelity that has passed through the work of mourning performed by Steyerl and Loridan-Ivens; perhaps that is what we find emerging in the still-embattled terrain of Kurdistan.

Conclusion

Transfiguring Implication

This book has introduced a new figure to critical theory and to the political imagination: the implicated subject. By referring to the implicated subject as a figure, I draw attention to the tensions at the heart of that concept: the resonances of both figurative art—"art that retains strong references to the real world and particularly to the human figure"—and figurative language: language that diverges from the literal.[1] An implicated subject is a figure insofar as it both alludes to human beings located in a real, material world and serves as a trope for describing a contingent, shifting, and socially constituted position in that world. The implicated subject is not an identity, but rather a figure to think with and through.

This book has presented various figures of implication, many derived from works of visual art. Indeed, the visual realm has proven ripe for the investigation of implication because of the possibilities it offers for the figurative exploration of structural problems, that is, for making tangible and perceptible the large-scale histories and social dynamics that produce implication. We have met such figures as Kentridge's alter egos Felix and Soho, Steyerl's Andrea Wolf and her own staged self, Schechner's visually manipulated Warsaw Ghetto and Palestinian boys, and in nonvisual but still embodied realms, Kincaid's imaginary white tourist and the contributors to the "We are not Trayvon Martin" website. Although found in different media, in different national contexts, and in both fictional and nonfictional discourses, these implicated subjects are nevertheless all figures of implication, imaginative representations of real but difficult-to-pin-down social forces. The examples of visual manipulation we find in many of the artworks analyzed here—those of Kentridge, Schechner, and Steyerl, most obviously—emphasize the significance of the nonliteral dimensions of these human forms: the fact that they offer allegories of social relations rather than essential or fixed individual identities. The hyperbolic nature of Kincaid's address to the white reader and the twists and turns of her rhetoric function similarly.

The implicated subject is not something to celebrate. On the contrary, the implicated subject represents, above all, not a solution but a problem. Implicated subjects inhabit the machinery of political violence, economic exploitation, and ecological devastation. This is not to say, however, that implicated subjects serve merely as "cogs" in that machinery. Rather, they are, in the words I have adopted from Simona Forti, "transmission belts" of domination—a more active notion than that implied by the misleadingly passive "cog." The stress on rethinking historical and political responsibility as implication highlights the need to hold implicated subjects accountable in both moral and political registers. If there is a potential "solution" in positing the existence of an implicated subject and drawing attention to the breadth of implication in a globally connected world, it derives from the impetus to combat and *transfigure* implication by self-consciously grasping one's position as an implicated subject and joining with others in collective action. In other words, I do believe that individual subjects matter, but I believe they become effective agents—for good or ill—primarily by acting in concert with others. Implication derives from one form of acting in concert: the kind we undertake without being conscious of our actions' impact or that we perform while engaging in more active forms of disavowal. Socially constituted ignorance and denial are essential components of implication; as such, they are also potential starting points for those who want to transform implication and refigure it as the basis of a differentiated, long-distance solidarity.

Implication is widespread. The interlocking systems of oppression that intersectional feminists such as the members of the Combahee River Collective have illuminated ensure that degrees of implication pervade the social worlds of most inhabitants of the planet. Emphasizing the figural dimension of implicated subjects casts light on the diversity of figures of responsibility in critical discourse without reifying or essentializing differences and dynamic social relations. Indeed, implication comes in diverse forms: it describes beneficiaries and descendants, accomplices and perpetuators, and it can even attach to people who have had shattering experiences of trauma or victimization and are thus situated within "complex implication." Throughout the book, we have seen that implication emerges from genealogies and structures: from the different ways that historical legacies and contemporary conflicts, intimate inheritances and diffuse social forces, intertwine.

Despite its pervasive character, however, implication is not evenly distributed. Responsibility for the manifold injustices that confront us in the daily news and in our history books lies disproportionately with certain populations who live in certain locations. Ours is an uneven world, and that unevenness manifests itself in local neighborhoods as well as global flows. I thus side, for example, with those who are skeptical about the homogenizing and universalizing dimensions of categories like the "Anthropocene" and prefer to highlight instead the asymmetries of the "Capitalocene." Assessing degrees and kinds of implication—whether in the Capitalocene, in the wake of racial slavery, or in the ongoing dispossessions of settler colonialism—demands political judgment, a sense of proportion and scale, and an ability to both distinguish and hold together different claims for justice.

The ultimate point, though, is not to dwell on or in implication but to transfigure it: to acknowledge and map implication in order to reopen political struggles beyond the defensive purity of self-contained identities. While dwelling in implication involves closing off the self from its responsibilities, complicities, and debts, transfiguring implication opens the self to others—and to one's own otherness, prosthetic agency, and unacknowledged capacity to wound. As the examples of Loridan-Ivens and Steyerl illustrate, the movement from implication to solidarity does not follow a direct path; it often involves ambivalence, error, and unintended consequences. Differentiated forms of long-distance solidarity are necessary to implication's transfiguration, but neither histories of violence nor structures of inequality release their hold on implicated subjects without a fight.

The struggle against implication and the injustices it brings into view has deadly literal (literally deadly) dimensions to it, as the case of Andrea Wolf, among others, reminds us, but it also involves a struggle at the level of concepts and figures. It matters, I have argued, how we construct figures of solidarity, just as it matters how we figure responsibility. Are we Trayvon Martin or are we not? Is Gaza Warsaw or is it something else? What is the difference between a "Kurdish terrorist" and a "Kurdish protestor"? I doubt we will all agree on the answers to such questions; indeed, the answers will vary depending on how we're situated in relation to the problems they seek to address.

But for those who are committed to addressing the kinds of injustices invoked by names such as "Trayvon Martin," "Gaza," and "Kurdistan," I have put forward several propositions over the course of this book that I synthesize here as the point of departure for further discussion and debate:

1. We must enlarge our understanding of the actors involved in injustices beyond the most often invoked figures of victims, perpetrators, and bystanders.

2. Interlocking systems of oppression produce implicated subjects as well as victims and perpetrators. The innocent, uninvolved bystander is, in most cases, an idealized myth.

3. Implicated subjects take a variety of forms in relation to distinct, if often overlapping, forms of injustice. The increasing prominence of the beneficiary in critical discourse represents important conceptual progress but requires further elaboration and nuance: the beneficiary belongs to a cohort of implicated subjects.

4. Interlocking systems of oppression create dilemmas of collective political responsibility that cannot be reduced to assignations of legalistic individual guilt.

5. Those dilemmas of responsibility involve both historical legacies and contemporary inequalities. Such legacies and inequalities are intertwined, but analytic attention to both diachronic and synchronic axes can help sort out the nature of their entanglement.

6. On both of those intertwined axes, implicated subjects—subjects who are neither purely victim nor perpetrator—play essential roles in producing and reproducing violence and inequality.

7. Many people find themselves "complexly" implicated: with lines of direct or indirect connection to histories of both victimization and perpetration. Thinking about implication complements thinking about postmemory.

8. In the face of complex implication, a multidirectional politics of differentiated, long-distance solidarity has greater purchase than a politics premised on identification, purity, or the absolute separation between locations and histories.

9. Yet the forging of long-distance solidarity comes with its own risks: risks of adventurism, misunderstanding, appropriation, and ideological rigidity.

10. The best way to combat the risks of solidarity is not to retreat into local or identity-based certainties, but rather to confront directly socially sanctioned denial and ignorance and conscious and unconscious investments in privilege and hierarchy. The self-reflexivity of implicated subjects is not sufficient for the construction of durable solidarities, but it remains a necessary component of coalition building.

11. Scholars and activists need both to interpret implication and to transfigure it.

Notes

INTRODUCTION: FROM VICTIMS AND PERPETRATORS TO IMPLICATED SUBJECTS

1. See Hannah Arendt, "Collective Responsibility," in *Responsibility and Judgment*, ed. Jerome Kohn (New York: Schocken, 2003), 157.

2. See the *OED* entries for *implication, implicate, implicated*. For an emphasis on complicity as folding, see Mark Sanders, *Complicities: The Intellectual and Apartheid* (Durham, NC: Duke University Press, 2002). I return to the relation of implication and complicity below.

3. Black Lives Matter is a decentralized movement catalyzed for the most part by black women (and especially queer black women). Thinking about implication can contribute indirectly to such a movement by offering an analytic perspective to those who are not generally victims of racist violence, but rather are enmeshed in the culture of white supremacy against which Black Lives Matter struggles. For extended considerations of the history and politics of Black Lives Matter, see Keeanga-Yamahtta Taylor, *From #BLACKLIVESMATTER to Black Liberation* (Chicago: Haymarket, 2016); Christopher Lebron, *The Making of Black Lives Matter: A Brief History of an Idea* (New York: Oxford University Press, 2017); and Barbara Ransby, *Making All Black Lives Matter: Reimagining Freedom in the Twenty-First Century* (Berkeley: University of California Press, 2018).

4. Among many possible examples, see http://iamtrayvonmartin.tumblr.com; "'We Are All Trayvon Martin': Photos and Video from the Million Hoodie March," *Mother Jones* (March 21, 2012), http://www.motherjones.com/mojo/2012/03/photos-million-hoodie-march-trayvon-martin; and Otis Moss III, "We Are All Trayvon Martin," *The Daily Beast* (April 13, 2012), http://www.thedailybeast.com/articles/2012/04/13/we-are-all-trayvon-martin.html. The cover of Claudia Rankine's award-winning poetry collection *Citizen: An American Lyric* (Minneapolis: Graywolf, 2014) also features a work of hoodie art. Although created before Trayvon Martin's murder, the choice of that image for the cover clearly references Martin's recent killing. The volume itself focuses especially on the kinds of everyday racism that implicate privileged white subjects on an ongoing basis. I'm grateful to Bill Maxwell for reminding me of the relevance of Rankine's cover image.

5. Cohn-Bendit was born in France to German-Jewish refugee parents and was educated in both Germany and France. Alain Finkielkraut has famously criticized the May '68 slogan in his book *Le juif imaginaire* (Paris: Seuil, 1983). For defenses of that claim to identification, see Jacques Rancière, "Politics, Identification, and Subjectivization," *October* 61 (1992): 58–64, esp. 61–62; and Sarah Hammerschlag, *The Figural Jew: Politics and Identity in Postwar French Thought* (Chicago: University of Chicago Press, 2010). As Rancière asserts, "Politics is about 'wrong' names—misnomers that articulate a gap and connect with a wrong" (62). Neil Levi offers a critical perspective on this politics of identification with the figure of the Jew that is consonant with my own stress on implicated subjects. See his *Modernist Form and the Myth of Jewification* (New York: Fordham University Press, 2013), 202–3n20.

6. See, for example, the anonymous YouTube video posted by 13emcha (a young white woman) on March 31, 2013, called "I Am Not Trayvon Martin," http://www.youtube.com/watch?v=TBRwiuJ8K7w. Asam Ahmad goes even further and offers a critique of the identification of non–African American people of color with Martin. See Ahmad, "We Are NOT All Trayvon: Challenging Anti-Black Racism in POC Communities," *Black Girl Dangerous*, July 16, 2013, http://blackgirldangerous.org/new-blog/2013/7/16/we-are-not-all-trayvon-challenging-anti-black-racism-in-poc-communities.

7. Mark Danner, "We Are All Torturers Now," *New York Times*, January 6, 2005, http://www.nytimes.com/2005/01/06/opinion/we-are-all-torturers-now.html?_r=0.

8. Timothy Kaufman-Osborn, "'We Are All Torturers Now': Accountability after Abu Ghraib," *Theory and Event* 11.2 (2008): n.p. Kaufman-Osborn offers an incisive critique of the logic of Danner's approach.

9. While certainly not frequent, the claim "I am George Zimmerman" was not completely absent from antiracist arguments. See, for example, http://wearenottrayvonmartin.tumblr.com/post/56222710418/i-am-george-zimmerman, July 23, 2013. The YouTube video by 13emcha cited above also offers "I am George Zimmerman" as a "more accurate" slogan than "I am Trayvon Martin."

10. See http://wearenottrayvonmartin.tumblr.com. The website describes its mission this way: "It's not enough to know you aren't Trayvon. What will you do to change our country? Hi, we are Joseph and Tobias and we are here to recruit YOU in the fight against racism." Originally found at the address wearenottrayvonmartin.com, the website eventually moved to a tumblr site.

11. See also those campaigns organized under the slogan "Not in my name," a refusal of identification that has been used by everyone from Jewish critics of Zionism to Muslim critics of the Islamic State. By distancing itself from forces considered oppressive, "Not in my name" lies closer to explicit disidentification than does "We are not Trayvon Martin," which seeks to avoid appropriation of the experience of a victim of racism. Yet, as in the Trayvon Martin case, "Not in my name" also implicitly suggests the speaker's proximity to the problem it "names" and thus the

inability to fully disengage oneself from it. In other words, the productivity of the assertion "Not in my name" derives from the implication that in fact something *is* being done in my name.

12. By "disidentification" I mean something different from what José Muñoz has theorized. Muñoz shows how disidentificatory practices function as "a survival strategy" that allows minority subjects "to resist and confound socially prescriptive patters of identification" by "work[ing] on and against dominant ideology." In contrast, I invoke disidentification as a possibility for the dominant subject. The dominant subject does not have the same access to the subversive form of disidentification described by Muñoz; rather, I suggest, privileged subjects can foster a productive nonidentification that creates critical distance between their position and those of both minority subjects and dominant ideologies. It thus brings the zone of implication into view. See José E. Muñoz, *Disidentifications: Queers of Color and the Politics of Performance* (Minneapolis: University of Minnesota Press, 1999).

13. See http://wearenottrayvonmartin.tumblr.com/post/56227679579/i-am-not-trayvon-martin-i-am-the-poster-girl-for, July 23, 2013.

14. The victim-perpetrator-bystander categorization derives from Holocaust studies but has a more extended influence in popular understandings of trauma and violence. This book contests the individualizing and reifying nature of this categorization even as it recognizes the usefulness of those categories in certain circumstances and for certain purposes. In Mahmood Mamdani's account, the individualizing approach derives from the focus on particular, high-ranking perpetrators in the Nuremberg trials. See his critical account in "Beyond Nuremberg: The Historical Significance of the Post-Apartheid Transition in South Africa," *Politics & Society* 43.1 (2015): 61–88.

15. See http://wearenottrayvonmartin.tumblr.com/post/56143401288/i-am-not-trayvon-martin-because-i-pass, July 22, 2013.

16. I do not assume that "victim" and "perpetrator" are fixed or clear-cut categories; rather, they are abstractions and generalizations, albeit useful ones. The point of introducing the "implicated subject" is to draw attention to ambiguous spaces that do not fit neatly into our scripts for explaining violence and injustice. To assert the importance of interrogating the space between and beyond the categories of victims and perpetrators, however, should not be taken as a call to forgo these categories or to collapse them into each other (though it is possible to occupy both in succession). It is sometimes, especially in the legal realm, essential to hold on to clear-cut distinctions; yet, much remains to be explained beyond those categories.

17. Writing about the John Crawford and Tamir Rice cases, Cobb emphasizes how a broader public—that is, implicated subjects—contributes to the disproportionate number of black people killed by police officers: "It's easy to think of these circumstances as matters of policing, but in both cases the police were acting upon the perceptions of callers who saw armed black men and deduced

a criminal threat." See Jelani Cobb, "Tamir Rice and America's Tragedy," *New Yorker*, December 29, 2015, http://www.newyorker.com/news/daily-comment/tamir-rice-and-americas-tragedy.

18. Aliza Luft offers a "dynamic theory of action" to explain how people move in and out of roles such as perpetrator in genocidal situations. Even in a genocidal context, she shows, the position of "perpetrator" does not remain fixed. Although she does not discuss questions of implication directly, her relational account of genocide demonstrates how those who do not directly participate can nonetheless be implicated in the unfolding events. See Aliza Luft, "Toward a Dynamic Theory of Action at the Micro Level of Genocide: Killing, Desistance, and Saving in 1994 Rwanda," *Sociological Theory* 33.2 (2015): 148–72.

19. On denial, see Stanley Cohen, *States of Denial: Knowing about Atrocities and Suffering* (Malden, MA: Blackwell, 2001); and Catherine Hall and Daniel Pick, "Thinking about Denial," *History Workshop Journal* 84 (Autumn 2017): 1–23. Ann Laura Stoler usefully conceptualizes "colonial aphasia" as a means of discussing "the confused and clogged spaces in between" knowledge and ignorance. See "Colonial Aphasia: Race and Disabled Histories in France," *Public Culture* 23.1 (2011): 121–56; 122.

20. See Berber Bevernage, *History, Memory, and State-Sponsored Violence* (New York: Routledge, 2012).

21. For controversies about reparations, see, for example, the claims by the Caricom Reparations Commission and the controversy that erupted when British Prime Minister David Cameron visited Jamaica in 2015, or the attention garnered by the journalist Ta-Nehisi Coates's writings on reparations and his critique of Democratic candidate Bernie Sanders. I return to the question of reparations in Chapter 1. On Caricom and Cameron, see Rowena Mason, "Jamaica Calls for Britain to Pay Billions of Pounds in Reparations for Slavery," *The Guardian*, September 28, 2015, http://www.theguardian.com/world/2015/sep/29/jamaica-calls-britain-pay-billions-pounds-reparations-slavery. For Coates and Sanders, see Ta-Nahisi Coates, "The Case for Reparations," *The Atlantic*, June 2014, http://www.theatlantic.com/magazine/archive/2014/06/the-case-for-reparations/361631/; and Coates, "Why Precisely Is Bernie Sanders against Reparations?," *The Atlantic*, January 19, 2015, http://www.theatlantic.com/politics/archive/2016/01/bernie-sanders-reparations/424602/. The Coates-Sanders debate led the *New York Times* to offer a "Room for Debate" forum on the topic. See "Racial Reparations and the Limits of Economic Policy," *New York Times*, January 28, 2016, http://www.nytimes.com/roomfordebate/2016/01/28/racial-reparations-and-the-limits-of-economic-policy.

22. Paul Gilroy, *The Black Atlantic: Modernity and Double Consciousness* (Cambridge, MA: Harvard University Press, 1993). In "Case for Reparations," Coates emphasizes the links between slavery and postslavery histories of segregation and housing discrimination. On the actuality of slavery's legacies, see also Saidiya Hartman, *Lose Your Mother: A Journey along the Atlantic Slave Route* (New York: Farrar, Straus and Giroux, 2007); and Christina Sharpe, *In the Wake: On Blackness and Being*

(Durham, NC: Duke University Press, 2016). Neither Hartman nor Sharpe poses reparations as the most adequate response to slavery's ongoing presence. Despite their many differences, Coates, Hartman, and Sharpe all demonstrate a commitment to the "irrevocable" nature of the past conceptualized by Beverage, a conception that disrupts the binary opposition between past and present.

23. Berlant uses this phrase in "Without Exception: On the Ordinariness of Violence," an interview with Brad Evans published in the *Los Angeles Review of Books*, July 30, 2018, https://lareviewofbooks.org/article/without-exception-on-the-ordinariness-of-violence/#!. See also Berlant, *Cruel Optimism* (Durham, NC: Duke University Press, 2011), for more extended reflection on the "structural and ongoing" nature of violence (7).

24. Otto Kerner et al., *Report of the National Advisory Commission on Civil Disorders* (Washington, DC: 1968), 1. For a history of the commission released on its fiftieth anniversary, see Steven M. Gillon, *Separate and Unequal: The Kerner Commission and the Unraveling of American Liberalism* (New York: Basic Books, 2018). The report offered a more radical indictment of white racism and the "separate and unequal" conditions of American society than President Johnson had anticipated in establishing the commission. While Black Power advocates initially dismissed the commission, H. Rap Brown later wrote: "They're saying essentially what I've been saying." Quoted in Justin Driver, "The Report on Race That Shook America," *The Atlantic*, May 2018, https://www.theatlantic.com/magazine/archive/2018/05/the-report-on-race-that-shook-america/556850/.

25. Driver, "Report on Race."

26. See also Richard Rothstein's account of the enduring legacies of de jure (not just de facto) segregation in *The Color of Law: A Forgotten History of How Our Government Segregated America* (New York: Liveright, 2017).

27. I discuss the cases of globalized labor and climate change at somewhat greater length in "Beyond Tancred and Clorinda: Trauma Studies for Implicated Subjects," in *The Future of Trauma Theory: Contemporary Literary and Cultural Criticism*, ed. Gert Buelens, Sam Durrant, and Robert Eaglestone (New York: Routledge, 2013), xi–xviii. See also Richard Crownshaw, "Cultural Memory Studies in the Age of the Anthropocene," in *Memory Unbound: Tracing the Dynamics of Memory Studies*, ed. Lucy Bond, Stef Craps, and Pieter Vermeulen (New York: Berghahn, 2017), 242–57.

28. Debarati Sanyal, *Memory and Complicity: Migrations of Holocaust Remembrance* (New York: Fordham University Press, 2015), 17. In formulating a new concept of complicity, Sanyal draws on several works that have also proven valuable for my work, including Sanders, *Complicities*; Christopher Kutz, *Complicity: Ethics and Law for a Collective Age* (New York: Cambridge University Press, 2000); and Naomi Mandel, *Against the Unspeakable: Complicity, the Holocaust, and Slavery in America* (Charlottesville: University of Virginia Press, 2007).

29. Kaufman-Osborn, "'We Are All Torturers Now,'" n.p.; my emphasis. Kaufman-Osborn is drawing on Kutz, *Complicity*.

30. Numerous other examples, also from work that has inspired my own, could be added here. For instance, in outlining her project on the "burdens of political responsibility," Jade Larissa Schiff concludes: "I seek to understand how the stories we tell, and how we listen to them, mediate our encounters with the face of the Other; and how those stories operate not as commands (as they might for him), but as invitations to face up to our *implication* in others' suffering." See Schiff, *Burdens of Political Responsibility: Narrative and the Cultivation of Responsiveness* (New York: Cambridge University Press, 2014), 26; my emphasis. Such examples, which could easily be multiplied, suggest to me that critics recognize the ubiquity of implication but have yet to formulate it as a problematic deserving its own conceptualization.

31. Iris Marion Young, *Responsibility for Justice* (New York: Oxford University Press, 2011), 103–4.

32. Consider the frequently referenced example of non-Jewish Germans growing up after the Holocaust. Not only does it make no sense to describe them as "guilty" of the Holocaust; it also makes no sense to say that they are "complicit" in it—although they could, for example, be complicit in Holocaust memory's relativization, denial, or instrumentalization. Note, however, that these last actions are all ones that involve the current image of the Holocaust and not the weight of the past as such. I think the distinction is worth maintaining. Drawing on Mandel, Sanyal makes a strong case for linking current practices of memory with complicity (see esp. 14), but a hypothetical connection between history and complicity remains elusive and less convincing to me.

33. See Marianne Hirsch, *The Generation of Postmemory: Writing and Visual Culture after the Holocaust* (New York: Columbia University Press, 2012); and Gabriele Schwab, *Haunting Legacies: Violent Histories and Transgenerational Trauma* (New York: Columbia University Press, 2010). For a comparative approach, see Erin McGlothlin, *Second Generation Holocaust Literature: Legacies of Survival and Perpetration* (Rochester, NY: Camden House, 2006).

34. Robert Meister, *After Evil: A Politics of Human Rights* (New York: Columbia University Press, 2011), 25–26.

35. Bevernage develops this insight in "The Past Is Evil / Evil Is Past: On Retrospective Politics, Philosophy of History, and Temporal Manichaeism," *History and Theory* 54 (October 2015): 333–52.

36. I make a related argument in response to the cultural theorist Ariella Azoulay in Chapter 4, where the matter at hand is the question of Israel and Palestine.

37. Bruce Robbins, *The Beneficiary* (Durham, NC: Duke University Press, 2017), 9.

38. Mahmood Mamdani, "Reconciliation without Justice," *Southern African Review of Books* (November/December 1996): 3–5; 5.

39. Since Robbins argues, as do I, that the category of the beneficiary is distinct from that of the perpetrator, this notion of causality must also be distinct from the notion associated with the perpetration of a deed. The causality of perpetration

accords with the direct form of responsibility that Karl Jaspers calls "criminal guilt" (and which I discuss in the next chapter), but the causality associated with beneficiary status must be more complex. See Young, *Responsibility for Justice*, and my discussion in the next chapter.

40. Robbins, in contrast, argues that the emphasis on the historical dimension of beneficiary status distracts from the (to him) more fundamental problem of current global inequality.

41. Zafer Şenocak and Bülent Tulay, "Germany—Home for Turks?," in Zafer Şenocak, *Atlas of a Tropical Germany: Essays on Politics and Culture, 1990–1998*, tr. and ed. Leslie A. Adelson (Lincoln: University of Nebraska Press, 2000), 6. I have slightly altered Adelson's translation in this case. See Z. Şenocak, *Atlas des tropischen Deutschland* (Berlin: Babel Verlag, 1993), 16.

42. The complex question of immigrants' relation to Holocaust memory in Germany is the subject of the book I am coauthoring with Yasemin Yildiz, *Inheritance Trouble: Migrant Archives of Holocaust Remembrance* (under contract with Fordham University Press).

43. In *The Beneficiary*, Robbins addresses his audience directly: "Who is a beneficiary? You are, probably. If you had not benefitted from some ambitious higher education, it seems unlikely that you would be dipping into a book with so earnest and unpromising a title as this one" (6). Although I do not seek to address my reader as directly as does Robbins, much the same could be said about the implicated subject: most (all?) readers of this book will be implicated subjects. Indeed, the institutions of higher education Robbins mentions are themselves vectors of implication, as recent explorations of American universities' complicity in the slave trade illustrate. More generally, universities—while serving as important, indeed necessary, sites of counterdiscourse—have traditionally produced knowledge that contributes to militarization, racial hierarchies, and more. Yet, this book is ultimately not addressed to "implicated subjects" as an identity group—one of my arguments is, in fact, that we shift in and out of positions of implication depending on context—but rather at those who are interested in exploring and contesting the fact of implication.

44. Carrie Tirado Bramen, *American Niceness: A Cultural History* (Cambridge, MA: Harvard University Press, 2017), 25. Bramen is drawing on the psychoanalyst Christopher Bollas's idea of "violent innocence." See Bollas, *Being a Character: Psychoanalysis and Self Experience* (New York: Hill and Wang, 1992).

45. Writing in the wake of the 2016 US election, artist and theorist Andrea Fraser draws on Bourdieu's account of the field of power to make a case for the uses of reflexivity on the political left. See Andrea Fraser, "Toward a Reflexive Resistance," *X-tra*, March 2018, http://x-traonline.org/article/artist-writes-no-2–toward-a-reflexive-resistance/.

46. I cite Walter Benjamin's well-known eighth thesis: "The current amazement that the things we are experiencing are 'still' possible in the twentieth century is

not philosophical. This amazement is not the beginning of knowledge—unless it is the knowledge that the view of history which gives rise to it is untenable." See Benjamin, "On the Concept of History," tr. Harry Zohn, in *Selected Writings*, vol. 4: *1938–1940*, ed. Howard Eiland and Michael W. Jennings (Cambridge, MA: Harvard University Press, 2006), 392.

47. Simona Forti, *New Demons: Rethinking Power and Evil Today* (Stanford, CA: Stanford University Press, 2014). See also Robert Eaglestone's complementary discussion of Arendt and the banality of evil in *The Broken Voice: Reading Post-Holocaust Literature* (Oxford: Oxford University Press, 2017), 31–40.

48. This book arises out of continued reflection on issues I began thinking about in *Multidirectional Memory: Remembering the Holocaust in the Age of Decolonization* (Stanford, CA: Stanford University Press, 2009), and to some extent in *Traumatic Realism: The Demands of Holocaust Representation* (Minneapolis: University of Minnesota Press, 2000). Indeed, some of the examples that ground *Multidirectional Memory* return here in new contexts. In *Multidirectional Memory*, I pursued mnemonic links between the Nazi genocide and European colonialism that usually involved experiences of victimization perceived as shared or shareable across contexts. Engaging with this archive, I made a more general argument about the productive and dialogic nature of cultural memory: while the public articulation of memory takes place in a space of contestation, it does not obey the logic of a zero-sum game, but rather emerges via echo, ricochet, and cross-cultural borrowing. In moving from *Multidirectional Memory* to *The Implicated Subject*, I have maintained my interest in the way histories and memories overflow the borders of nations and identities, but I have shifted attention to different valences of connection. In place of the intervictim group "minor transnationalism" (in Lionnet and Shih's useful term) out of which the previous book sought to construct a new theory of memory, the present book pursues the implication of those proximate to power in historically or spatially distant events and in impersonal structures.

49. Robbins, *The Beneficiary*, 10. See also Bruce Robbins, *Perpetual War: Cosmopolitanism from the Viewpoint of Violence* (Durham, NC: Duke University Press, 2012).

50. In addition to thinkers discussed elsewhere, several other scholars have been important to my conceptualization of implication. Historian Tessa Morris-Suzuki offers a notion of implication close to mine in her book *The Past within Us*. Morris-Suzuki's primary focus, however, involves investigating how different media construct historical consciousness and the importance of a notion of historical "truthfulness" as opposed to a fetishized "truth." Both complicity and implication are keywords in sociologist Alexis Shotwell's book *Against Purity*, but Shotwell does not attempt to distinguish them or put forward a theory of implication as such. I share Shotwell's critique of purism, but I primarily foreground the limits of the victim/perpetrator binary. In *The Broken Voice*, literary critic Robert Eaglestone investigates the role of public secrets in the construction of complicity in genocide in a way that complements my own approach. Michael Lazzara's *Civil Obedience* offers a nuanced account of "complicity

and complacency" in neoliberal Chile whose argument is generally in line with my own. See Tessa Morris-Suzuki, *The Past within Us: Media, Memory, History* (London: Verso, 2005); Alexis Shotwell, *Against Purity: Living Ethically in Compromised Times* (Minneapolis: University of Minnesota Press, 2016); Robert Eaglestone, *The Broken Voice*; and Michael Lazzara, *Civil Obedience: Complicity and Complacency in Chile since Pinochet* (Madison: University of Wisconsin Press, 2018).

51. Sanyal calls these pitfalls "dangerous intersections" and explores the advantages and disadvantages of multidirectional memory with great nuance and tact in *Memory and Complicity*. See also Tzvetan Todorov, *Hope and Memory: Lessons from the Twentieth Century*, tr. David Bellos (Princeton, NJ: Princeton University Press, 2003), esp. 159–76.

CHAPTER 1: THE TRANSMISSION BELT OF DOMINATION

1. Samuel Moyn, "Human Rights Are Not Enough," *The Nation*, April 9, 2018, https://www.thenation.com/article/human-rights-are-not-enough/. For a full account, see Moyn, *Not Enough: Human Rights in an Unequal World* (Cambridge, MA: Belknap Press of Harvard University Press, 2018).

2. Robert Meister, *After Evil: A Politics of Human Rights* (New York: Columbia University Press, 2011); Bruce Robbins, *The Beneficiary* (Durham, NC: Duke University Press, 2017).

3. Charles Mills, *Black Rights / White Wrongs: The Critique of Racial Liberalism* (New York: Oxford University Press, 2017), 49.

4. For the initial use of the concept of intersectionality, see Kimberlé Crenshaw, "Demarginalizing the Intersection of Race and Sex: A Black Feminist Critique of Antidiscrimination Doctrine, Feminist Theory and Antiracist Politics," *University of Chicago Legal Forum* (1989): 139–67. For a recent review essay that interrogates the often fierce debates over intersectionality, the question of its institutionalization in the US academy, and the frequent attempts to establish a definitive genealogy of the concept, see Jennifer C. Nash, "Intersectionality and Its Discontents," *American Quarterly* 69.1 (2017): 117–29.

5. A new edition, with a contextualizing introduction and interviews with the original authors, marks the fortieth anniversary of the statement. See Keeanga-Yamahtta Taylor, ed., *How We Get Free: Black Feminism and the Combahee River Collective* (Chicago: Haymarket, 2017). Further references to the statement are from this edition.

6. Quoted in Asad Haider, *Mistaken Identity: Race and Class in the Age of Trump* (New York: Verso, 2018), 9. Haider emphasizes throughout his book the need to create something like what I call "long-distance solidarity"—that is, solidarity that transcends fixed identity categories.

7. Primo Levi, "The Gray Zone," in *The Drowned and the Saved*, tr. Michael F. Moore, *The Complete Works of Primo Levi*, vol. 3, ed. Ann Goldstein (New York: Liveright, 2015), 2414–15.

8. The question of how far one can justly take the concept of the gray zone away from the Nazi camps is a major bone of contention in writings on Levi. My position is that Levi invites translation of his concept outside the context of the concentrationary universe, but that such translations demand care and a nuanced approach to comparison.

9. I take the phrase "extreme duress" from the philosopher Claudia Card. For Card, extreme duress constitutes one of the necessary but not sufficient conditions of the gray zone. See Claudia Card, "Groping through Gray Zones," in *On Feminist Ethics and Politics*, ed. C. Card (Lawrence: University Press of Kansas, 1999), 3–26.

10. For an understanding of the mass incarceration of people of color as genocide, see Laura Whitehorn, "Black Power Incarcerated: Political Prisoners, Genocide, and the State," *Socialism and Democracy* 28.3 (2014): 101–17. Whitehorn also refers to the *Black Agenda Report*, edited by Glen Ford: https://www.blackagendareport.com/content/mass-black-incarceration-damn-right-we-charge-genocide.

11. Gilles Deleuze, "Postscript on the Societies of Control," *October* 59 (1992): 3–7. For Foucault's classic work on disciplinary societies, see esp. Michel Foucault, *Discipline and Punish: The Birth of the Prison*, tr. Alan Sheridan (New York: Vintage, 1979), and *Power/Knowledge: Selected Interviews and Other Writings, 1972–1977*, ed. Colin Gordon (New York: Pantheon, 1980). Even as Foucault was theorizing disciplinary power, he was also illuminating biopower and biopolitics—more dispersed, higher-level forms of power that operate at the level of the population.

12. Levi's discussion of the perpetrators also remains minimal in "The Gray Zone." The one example he discusses at any length is the story of the SS man Muhsfeld, who exhibits a brief moment of compassion in the face of a young victim who has not died, as she was meant to, in the gas chamber. As Levi writes, this hesitation is enough to place Muhsfeld at the outer edge of the gray zone (2446–47).

13. I return to the importance of consent in my discussion below of the philosopher Simona Forti. On the power associated with "unknowing" and ignorance, see Eve Kosofsky Sedgwick, "Privilege of Unknowing," *Genders* 1 (1988): 102–24, and *Epistemology of the Closet* (Berkeley: University of California Press, 1990). For more recent discussions, see Shannon Sullivan and Nancy Tuana, eds., *Race and Epistemologies of Ignorance* (Albany: SUNY Press, 2007); Robert Proctor and Londa Schiebinger, eds., *Agnotology: The Making and Unmaking of Ignorance* (Stanford, CA: Stanford University Press, 2008); and Mills, *Black Rights / White Wrongs*.

14. Karl Jaspers, *Die Schuldfrage* (Heidelberg: Lambert Schneider, 1946); English version: *The Question of German Guilt*, tr. E. B. Ashton (New York: Fordham University Press, 2000). Subsequent references are to the English version.

15. For a rich discussion of the content and context of Jaspers's lectures with a focus on their affective dimensions, see Anna Parkinson, *An Affective State: The Politics of Emotion in Postwar West German Culture* (Ann Arbor: University of Michigan Press, 2015).

16. See the discussions of Jaspers in Anson Rabinbach, *In the Shadow of Catastrophe: German Intellectuals between Apocalypse and Enlightenment* (Berkeley: University of California Press, 1997), 129–65; and in Andrew Schaap, *Political Reconciliation* (New York: Routledge: 2005), esp. 118–20. Both of these works have helped me in parsing Jaspers's text in the following paragraphs.

17. Mahmood Mamdani, "Beyond Nuremberg: The Historical Significance of the Post-Apartheid Transition in South Africa," *Politics & Society* 43.1 (2015): 61–88. Reflecting on the negotiated settlement that ended apartheid, Mamdani concludes: "Neither victors' justice nor victims' justice, CODESA shed the zero-sum logic of criminal justice for the inclusive nature of political justice, inclusion through the reform of the political community in which yesterday's victims, perpetrators, bystanders, and beneficiaries may participate as today's survivors" (82).

18. Arendt to Jaspers, August 17, 1946, in Hannah Arendt and Karl Jaspers, *Correspondence, 1926–1969*, ed. Lotte Kohler and Hans Saner, tr. Robert and Rita Kimber (New York: Harcourt Brace Jovanovich, 1992), 54.

19. For astute reflections on Arendt, judgment, and justice in the Nuremberg- and Eichmann-trial eras, see Lyndsey Stonebridge, *The Judicial Imagination: Writing after Nuremberg* (Edinburgh: Edinburgh University Press, 2011).

20. Hannah Arendt, "Collective Responsibility," in *Responsibility and Judgment*, ed. Jerome Kohn (New York: Schocken, 2003), 147.

21. "Personal Responsibility under Dictatorship," in *Responsibility and Judgment*, ed. Jerome Kohn (New York: Schocken, 2003), 24.

22. Arendt goes on to argue that refugees, in contrast, do not bear any political responsibility because they are "truly outcasts, belonging to no internationally recognizable community whatever" ("Collective Responsibility" 150). Her distinctions thus describe a political space that encompasses the guilt of the perpetrator, the innocence of the refugee, and the collective responsibility of the vast majority of members of society in between. Although useful, Arendt's account simplifies the position of immigrants in relation to national responsibilities. On the one hand, it is not clear that one simply leaves such responsibilities behind by emigrating. On the other hand, the taking on of responsibilities in the land of immigration will depend on a variety of factors, including the imagination of peoplehood or national identity in the new home. For more on these questions, with a particular focus on immigrants to Germany in relation to responsibility for the Holocaust, see Michael Rothberg and Yasemin Yildiz, "Memory Citizenship: Migrant Archives of Holocaust Remembrance in Contemporary Germany," *Parallax* 17.4 (2011): 32–48, and our forthcoming book *Inheritance Trouble: Migrant Archives of Holocaust Remembrance* (under contract with Fordham University Press).

23. Jasbir K. Puar, *Terrorist Assemblages: Homonationalism in Queer Times* (Durham, NC: Duke University Press, 2007), 23–24. For more on the contrast between intersectionality and Puar's preferred assemblage theory, see 211–16. Radically rejecting the category of the subject, Puar would probably not follow me in highlighting

the position of the implicated subject, but her approach helps me to map its sites of emergence. Like me—and like Levi—Puar "deprivileges . . . binary opposition" and "underscores contingency and complicity with dominant formations" (205).

24. Iris Marion Young, *Responsibility for Justice* (New York: Oxford University Press, 2011).

25. Even in an extreme case such as the Nazi genocide of European Jews, such an approach to structural injustice resonates. In her local study of a town near Auschwitz, Mary Fulbrook concludes that "the Holocaust was made possible by the actions of so many, yet [was] actually intended by so few." It was even possible that "some people could later claim that they had 'always been against it' with varying degrees of honesty." See Mary Fulbrook, *A Small Town near Auschwitz: Ordinary Nazis and the Holocaust* (New York: Oxford University Press, 2012), 356. Here we see how the category of the implicated subject can open up the conventional triad of perpetrators-victims-bystanders that has organized much work on the Holocaust.

26. Controversially, perhaps, Young argues that, in the social connection model, even those conventionally considered victims of particular structural injustices bear political responsibility for transforming the conditions in which they live. Young's point is to distinguish responsibility from guilt, so her purpose in making this part of the argument is not to claim that people are "guilty" for their own suffering; rather, she is trying to provide space for collective action that would not primarily involve paternalistic "humanitarianism" from outside, but rather would include those most intimately impacted by injustice alongside those whose privilege derives from the unjust conditions at stake but who are not "guilty" of producing those conditions.

27. Although I appreciate the larger framework Young develops here, I do not necessarily follow her opposition to reparations. I discuss this complex issue at greater length in the next chapter, on the legacies of transatlantic slavery.

28. Simona Forti, *New Demons: Rethinking Power and Evil Today*, tr. Zakiya Hanafi (Stanford, CA: Stanford University Press, 2015), 308.

29. On the relation between these two movements, see Daniel Levy and Natan Sznaider, *Human Rights and Memory* (University Park: Penn State University Press, 2010). I return to their work in Chapter 5.

CHAPTER 2: ON (NOT) BEING A DESCENDANT

1. In "Fugitive Justice," Stephen Best and Saidiya Hartman offer a powerful account of the limits of liberal legal paradigms that privilege the individual, rights-bearing subject. They write, "The paradigm of individual rights presents African Americans with particular obstacles. First, this paradigm's standard of accountability renders all claims for black reparations null and void, as the victims and perpetrators of slavery have been long dead. Second, the focus on the individual in liberal legal formulas for remedy makes difficult an account of group oppression and structural inequalities. Third, and finally, the focus on identifiable victims and perpetrators foregrounds the law's indifference to tangled and complicated webs of causation." Best

and Hartman's account reveals the terrain on which a theory of implication and the implicated subject in the aftermath of slavery must seek to intervene. Such a theory must be able to respond to all three of the obstacles they outline: it must be able to account for temporal delay, collective identities, and structural inequalities, and in doing so, it must leave behind the comfort of identifiable identity categories and enter into the more difficult and tangled arena of indirect causality. See Stephen Best and Saidiya Hartman, "Fugitive Justice," *Representations* 92 (2006): 1–15; 8.

2. Ta-Nehisi Coates, "The Case for Reparations," *The Atlantic*, June 2014, https://www.theatlantic.com/magazine/archive/2014/06/the-case-for-reparations/361631/.

3. Although it is not the focus of this chapter, it is worth remembering that the university is among the structures and institutions that have been intertwined with the history of slavery. Recent research, both by universities themselves and scholars such as Craig Wilder, have demonstrated the extent to which North American universities, among others, were founded with support from and in proximity to slavery and the slave trade. This is significant in at least two ways: because universities have played a central role in shaping subjectivities and because they are the centers where knowledge production and scholarship such as my own takes place. Our university-based scholarship, in other words, is always already implicated in the aftermath of slavery, although the nature of this implication is not necessarily simple to trace. One of the first university inquiries was *Slavery and Justice: Report of the Brown University Steering Committee on Slavery and Justice* (Providence, RI: Brown University, 2006). See also Craig Steven Wilder, *Ebony and Ivy: Race, Slavery, and the Troubled Histories of America's Universities* (New York: Bloomsbury, 2013). For a thoughtful introduction to the issue—with important reflections on the limits of a purely historical approach to the question of universities' entanglement with slavery—see Alex Karp, "Slavery and the University," *New York Review of Books*, February 7, 2018, http://www.nybooks.com/daily/2018/02/07/slavery-and-the-american-university/.

4. The literature on reparations for slavery alone is enormous. One of the best-known interventions is Randall Robinson, *The Debt: What America Owes to Blacks* (New York: Dutton, 2000). See also Robert Westley, "Many Billions Gone: Is it Time to Reconsider the Case for Black Reparations?," *Boston College Law Review* 40 (1998); Robin D. G. Kelley, *Freedom Dreams: The Black Radical Imagination* (Boston: Beacon Press, 2002); John Torpey, *Making Whole What Has Been Smashed: On Reparations Politics* (Cambridge, MA: Harvard University Press, 2006), esp. 107–32; and Salamishah Tillet, *Sites of Slavery: Citizenship and Racial Democracy in the Post–Civil Rights Imagination* (Durham, NC: Duke University Press, 2012), esp. 133–67. For a comprehensive history of claims for reparation in the context of slavery, see Ana Lucia Araujo, *Reparations for Slavery and the Slave Trade* (New York: Bloomsbury, 2017).

5. Elazar Barkan, *The Guilt of Nations: Restitution and Negotiating Historical Injustices* (Baltimore: Johns Hopkins University Press, 2000), xviii. Barkan defines restitution as a comprehensive category that involves "the entire spectrum of attempts

to rectify historical injustices," including actions that fall under related categories such as reparation and apology (xix). For an illuminating introduction to the ways that questions of remembrance intersect with matters of restitution and reconciliation, see Ann Rigney, "Reconciliation and Remembering: (How) Does It Work?," *Memory Studies* 5.3 (2012): 251–58.

6. Marianne Hirsch, *The Generation of Postmemory: Writing and Visual Culture after the Holocaust* (New York: Columbia University Press, 2012); Nicole L. Immler, "'Too Little, Too Late'? Compensation and Family Memory: Negotiating a Holocaust Past," *Memory Studies* 5.3 (2012): 270–81. See also Susan Slyomovics, *How to Accept German Reparations* (Philadelphia: University of Pennsylvania Press, 2015), a brilliant exploration that is both scholarly and personal insofar as it focalizes its reflections on reparations through the story of the author's mother and grandmother. Slyomovics links debates about reparations for the Nazi genocide primarily to debates about settler colonialism rather than slavery.

7. Erin McGlothlin, *Second-Generation Holocaust Literature: Legacies of Survival and Perpetration* (Rochester, NY: Camden House, 2006); Gabriele Schwab, *Haunting Legacies: Violent Histories and Transgenerational Trauma* (New York: Columbia University Press, 2010).

8. In a column in the *New York Times*, the historian of slavery Walter Johnson writes, "We are accustomed to reckoning the legacy of slavery in the United States in terms of black disadvantage. The centrality of slavery to the nation's economic development, however, suggests that any calculation of the nation's unpaid debt for slavery must include a measure of the wealth it produced, of advantage as well as disadvantage." See Walter Johnson, "King Cotton's Long Shadow," *Opinionator* (blog), *New York Times*, March 30, 2013, http://opinionator.blogs.nytimes.com/2013/03/30/king-cottons-long-shadow/. As Saidiya Hartman illustrates in a powerful passage in *Lose Your Mother*, slavery remains—despite the temporal distance from emancipation—just within the realm of communicative memory: she recounts hearing about her great-great-grandmother Ella, who was born in slavery, from her great-grandfather, but the details she garners remain sparse. As she writes, "The gaps and silences of my family were not unusual: slavery made the past a mystery, unknown and unspeakable." See Saidiya Hartman, *Lose Your Mother: A Journey along the Atlantic Slave Route* (New York: Farrar, Straus and Giroux, 2007), 13–14.

9. The discussion of the semantics of *legacy*, *inheritance*, and *descent* is based on entries in the online *OED*.

10. Orlando Patterson, *Slavery and Social Death: A Comparative Study* (Cambridge, MA: Harvard University Press, 1985), 5.

11. Cited in Ron Eyerman, "The Past in the Present: Culture and the Transmission of Memory," *Acta Sociologica* 47.2 (2004): 159–69; 165. Garvey's language also echoes that of the Jewish Passover seder.

12. Michelle Alexander, *The New Jim Crow: Mass Incarceration in the Age of Colorblindness* (New York: New Press, 2012).

13. Stephen Best, "On Failing to Make the Past Present," *Modern Language Quarterly* 73.3 (2012): 453–74; 453, 455.

14. Nicholas Draper, *The Price of Emancipation: Slave-Ownership, Compensation and British Society at the End of Slavery* (New York: Cambridge University Press, 2010), 276.

15. Jamaica Kincaid, *A Small Place* (New York: Plume, 1988), 80–81.

16. This conflation can also be found elsewhere in the text: "In accounts of the capture and enslavement of black people almost no slave ever mentions who captured and delivered him or her to the European master. In accounts of their corrupt government, Antiguans neglect to say that in twenty years of one form of self-government or another, they have, with one five-year exception, placed in power the present government" (55–56). Here Kincaid evokes other forms of implication in the wake of slavery: those that arise from local African complicity in the slave trade and from corrupt forms of postcolonial governance. I return to the question of postcolonial and neocolonial corruption later in this chapter, in the section on Kincaid and the Codrington family. While the question of African complicity in the slave trade is beyond the scope of this chapter, it is taken up in two powerful works of creative nonfiction that address slavery's uneven transnational legacies and have influenced my thinking on these matters: Caryl Phillips's *The Atlantic Sound* (New York: Vintage: 2001) and Hartman's *Lose Your Mother*.

17. Frantz Fanon, *Black Skin, White Masks*, tr. Charles Lam Markham (New York: Grove Press, 1967), 219.

18. In Sabine Broeck's reading of these rhetorical strategies, "Kincaid's exhortation 'invites' us in no uncertain terms to cross the critical distance between a disinterested condemnation of colonialism, and a recognition of our readerly self being implicated in white ethnocentric practices/habits/fantasies of control, ignorance, and willful exercise of privilege." See Sabine Broeck, "When Light Becomes White: Reading Enlightenment through Jamaica Kincaid's Writing," *Callaloo* 25.3 (2002): 821–43; 841–42.

19. For a relevant concept of the "implicated reader," see Joseph Slaughter, "One Track Minds: Markets, Madness, Metaphors, and Modernism in Postcolonial Nigerian Fiction," in *African Writers and Their Readers: Essays in Honor of Bernth Lindfors*, ed. Toyin Falola and Barbara Harlow (Trenton, NJ: Africa World Press, 2002), 2:55–89, and *Human Rights, Inc.: The World Novel, Narrative Form, and International Law* (New York: Fordham University Press, 2007).

20. See Wendy Brown, *States of Injury: Power and Freedom in Late Modernity* (Princeton, NJ: Princeton University Press, 1995).

21. For references to Syrian and Lebanese businessmen, see, e.g., Kincaid 62–63. The narrator often sounds xenophobic and nativist notes in such passages, as when she suggests that the world would have been better if the colonizer had simply "stayed at home." I take the concept of "surrogation" from Joseph Roach. See his *Cities of the Dead: Circum-Atlantic Performance* (New York: Columbia University Press, 1996). See also Alexander's discussion of the serial constitution of a racial caste system in

the US from slavery through Jim Crow and on to the current prison system, as well as Coates's "Case for Reparations."

22. Such a melancholic view of history bears more than a passing resemblance to that of Walter Benjamin's "angel of history," who sees history as "one single catastrophe which keeps piling wreckage upon wreckage and hurls it in front of his feet." Walter Benjamin, "Theses on the Philosophy of History," in *Illuminations*, ed. Hannah Arendt and tr. Harry Zohn (New York: Schocken, 1968), 257.

23. What it means for former victims or their descendants to be implicated in new forms of violence and perpetration—which I call "complex implication"—will also be at the center of the two chapters in the next section, which concern diasporic Jewish responses to South African apartheid and the Israeli occupation of Palestine, respectively.

24. Bruce Robbins, *The Beneficiary* (Durham, NC: Duke University Press, 2017), 39.

25. Paul Ricoeur, *Memory, History, Forgetting*, tr. Kathleen Blamey and David Pellauer (Chicago: University of Chicago Press, 2006).

26. Christina Sharpe, *Monstrous Intimacies: Making Post-Slavery Subjects* (Durham, NC: Duke University Press, 2010), 3.

27. In Robbins's reading of this passage, "What Kincaid is saying to 'you' . . . is that your most intimate bodily identity is constituted by your relations with distant places." He then goes on to argue that the passage also illustrates how Kincaid herself is a beneficiary of the system she denounces (39). Taking account of the last sentence I quoted, evoking slavery—which Robbins leaves out—complicates this picture, without undermining Robbins's point. For more on Robbins's reading of this passage, see my review essay, "Of Beneficiaries and Other Implicated Subjects," *Contemporary Literature* (forthcoming).

28. The sea as trope is also used powerfully to evoke the past's continued hold on the present in Christina Sharpe's *In the Wake: On Blackness and Being* (Durham, NC: Duke University Press, 2016).

29. Timothy Morton, *Hyperobjects: Philosophy and Ecology after the End of the World* (Minneapolis: University of Minnesota Press, 2013).

30. For the Legacies of British Slave-Ownership project, see the website: http://www.ucl.ac.uk/lbs. In his commentary on Draper's *The Price of Emancipation*, Christer Petley also briefly links the questions raised by the legacies of British slave-ownership with the final passage of *A Small Place*. Although he does not develop this link, the connection is in the spirit of my argument here. See Christer Petley, "British Fortunes and Caribbean Slavery," *Small Axe* 37 (2012): 144–53, esp. 153. Petley's article is part of a forum that includes an introduction by *Small Axe* editor David Scott, another response from Susan Thorne, and a reply by Draper.

31. In her references to the family, Kincaid consistently misspells their name as "Condrington," but the reference to the Codringtons is clear.

32. Unless otherwise noted, the information in this paragraph and the next

comes from the entry on the Legacies of British Slave-Ownership website: http://www.ucl.ac.uk/lbs/person/view/470.

33. Simon Gikandi, *Slavery and the Culture of Taste* (Princeton, NJ: Princeton University Press, 2011), xiv, 124.

34. The information in this sentence comes from the website of the Museum of Antigua and Barbuda: http://antiguahistory.net/Museum/BettysHopeHome.htm. See also the Wikipedia entry: en.wikipedia.org/wiki/Betty%27s_Hope.

35. Hall made this statement during a presentation at the conference "The Colonial Legacy of the Treaty of Utrecht, 1713–1863–2013," Utrecht, June 2013.

36. See the Museum of Antigua and Barbuda website: http://www.antiguamuseum.org/About.html.

37. This claim about breeding is discussed in the BBC documentary *From Codrington to Codrington*, where it is described as controversial but based on some evidence.

38. Benjamin, "Theses," 256. Recall also that Benjamin values "the image of enslaved ancestors rather than of liberated grandchildren" (260).

39. My hypothesis here is inspired by Dominick LaCapra's important distinction between structural and historical trauma, but tries to take that distinction to the other side of the victim/perpetrator dyad. See Dominick LaCapra, "Trauma, Absence, Loss," in *Writing History, Writing Trauma* (Baltimore: Johns Hopkins University Press, 2000).

40. Tessa Morris-Suzuki, *The Past within Us: Media, Memory, History* (London: Verso, 2005), 26–27.

41. Jacques Lacan, *The Seminar of Jacques Lacan, Book VII: The Ethics of Psychoanalysis, 1959–1960*, ed. J.-A. Miller, tr. Dennis Porter (New York: Norton, 1992), 139.

42. For a classic, influential analysis of the intimacy of race and property, see Cheryl I. Harris, "Whiteness as Property," *Harvard Law Review* 106 (1993): 1709–91. Harris explores the emergence of racialized identity in the Americas in relation to both slavery and the dispossession of Native Americans.

43. Nancy Fraser, *Justice Interruptus: Critical Reflections on the "Postsocialist" Condition* (New York: Routledge, 1997), and *Scales of Justice: Reimagining Political Space in a Globalizing World* (New York: Columbia University Press, 2009).

44. Nancy Fraser, "Abnormal Justice," *Critical Inquiry* 34 (2008): 393–422. See also Fraser, *Scales of Justice*.

45. The inclusion in this chapter of materials pertaining to slavery in the US, the Caribbean, and Britain should be taken as an indication that the question of geographical scale is also pertinent to a transnational history such as the one at stake here and would thus also complicate the question of justice in its aftermath.

46. My thinking here is inspired by Robert Meister's distinction between "loss-based" and "gain-based" remedies: "a gain-based approach to reparative justice . . . directly addresses the circumstances in which the benefits of past injustice have been cumulative, in which an ever decreasing number of the direct

victims survive, and in which individual victims would have difficulty proving losses on the scale of the cumulative gains that were thereby produced. In this respect, gain-based remedies differ from loss-based remedies, which typically require proof of direct causation to establish liability—my action (whether gainful or not) must be shown to have caused your loss. Freed of this constraint, a gain-based approach to restitution would allow recovery from the beneficiaries of past injustice long after the perpetrators are gone, sometimes even generations later." See Meister, *After Evil: A Politics of Human Rights* (New York: Columbia University Press, 2011), 234–35.

47. My point here is again influenced by Meister as well as Fraser. Meister writes: "The remedial equality I have in mind does not rest on an ethical defense of egalitarianism as an ideal. It simply assumes that most inequality is a result of history and that most of history was bad" (258).

CHAPTER 3: PROGRESS, PROGRESSION, PROCESSION

1. Walter Benjamin, *Illuminations*, tr. Harry Zohn (New York: Schocken, 1968), 256.

2. Dan Cameron, "A Procession of the Dispossessed," in *William Kentridge*, ed. Dan Cameron, Carolyn Christov-Bakargiev, and J. M. Coetzee (London: Phaidon, 1999), 47.

3. Quoted in Aiden Whitman, "Haile Selassie of Ethiopia Dies at 83," *New York Times*, August 28, 1975.

4. The moderated, gradual progress in which Selassie believed will be relevant to our later discussion of liberal narratives of transitional justice. Selassie's *New York Times* obituary includes a description of the emperor that seems pertinent to *Arc/Procession*: "Around the clock, he was guarded by lions and cheetahs, protected by Imperial Bodyguards, trailed by his pet papillon dogs, flanked by a multitude of chamberlains and flunkies and sustained by a tradition of reverence for his person." See Whitman, "Haile Selassie." *Arc/Procession* may represent an ironized version of this royal procession as well as a counternarrative to the Roman *Triumphzug*.

5. Gordimer cites Gramsci in an epigraph to her 1981 novel *July's People* and takes it as the inspiration for her 1983 essay "Living in the Interregnum." See "Living in the Interregnum," in *The Essential Gesture: Writing, Politics, and Places*, ed. Stephen Clingman (New York: Knopf, 1988), 261–84.

6. Kentridge's father Sydney was a prominent antiapartheid lawyer who represented Nelson Mandela in the treason trials of the 1950s, was involved in the Stephen Biko inquest, and served as an acting justice of the South African Constitutional Court in the mid-1990s. Kentridge's mother Felicia was also a prominent antiapartheid lawyer who cofounded the Legal Resources Centre in 1979. See the brief mention of the Kentridge parents in Gideon Shimoni, *Community and Conscience: The Jews in Apartheid South Africa* (Hanover, NH: University Press

of New England, 2003), 61, 191. See also the Wikipedia entries for Sydney and Felicia Kentridge.

7. Much has been written about persistent inequality in postapartheid South Africa. For one recent scholarly overview, see Marlea Clarke and Carolyn Bassett, "The Struggle for Transformation in South Africa: Unrealized Dreams, Persistent Hopes," *Journal of Contemporary African Studies* 34.2 (2016): 183–89.

8. The literature on transitional justice is recent but vast. For a basic definition, see Louis Bickford, "Transitional Justice," in *The Encyclopedia of Genocide and Crimes against Humanity*, ed. Dinah Shelton (Detroit: Macmillan Reference USA, 2004), 3:1045–47. For a lucid and more detailed account, see Ruti Teitel, *Transitional Justice* (New York: Oxford University Press, 2001). For a deeper historical approach, see Jon Elster, *Closing the Books: Transitional Justice in Historical Perspective* (New York: Cambridge University Press, 2004).

9. A narratology of transitional justice evokes both work on narrative and law and emergent interest in postcolonial narration. For a seminal essay in legal narratology, see Robert M. Cover, "Nomos and Narrative," *Harvard Law Review* 97.4 (1983): 4–68; on postcolonial narratology, see Gerald Prince, "On a Postcolonial Narratology," in *A Companion to Narrative Theory*, ed. James Phelan & Peter J. Rabinowitz (Malden, MA: Blackwell, 2005), 372–81.

10. A year after my article on Kentridge's processions appeared in the journal *Narrative*, the art historian Leora Maltz-Leca published an insightful parallel study of Kentridge. Maltz-Leca confirms my linkage of the form of the procession to the historical context of transitional South Africa and provides a rich archive of imagery that has served as the basis of Kentridge's engagement with the form (including a film about the release of Mandela for which Kentridge served as assistant producer). Maltz-Leca does not, however, explore at length the way Kentridge depicts his own implication in the scenes of injustice he renders. See Leora Maltz-Leca, "Process/Procession: William Kentridge and the Process of Change," *Art Bulletin* 95.1 (2013): 139–65. Another illuminating recent essay that explores the procession form is Homi Bhabha, "Processional Ethics," *Artforum*, October 2016, 230–37, 292. I return to Bhabha below.

11. Ruti Teitel, "Transitional Justice as Liberal Narrative," in *Experiments with Truth: Transitional Justice and the Processes of Truth and Reconciliation, Documenta11_Platform2*, ed. Okwui Enwezor et al. (Ostfildern-Ruit, Germany: Hatje Cantz, 2002), 249. For approaches that emphasize literature and culture without slighting institutional dimensions, see also Paul Gready, "Novel Truths: Literature and Truth Commissions," *Comparative Literature Studies* 46.1 (2009): 156–76, and *The Era of Transitional Justice: The Aftermath of the Truth and Reconciliation Commission in South Africa and Beyond* (New York: Routledge, 2011); and Mark Sanders, *Ambiguities of Witnessing: Law and Literature in the Time of a Truth Commission* (Stanford, CA: Stanford University Press, 2007).

12. On time consciousness, the space of experience, and the horizon of expectations, see Reinhart Koselleck, *Futures Past: On the Semantics of Historical Time* (New York: Columbia University Press, 2004).

13. For the concept of "masterplot," see H. Porter Abbott, *The Cambridge Introduction to Narrative* (New York: Cambridge University Press, 2008).

14. Robert Meister, *After Evil: The Politics of Human Rights* (New York: Columbia University Press, 2011), 25.

15. See also Meister's critique of transitional narratives: "The rule of law in the aftermath of evil is expressly meant to decollectivize both injury and responsibility and to redescribe systemic violence as a series of individual crimes" (28).

16. For a related argument, see Mahmood Mamdani, "Amnesty or Impunity? A Preliminary Critique of the Report of the Truth and Reconciliation Commission of South Africa (TRC)," *Diacritics* 32.3–4 (2002): 33–59.

17. See David Smith, "South African Rugby Team Still Looking for Happy Ending Despite Film Portrayal," *The Guardian*, December 7, 2009, https://www.theguardian.com/world/2009/dec/07/south-africa-rugby-team-film.

18. Eric Santner, "History beyond the Pleasure Principle: Some Thoughts on the Representation of Trauma," in *Probing the Limits of Representation: Nazism and the "Final Solution,"* ed. Saul Friedlander (Cambridge, MA: Harvard University Press, 1992), 143–54. I characterize such narratives as "neoliberal" in order to recognize the diversity of stories that can be told within a liberal framework. The neoliberal variety seeks to produce subjects as "free agents" disembedded from social implication, while other varieties of liberalism can sustain visions of communality and sociality. I take the idea of neoliberalism as a form of disembedding from Yasemin Yildiz, "Governing European Subjects: Tolerance and Guilt in the Discourse of 'Muslim Women,'" *Cultural Critique* 77 (Winter 2011): 70–101.

19. Stanley Cohen, *States of Denial: Knowing about Atrocities and Suffering* (Cambridge, UK: Polity Press, 2001), 9.

20. Bakhtin's definition of the chronotope is apposite for Kentridge's work. In chronotopes, "time, as it were, thickens, takes on flesh, becomes artistically visible; likewise, space becomes charged and responsive to the movements of time, plot and history." See Mikhail Bakhtin, "Forms of Time and of the Chronotope in the Novel," in *The Dialogic Imagination: Four Essays*, tr. Caryl Emerson and Michael Holquist (Austin: University of Texas Press, 1981), 84. "Thick time" is a Bakhtin-inspired phrase used by Kentridge and applies especially to his works of animation.

21. Benedict Anderson, *Imagined Communities: Reflections on the Origin and Spread of Nationalism* (New York: Verso, 1991), 26.

22. See James Phelan, *Experiencing Fiction: Judgments, Progressions, and the Rhetorical Theory of Narrative* (Columbus: Ohio State University Press, 2007), and *Reading People, Reading Plots: Character, Progression, and the Interpretation of Narrative* (Chicago: University of Chicago Press, 1989). For a relevant and nuanced account of a "narrative ethics of implication," inspired in part by my own earlier work on

implication, see Hanna Meretoja, *The Ethics of Storytelling: Narrative Hermeneutics, History, and the Possible* (New York: Oxford University Press, 2017), 179–216.

23. William Kentridge, "Director's Note," in Jane Taylor, *Ubu and the Truth Commission* (Cape Town: University of Cape Town Press, 1998), xi.

24. The concept of "thick time" is one of the ordering principles of *William Kentridge: Five Themes*, ed. Mark Rosenthal (New Haven, CT: Yale University Press, 2009).

25. For Krauss's reading of Kentridge, see Rosalind Krauss, "'The Rock': William Kentridge's Drawings for Projection," *October* 92 (2000): 3–35, and *Perpetual Inventory* (Cambridge, MA: MIT Press, 2010). On the procession in Kentridge, see also Cameron, "A Procession of the Dispossessed."

26. The most recent of the series is *Other Faces*, which premiered at the Marian Goodman Gallery in New York in 2011; the previous film, *Tide Table*, had been created in 2003. The irregular nature of the series reinforces the "nonhomogeneous" time of Kentridge's narratives.

27. See Krauss's essay "'The Rock'" for an affirmation of Kentridge's own views on the necessity of an indirect approach to apartheid.

28. For a "thick description" of this technique, see Tom Gunning, "Doubled Vision: Peering through Kentridge's 'Stereoscope,'" *Parkett* 63 (2001): 66–73.

29. Kentridge's depiction of mines seems inspired in part by David Goldblatt and Nadine Gordimer's collection *On the Mines* (Cape Town: C. Struik, 1973). Some of Goldblatt's more hallucinatory photographs in the section "Shaftsinking" (plates 28–38) anticipate images in the film *Mine* I will discuss below. Gordimer's introduction emphasizes the amnesiac qualities of the mining landscape that Kentridge both confirms and contests. On Kentridge's landscapes, see also Okwui Enwezor, "(Un)Civil Engineering: William Kentridge's Allegorical Landscapes," in *William Kentridge: Tapestries*, ed. Carlos Basulado (New Haven, CT: Philadelphia Museum of Art in association with Yale University Press, 2008), 87–95.

30. William Kentridge, "Landscape in a State of Siege (extract)," in *William Kentridge*, ed. Dan Cameron, Carolyn Christov-Bakargiev, and J. M. Coetzee (London: Phaidon, 1999), 126.

31. Much of Kentridge's work clearly engages the question of environmental justice, which—like transitional justice—involves concerns about narration and temporality. On the difficult-to-narrate temporality of ecological devastation, see Rob Nixon, *Slow Violence and the Environmentalism of the Poor* (Cambridge, MA: Harvard University Press, 2011).

32. For insightful reflections on memory and forgetting in Kentridge that are close to my own, see the short book of Andreas Huyssen, *William Kentridge, Nalini Malani: The Shadow Play as Medium of Memory* (Milan: Charta, 2013).

33. Michael Rothberg, *Traumatic Realism: The Demands of Holocaust Representation* (Minneapolis: University of Minnesota Press, 2000). For an exemplary reading of trauma and South Africa's transition, see Jessica Dubow and Ruth Rosengarten,

"History as the Main Complaint: William Kentridge and the Making of Post-Apartheid South Africa," *Art History* 27.4 (2004): 671–90.

34. William Kentridge, "'Fortuna': Neither Programme nor Chance in the Making of Images," in Carolyn Christov-Bakargiev, *William Kentridge* (Brussels: Société des Expositions du Palais des Beaux-Arts de Bruxelles, 1998), 67.

35. Krauss also makes a connection between the metamorphic possibilities of animation and capital's deployment of universal equivalence ("'Rock'," 16).

36. Jonathan Crush, "Scripting the Compound: Power and Space in the South African Mining Industry," *Society and Space* 12 (1994): 301–24; 303–4. In a further turn, however, Crush shows that contemporary research emphasizes instead the porous nature of control and discipline in the mines and the variety of forms of miners' self-organization and resistance. The references to the medieval and to slavery are taken from a 1942 submission of the African Mine Workers' Union to the Native Mine Wages Commission. The reference to the "supreme dictator" comes from the work of Michael Burawoy, and the concept of the "total institution" is taken from Erving Goffman. See also Rosalind C. Morris's evocation of the South African mines in "The Miner's Ear," *Transition* 98 (2008): 96–114. Morris writes that the mines have rarely been the site of an ameliorative biopolitics: "One is tempted to say that, for black miners, the mines were like death camps, the spaces in which these men lived in anticipation of their own deaths" (111).

37. Claudia Braude, introduction to *Contemporary Jewish Writing in South Africa: An Anthology*, ed. Claudia Braude (Lincoln: University of Nebraska Press, 2001), xviii.

38. Quoted in Daniel Belasco, "Vexed Lives: A Retrospective of the Art of William Kentridge Looks at Paradoxes for Jews in South Africa," *New York Jewish Week*, June 15, 2001, 35. Kentridge makes even more explicit comments about the ironies of Jewish privilege in South Africa in Eric Herschthal, "Out of South Africa," *New York Jewish Week*, March 11, 2010, http://jewishweek.timesofisrael.com/out-of-south-africa/. For more on the position of Jews in South Africa, see Braude, *Contemporary Jewish Writing in South Africa*, and Shimoni, *Community and Conscience*.

39. See Diana Ketcham, "Writing on the Wall: William Kentridge in Rome," *Art in America*, May 13, 2016, https://www.artinamericamagazine.com/news-features/news/writing-on-the-wall-william-kentridge-in-rome/.

40. *More Sweetly Play the Dance* was commissioned by EYE Filmmuseum in Amsterdam and shown at the Lichtsicht—Projection Biennale in Bad Rothendfelde, Germany, where it was projected on a huge wall of blackthorn brushwood. It was the title piece of an exhibit at the Marian Goodman Gallery in London (2015) and has been displayed in various other exhibition contexts. I saw it first at the *No It Is!* exhibition at the Martin-Gropius-Bau in Berlin in the summer of 2016. See William Kentridge, *More Sweetly Play the Dance*, ed. Marente Bloemheuvel and Jaap Guldemond (Amsterdam: EYE Filmmuseum and nai010, 2015).

41. For a partial account of the creation of the piece, see the artist's production notes in Kentridge, *More Sweetly*.

42. For an extended reflection on the place of the gaps between screens in this work, see Bhabha, "Processional Ethics."

43. See, for instance, Anna Heyward "More Sweetly Play the Dance," *Paris Review*, October 6, 2015, https://www.theparisreview.org/blog/2015/10/06/more-sweetly-play-the-dance/. In reference to the procession in Plato's allegory of the cave, Kentridge writes: "This again feels like a contemporary phenomenon. The flickering projections we see in the news of people fleeing floods, civil war, refugees, migrations, refugees returning, displacements—still, two and a half thousand years later, so largely on foot, individual human power still the central means of locomotion, handcarts, wheelbarrows, shopping carts, the only aids." Although created a few years later, *Dance* offers just such a vision. See William Kentridge, *Six Drawing Lessons: The Charles Eliot Norton Lectures* (Cambridge, MA: Harvard University Press, 2014), 28.

44. Paul Celan, *Poems of Paul Celan*, tr. Michael Hamburger (New York: Persea, 1989), 60–63.

45. Antjie Krog, *Country of My Skull: Guilt, Sorrow, and the Limits of Forgiveness in the New South Africa* (Portland, OR: Broadway Books, 2000), 311. In his studio notes, Kentridge includes "Death Is a Master from Germany" as a possible title for what became *Dance*. See *More Sweetly Play the Dance*, 41.

46. On this scene, see also Sanders, *Ambiguities*, 147–48.

47. See Jacques Rancière, *The Politics of Aesthetics: The Distribution of the Sensible*, tr. Gabriel Rockhill (London: Continuum, 2004).

CHAPTER 4: FROM GAZA TO WARSAW

1. Steven Levitsky and Glen Weyl, "We Are Lifelong Zionists. Here's Why We've Chosen to Boycott Israel," *Washington Post*, October 23, 2015, http://www.washingtonpost.com/oinions/a-zionist-case-for-boycotting-israel/2015/10/23.

2. As Naomi Taub pointed out to me, "affect actually *is* the ideology that the Israeli state attempts to cultivate transnationally: love for Israel, hatred for its perceived enemies, fear of what a world without Israel would mean, suspicion of anyone who criticizes it." Clearly, the range of affects at stake extends well beyond the "love" that Levitsky and Weyl proclaim. Personal communication, August 3, 2018.

3. On long-distance nationalism, see Benedict Anderson, "Exodus," *Critical Inquiry* 20.2 (1994): 314–27.

4. Of course, not "all" Jews are treated equally by the State of Israel. Questions of race, religion, and ideology play an increasingly differentiating role.

5. Quoted in John Quigley, *Palestine and Israel: A Challenge to Justice* (Durham, NC: Duke University Press, 1990), 129.

6. Saree Makdisi, "Apartheid / Apartheid / []," *Critical Inquiry* 44 (2018): 304–30; 311.

7. I am reminded here of Hannah Arendt's response to Gershom Scholem during their epistolary exchange in the wake of *Eichmann in Jerusalem*. Shocked by the tone of Arendt's account of the Eichmann trial, Scholem accused Arendt of possessing "no trace" of "love for the Jewish people." Arendt responded by confirming that she loved neither the Jewish people nor any other "nation or collective," but only her friends. Although the question of love in politics demands more extensive consideration, in the Levitsky/Weyl column "love" serves primarily to mark continued attachment to and implication in an unjust project.

8. Bashir Bashir and Amos Goldberg, "The Holocaust and the Nakba: A New Syntax of History, Memory, and Political Thought," in *The Holocaust and the Nakba: A New Grammar of Trauma and History*, ed. Bashir and Goldberg (New York: Columbia University Press, 2019), 2.

9. On Holocaust memory in the Israeli context, see Tom Segev, *The Seventh Million: The Israelis and the Holocaust*, tr. Haim Watzman (New York: Hill and Wang, 1993); and Idith Zertal, *Israel's Holocaust and the Politics of Nationhood* (New York: Cambridge University Press, 2005). For a collection of essays on the memory of the Palestinian catastrophe, see Ahmad H. Sa'di and Lila Abu-Lughod, eds., *Nakba: Palestine, 1948, and the Claims of Memory* (New York: Columbia University Press, 2007). See also Gilbert Achcar, *The Arabs and the Holocaust: The Arab-Israeli War of Narratives*, tr. G. M. Goshgarian (New York: Metropolitan Books, 2010); and Jo Roberts, *Contested Land, Contested Memory: Israeli's Jews and Arabs and the Ghosts of Catastrophe* (Toronto: Dundurn, 2013).

10. See Michael Rothberg, *Multidirectional Memory: Remembering the Holocaust in the Age of Decolonization* (Stanford, CA: Stanford University Press, 2009).

11. In thinking through these issues, I draw on Judith Butler, *Frames of War: When Is Life Grievable?* (New York: Verso, 2009); Nancy Fraser, *Scales of Justice: Reimagining Political Space in a Globalizing World* (New York: Columbia University Press, 2009); and Iris Marion Young, *Intersecting Voices: Dilemmas of Gender, Political Philosophy, and Public Policy* (Princeton, NJ: Princeton University Press, 1997).

12. *Human Rights in Palestine and Other Occupied Arab Territories: Report of the United Nations Fact Finding Mission on the Gaza Conflict*, United Nations Human Rights Council, September 15, 2009.

13. On Churchill's short play, see Stef Craps, "Holocaust Memory and the Critique of Violence: Caryl Churchill's *Seven Jewish Children: A Play for Gaza*," in *The Future of Testimony: Interdisciplinary Perspectives on Witnessing*, ed. Jane Kilby and Antony Rowland (Abdingdon, UK: Routledge, 2014), 179–92.

14. By way of comparison, the Gaza Strip had a population of 1.795 million as of July 2017 and an area of 139 square miles (360 square kilometers). Its population is growing at three times the world rate, and the median age for residents is 17.2 years, with 44.78 percent of the population 14 or younger. CIA World Factbook, https://www.cia.gov/library/publications/the-world-factbook/.

15. In "A Poor Christian Looks at the Ghetto," the speaker concludes that he will be "count[ed] among the helpers of death: / The uncircumcised." The "helpers of death" in this case are not perpetrators, but precisely implicated bystanders. See Miłosz, *Selected Poems, 1931–2004* (New York: HarperCollins, 2006), 18.

16. W. E. B. Du Bois, "The Negro and the Warsaw Ghetto," *Jewish Life* (May 1952): 14–15; 15.

17. W. E. B. Du Bois, *The World and Africa: An Inquiry into the Part Which Africa Has Played in World History* (New York: Viking, 1947), 23. This passage is often used as evidence for the argument that the Nazi genocide simply repeated colonial violence on European victims, but Du Bois came to a more nuanced view in "The Negro and the Warsaw Ghetto."

18. Marguerite Duras, "Les deux ghettos," *France-Observateur*, November 9, 1961, 8–10.

19. Robinson sent his email on January 19, 2009, the day after the Israeli bombing campaign ended, although at a time when the situation in the Gaza Strip remained dire. For more on the Gaza bombing and the situation on the ground, see the report by Amnesty International, *Israel/Gaza: Operation "Cast Lead": 22 Days of Death and Destruction* (London: Amnesty International Publications, 2009), and the Report of the United Nations Fact Finding Mission on the Gaza Conflict (The Goldstone Report), *Human Rights in Palestine and Other Occupied Arab Territories*, September 15, 2009, available online.

A range of documents pertaining to the Robinson case can be found on the website created by his supporters in the Committee to Defend Academic Freedom at UCSB, http://sb4af.wordpress.com. Robinson and his supporters consistently describe the essay by the Jewish American writer as "recent" and imply that it is related to the current Gaza crisis. In fact, as far as I've been able to ascertain, the essay—"Quest for Justice" by Judith Stone—was published in the November 10, 2000, *Kansas City Jewish Chronicle*. Although the photo essay was not created by Finkelstein, it could still be found on his "official" website in August 2018 under the heading "Deutschland Uber Alles: The Grandchildren of Holocaust Survivors from World War II Are Doing to the Palestinians Exactly What Was Done to Them by Nazi Germany . . . " http://www.normanfinkelstein.com/deutschland-uber-alles/. According to contemporary news reports, a Norwegian diplomat created the photo essay in January 2009. See Cnaan Liphshiz, "Did Norway Promote a Diplomat Who Compared Israelis to Nazis?," *Haaretz*, July 22, 2009, https://www.haaretz.com/1.5080452. In the remainder of the essay, I will refer to this example simply as "the photo essay."

20. For an excellent account of threats to academic freedom for US-based academics critical of Israeli policy, see David Theo Goldberg and Saree Makdisi, "The Trial of Israel's Campus Critics," *Tikkun*, September/October 2009, http://www.tikkun.org/article.php/sept_oct_09_goldberg_makdisi. On the implications of the Robinson case for questions of academic freedom in the digital age, see Robert

O'Neil, "Academic Freedom in Cyberspace," *Academe Online* (September/October 2009), http://www.aaup.org/AAUP/pubsres/academe/2009/SO/Feat/onei.htm. Since this chapter was originally drafted as an article, the case of Steven Salaita has become the most well-known (and one of the most egregious) examples of such persecution of critics of Israel in the academy.

21. See Zertal, *Israel's Holocaust*.

22. Arye Naor, "Lessons of the Holocaust versus Territories for Peace, 1967–2001," *Israel Studies* 8.1 (2003): 130–52; 130. More recently and bizarrely, according to a 2002 *Ha'aretz* report, an Israeli officer claimed that with its occupation of Palestinian lands in mind, the Israeli army had "analyze[d] and internalize[d] the lessons of earlier battles—even, however shocking it may sound, even how the German army fought in the Warsaw ghetto" (qtd. by Amir Oren in *Ha'aretz*, January 25, 2002).

23. Oona King, "Israel Can Halt This Now," *The Guardian*, June 11, 2003. For a critique of King by an Israeli critic of the occupation, see Amira Hass, "Making Stupid Comparisons," *Ha'aretz*, July 9, 2003.

24. See for example, George Galloway, Talksport Radio, January 2, 2009, http://www.youtube.com/watch?v=DrK9oLvqbRk.

25. See Jacques Rancière, *The Politics of Aesthetics: The Distribution of the Sensible*, tr. Gabriel Rockhill (London: Continuum, 2004).

26. No captions identify the photographs in the photo essay. However, the image of the Huwara checkpoint can be found on the website of the International Committee of the Red Cross and bears the copyright of the Associated Press / N. Ishtayeh; see http://www.icrc.org/Web/eng/siteengo.nsf/html/palestine-report-131207. On www.remember.org, the image of the selection at Auschwitz-Birkenau is identified as being held by the Dachau Museum.

27. On how to approach perpetrator images, see Marianne Hirsch, "Nazi Photographs in Post-Holocaust Art: Gender as an Idiom of Memorialization," in *Crimes of War: Guilt and Denial*, ed. Omer Bartov, Atina Grossman, and Molly Noble (New York: New Press, 2002). See also David Bathrick, Brad Prager, and Michael D. Richardson, eds., *Visualizing the Holocaust: Documents, Aesthetics, Memory* (Rochester, NY: Camden House, 2008).

28. Adi Ophir, *The Order of Evils: Toward an Ontology of Morals* (New York: Zone Books, 2005). It may be that other comparisons are more productive, however, such as that of the occupation to South African apartheid. See Makdisi, "Apartheid," and "The Architecture of Erasure," *Critical Inquiry* 36.3 (2010): 519–59.

29. In a talk given a few months after the controversy broke, Robinson clarifies that "the differences are numerous" between Nazi and Israeli policies and suggests that "drawing analogies between historical and contemporary events or processes is not intended to suggest they are identical." Rather, he continues, "such comparisons are a pedagogical tool meant to uncover patterns of human conduct—or better put, human misconduct." While Robinson's email may ultimately serve this purpose—and lead to more fine-grained comparisons—the original email and photo essay

seem to me to obey a different logic, that of equation. In the talk, Robinson also identifies Israeli actions as "Nazi-like" and reiterates that "there is a definite parallel between the Warsaw Ghetto and Gaza." See "Prof. Robinson Delivers Speech Addressing His Case," May 23, 2009, sb4af.wordpress.com.

30. See Giorgio Agamben, *Homo Sacer: Sovereign Power and Bare Life*, tr. Daniel Heller-Roazen (Stanford, CA: Stanford University Press, 1998).

31. It is precisely this most significant aspect of the Warsaw Ghetto that must be forgotten in order to produce the Gaza/Warsaw equation.

32. Although LeVine does not mention Robinson, it is clear from its date that his article references the Robinson affair. See "Crisis in Gaza: Gaza Is No Warsaw Ghetto," *Aljazeera*, February 2, 2009, http://english.aljazeera.net/focus/crisisingaza/2009/02/20092191518941246.html.

33. My position is close to that of Judith Butler, who, in rejecting the equation of Zionism and Nazism, goes on to say that "there are principles of social justice that can be derived from the Nazi genocide that can and must inform our contemporary struggles even though the contexts are different and the forms of subjugating power clearly distinct." See *Parting Ways: Jewishness and the Critique of Zionism* (New York: Columbia University Press, 2012), 121.

34. Naor, "Lessons of the Holocaust versus Territories for Peace," 130–52.

35. Keren Tenenboim-Weinblatt mentions this appropriation in "'We Will Get through This Together': Journalism, Trauma and the Israeli Disengagement from the Gaza Strip," *Media, Culture & Society* 30.4 (2008): 507. Tenenboim-Weinblatt writes, "A group of settlers consciously imitated the unforgettable picture of the small boy being deported from the Warsaw Ghetto," but notes that the images was not given prominence in the Israeli press.

36. For more on Schwarz-Bart, see Rothberg, *Multidirectional Memory*, chap. 5.

37. On the Warsaw Ghetto boy, see Richard Raskin, *A Child at Gunpoint: A Case Study in the Life of Photo* (Aarhus, Denmark: Aarhus University Press, 2004); Frédéric Rousseau, *L'enfant juif de Varsovie: Histoire d'une photographie* (Paris: Seuil, 2009); and Marianne Hirsch, "Nazi Photographs in Post-Holocaust Art" and "Projected Memory: Holocaust Photographs in Personal and Public Fantasy," in *Acts of Memory: Cultural Recall in the Present*, ed. Mieke Bal, Jonathan Crewe, and Leo Spitzer (Hanover, NH: University Press of New England, 1999), 3–23.

38. Cited from Alan Schechner's website, www.dottycommies.com. Schechner's conjunction of "The Holocaust and the Intifada" is jarring—he seems to mean the Holocaust and the Occupation or Nakba. On *Legacy*, see Richard Raskin, *A Child at Gunpoint*; and Adrian Parr, "Deterritorialising the Holocaust," in *Deleuze and the Contemporary World*, ed. Ian Buchanan and Adrian Parr (Edinburgh: Edinburgh University Press, 2006), 125–45.

39. See Iris Marion Young, *Intersecting Voices*, 38–59.

40. In setting the two images in motion, Schechner's work might be understood to take part in what Ariella Azoulay calls the "civil contract of photography."

See her description of what it means to "watch" a photograph in *The Civil Contract of Photography* (New York: Zone Books, 2008), 14.

41. As Richard Raskin writes, "Schechner presents the two children as calling out to the viewer that each of them protests against the suffering inflicted on the other" (167).

42. Susannah Radstone, "Social Bonds and Psychical Order: Testimonies," *Cultural Values* 5.1 (January 2001): 59–78; 65.

43. These dimensions of Schechner's biography and motivations are discussed by the artist and other critics in various reviews, essays, and interviews included by the artist on his homepage. See http://www.dottycommies.com/reviews.html.

44. Ariella Azoulay, "Vulnerable Times, Perpetrators and Victims," *Profession* (2014): n.p., http://profession.commons.mla.org/2014/03/19/vulnerable-times-perpetrators-and-victims/. Azoulay's essay is part of the MLA's "Vulnerable Times" forum organized by Marianne Hirsch.

45. For me, Azoulay's formulation of the problem remains too much within the Nuremberg model that Mamdani argues against. See Mahmood Mamdani, "Beyond Nuremberg: The Historical Significance of the Post-Apartheid Transition in South Africa," *Politics & Society* 43.1 (2015): 61–88.

46. On the beneficiary in the context of Israel/Palestine, see Bruce Robbins, "The Logic of the Beneficiary: On Boycott, Divestment, and Sanctions," *N+1* 24 (Winter 2016): 13–23.

47. Judith Butler, *Precarious Life: The Powers of Mourning and Violence* (New York: Verso, 2004), 20.

48. See, for instance, Judith Butler, "Academic Freedom and the ASA's Boycott of Israel: A Response to Michelle Goldberg," *The Nation*, December 8, 2013, http://www.thenation.com/article/177512/academic-freedom-and-asas-boycott-israel-response-michelle-goldberg#.

49. Bruce Robbins, dir., *Some of My Best Friends Are Zionists*, 2013, http://www.bestfriendsfilm.com.

50. It is interesting that the question of Israel/Palestine does not figure prominently in Robbins's recent book *The Beneficiary* (Durham, NC: Duke University Press, 2017), except for a short discussion in the conclusion. Yet this makes sense from my perspective: being a beneficiary (as in the case of economic inequality) and being a perpetuator (in the case of Israel) are not identical, and yet both are forms of the implicated subject. The framework developed in this book might provide a home to these two seemingly separate sides of Robbins's concerns.

CHAPTER 5: UNDER THE SIGN OF SUITCASES

1. SLON stands for the "Société de Lancement des Oeuvres Nouvelles" (Society for the launching of new works). For details on the SLON collective, see François Lecointe, "The Elephant at the End of the World: Chris Marker and Third Cinema," *Third Cinema* 25.1 (2011): 93–104. On the film as a whole—including

a transcription of its text that I have consulted—see Laurent Véray, *Loin du Vietnam* (Paris: Paris Expérimental, 2004).

2. As Thomas Waugh writes, "In the discourse around the production of this film and within the narration of the film itself, [solidarity] designates both the film's objectives and self-conception as part of a documentary genre." See Waugh, "*Loin du Vietnam* (1967), Joris Ivens and Left Bank Documentary," *Jump Cut* 53 (2011), http://www.ejumpcut.org/archive/jc53.2011/WaughVietnam/index.html.

3. Distance joins solidarity as a favorite theme of Marker's. His *Lettre de Siberie* (*Letter from Siberia*; 1958), for instance, announces itself with the sentence "Je vous écris d'un pays lointain" (I write to you from a faraway country).

4. Castro reappears later in the film in an interview with Roger Pic, where he links the war in Vietnam to revolutions elsewhere in the world.

5. For a discussion of *Loin du Vietnam* that focuses on Godard's contribution and links the film back to Algerian War–era protest, see Matthew Croombs, "*Loin du Vietnam*: Solidarity, Representation and the Proximity of the French Colonial Past," *Third Text* 28.6 (2014): 489–505. Also relevant is Olivia C. Harrison's discussion of Godard's contribution in "Consuming Palestine: Anticapitalism and Anticolonialism in Jean-Luc Godard's *Ici et ailleurs*," *Studies in French Cinema* 18.3 (2017): 178–91.

6. Cited in Waugh, "*Loin du Vietnam*," who has taken the text from Ian Mundell.

7. The internationalist focus of the SLON collective continued over the next several years in a series of short films dubbed "On vous parle" (Speaking to you) that connected struggles around the globe, from Chile to Czechoslovakia, with working class struggles in the metropolis. Each title began with the same phrase: "On vous parle de . . . " As Lecointe observes, "the 'geographic framework' of a global enquiry was at the base of the construction of [*Loin du Vietnam*]" and "SLON became a refuge and a hub for images of the entire world" (95, 98).

8. On the SLON note, see Waugh, "*Loin du Vietnam*." For the tribunal, see "On Treatment of Civilians: Testimony by Joris Ivens and Marceline Loridan," in *Against the Crime of Silence: Proceedings of the Russell International War Crimes Tribunal*, ed. John Duffett (Flanders, NJ: O'Hare Books, 1968), 551–54.

9. Hito Steyerl, "A Thing like You and Me," in *Hito Steyerl*, exhibition catalogue, with texts by Pablo Lafuente, Hito Steyerl, and Maria Mühle (Høvikodden, Norway: Henie Onstad Art Centre, 2010), 61–71.

10. For an account of this period in France, see Kristin Ross, *May '68 and Its Afterlives* (Chicago: University of Chicago Press, 2002), esp. 80–90.

11. Daniel Levy and Natan Sznaider, *The Holocaust and Memory in a Global Age* (Philadelphia: Temple University Press, 2005).

12. See Michael Rothberg, *Multidirectional Memory: Remembering the Holocaust in the Age of Decolonization* (Stanford, CA: Stanford University Press, 2009), chap. 6. Multidirectional memory was also meant as an alternative to another theory of globalized Holocaust memory, that of Jeffrey Alexander. See my contribution to

Jeffrey Alexander, *Remembering the Holocaust: A Debate* (New York: Oxford University Press, 2009), 123–34.

13. For a history of internationalism, see Mark Mazower, *Governing the World: The History of an Idea, 1815 to the Present* (New York: Penguin, 2012). See also Mary Nolan's insightful review of Mazower's book, "The Rise and Fall of Internationalism," *Public Books*, July 10, 2013, http://www.publicbooks.org/nonfiction/the-rise-and-fall-of-internationalism.

14. See Manu Goswani, "Imaginary Futures and Colonial Internationalisms," *American Historical Review* 117.5 (2012): 1461–85.

15. Perry Anderson, "Internationalism: A Breviary," *New Left Review* 14 (March–April 2002): 5–6.

16. Samuel Moyn, *The Last Utopia: Human Rights in History* (Cambridge, MA: Harvard University Press, 2010), 85–86. The chapter from which I am quoting is called "Why Anticolonialism Wasn't a Human Rights Movement." Moyn's argument that the human rights movement only becomes significant in the post-1968 period lends support to my argument for alternative internationalisms in the pre-1968 period.

17. The work of Gary Wilder offers a distinct—and important—perspective on decolonization struggles. He argues that movements for decolonization should not simply be identified with national liberation struggles, but should rather be seen as having also experimented with nonstate visions of democratic federation. However, like Moyn, he wants to situate such movements outside the more recent turn to human rights (correctly, in my estimation). See Gary Wilder, *Freedom Time: Negritude, Decolonization, and the Future of the World* (Durham, NC: Duke University Press, 2015).

18. Daniel Levy and Natan Sznaider, *Human Rights and Memory* (University Park: Penn State University Press, 2010), 4.

19. Until recently there has been a consensus that memories of the Holocaust played a predominant role in this rearticulation of national sovereignty in relation to human rights, but new scholarship puts this claim into question. Scholars such as Samuel Moyn and Marco Duranti have shown that little evidence exists to buttress this consensus. As Duranti points out, there is no discussion of the specificity of the Holocaust in any of the documents or debates surrounding the Universal Declaration of Human Right in 1948. But even if the Holocaust did not motivate the turn to human rights in the late 1940s or 1970s, there is no doubt that its memory has now been articulated to the currently dominant form of internationalism. See Moyn, *Last Utopia*; and Duranti, "The Holocaust, the Legacy of 1789, and the Birth of International Human Rights Law: Revisiting the Foundation Myth," *Journal of Genocide Research* 14.2 (2012): 159–86.

20. Daniel Levy and Natan Sznaider, "Memory Unbound: The Holocaust and the Formation of Cosmopolitan Memory," *European Journal of Social Theory* 5.1 (2002): 87–106; 88. See also Levy and Sznaider, *The Holocaust and Memory*.

21. See Samuel Moyn, *Not Enough: Human Rights in an Unequal World* (Cambridge, MA: Belknap Press of Harvard University Press, 2018).
22. Bruce Robbins, *The Beneficiary* (Durham, NC: Duke University Press, 2017).
23. I will refer to Marceline Loridan-Ivens according to the name(s) she used at the time she took part in different cinematic and literary projects. When speaking generally about her, I will refer to her as Loridan-Ivens.
24. For the significance of 1961, see Annette Wieviorka, *The Era of the Witness*, tr. Jared Stark (Ithaca, NY: Cornell University Press, 2006); and Rothberg, *Multidirectional Memory*, parts 3 and 4.
25. María Lugones, "Playfulness, 'World'-Travelling, and Loving Perception," *Hypatia* 2.2 (1987): 3–19; 18.
26. Ibid., 16.
27. Jean Rouch and Edgar Morin, dir., *Chronique d'un été* (Paris: Argos, 1961).
28. For a discussion of this editing process as well as some of the footage treating these political themes, see Florence Dauman's documentary *Un été + 50* (Paris: Argos, 2011). For an analysis of the way politics was deliberately edited out of the film, see Sam DiIorio, "Total Cinema: *Chronique d'un été* and the End of Bazinian Film Theory," *Screen* 48.1 (2007): 25–43.
29. For my close reading of this scene, see *Multidirectional Memory*, chap. 6. Frédérique Berthet offers a deep reading of these scenes, together with many hours of audio rushes from *Chronicle* and other testimony provided by Loridan, in *La voix manquante* (Paris: P.O.L., 2018).
30. Writing forty years later, Loridan-Ivens describes the deportation in the following terms: "How could I have known, growing up as a little girl in a modern, happy family in Southern France, that history is so merciless. That my hard-working father, who had flown from anti-Semitism in Poland to France in 1920, would return on the same railway. We had both been arrested by the Gestapo in 1943 and transported to Poland, to the concentration camp Auschwitz. Of the fifty members of our family only a few would return. I arrived in France on the same cattle car, without him." See Marceline Loridan-Ivens, "The Wind of Tides," in *Cinema without Borders: The Films of Joris Ivens* (Nijmegen, The Netherlands: European Foundation Joris Ivens, 2002), 6.
31. My thinking on the mediation of memory is indebted to the work of Astrid Erll and Ann Rigney. See their jointly edited collection *Mediation, Remediation, and the Dynamics of Cultural Memory* (Berlin: Walter de Gruyter, 2009).
32. See the May 7, 1961, interview with Marceline Loridan for the television program *Reflets de Cannes*, now included in the 2103 Criterion edition of the *Chronicle of a Summer* DVD.
33. For the historical resonances of *Night and Fog*—including its links to decolonization—see Griselda Pollock and Max Silverman, eds., *Concentrationary Cinema: Aesthetics as Resistance in Alain Resnais's "Night and Fog"* (New York: Berghahn, 2012).
34. Marguerite Duras, "Les deux ghettos," *France-Observateur*, November 9,

1961, 8–10. See also Henri Kréa, "Le racism est collectif, la solidarité individuelle," *France-Observateur*, October 26, 1961, 14–15.

35. William Gardner Smith, *The Stone Face* (New York: Farrar, Straus, 1963).

36. Fiona C. Ross, "On Having a Voice and Being Heard: Some After-Effects of Testifying before the South African Truth and Reconciliation Commission," *Anthropological Theory* 3.3 (2003): 325–41.

37. This quotation is taken from the discussion of *Comment Yukong déplaça les montagnes* on the radio show *Le masque et la plume*, April 10, 1977, available on the website of INA: http://www.ina.fr/video/AFE09000133/les-echos-du-cinema-numero-23.fr.html. See also the press excerpts included in Jean-Pierre Sergent, "The Chinese Dream of Joris Ivens," *Studies in Documentary Film* 3.1 (2009): 61–68.

38. Joris Ivens and Marceline Loridan, *Le 17e parallèle: La guerre du peuple* (Paris: Argos, 1968). For a broader study of socialist solidarity in relation to documentary films about the Vietnam War (albeit one that does not mention Ivens and Loridan), see Christina Schwenkel, "Imaging Humanity: Socialist Film and Transnational Memories of the War in Vietnam," in *Transnational Memory: Circulation, Articulation, Scales*, ed. Chiara De Cesari and Ann Rigney (Berlin: De Gruyter, 2014), 219–44. For a nuanced, multiperspectival account of the memory of the war in Vietnam, see Viet Thanh Nguyen, *Nothing Ever Dies: Vietnam and the Memory of War* (Cambridge, MA: Harvard University Press, 2016).

39. In Loridan's words, the film was an attempt to capture "people's true lived experience." See Serge Daney, Thérèse Giraud, and Serge Le Péron, "Entretien avec Joris Ivens and Marceline Loridan," *Cahiers du cinéma* 266–67 (May 1976): 6–22; 7.

40. See the five-DVD collection Joris Ivens, *Cinéaste du monde* (Arte, 2009). The *Cahiers du cinéma* interview cited above gives a good sense of how Ivens and Loridan worked and portrays a fairly equitable collaboration.

41. See Loridan's comments on the relatively recent invention of the Coutant camera and the Nagra recorder in "Entretien avec Joris Ivens and Marceline Loridan," 14. Rouch and Morin's film and Ivens and Loridan's film also shared the same producer, Argos Films.

42. Sergent, "Chinese Dream," 63. My argument here is that the multidirectional links between *Chronicle of a Summer* and *The Seventeenth Parallel* are not primarily a matter of content (the histories at stake are, in fact, radically different from each other), but rather of genre (testimony, direct cinema), rhetoric ("never forget!"), and material form (technology and cinematic technique).

43. "On Treatment of Civilians," 551.

44. Marceline Loridan and Joris Ivens, *17e parallèle: La guerre du peuple (deux mois sous la terre)* (Paris: Les éditeurs Français Réunis, 1968), 51. It is relevant to the question of internationalism that the publishing house for this book was in the orbit of the French Communist Party.

45. Ibid., 54; my translation.

46. Ibid. This scene is not included in the film, although there is much footage of the underground schools, and children play a significant role (including giving testimony). The recordings Loridan describes in this scene are, however, similar to ones found in the final cut.

47. See, e.g., Ivens's comments in his preface to the book version of *17e Parallèle* (9). The filmmakers have also sometimes made contestable decisions about what footage to include—including scenes of corpses and of the capture and humiliation of an American soldier.

48. Steven Erlanger, "Jewish Deportee on Persecution, Past and Present," *New York Times*, January 2, 2016, http://www.nytimes.com/2016/01/02/books/a-french-deportee-life-at-auschwitz-and-history-repeating.html.

49. See also Pierre Haski, "Marceline Loridan a filmé la Chine de Mao: 'Je fus dupée par mon époque,'" *Rue89*, June 15, 2014, http://rue89.nouvelobs.com/2014/06/15/marceline-loridan-a-filme-chine-mao-jai-ete-dupee-epoque-252686.

50. See also Loridan-Ivens's remarks about the eternal nature of antisemitism on the occasion of the seventieth anniversary of the liberation of Auschwitz in Pierre Haski, "Auschwitz 70 ans après: Donner tort à Marceline Loridan," *Rue89*, January 27, 2015, http://rue89.nouvelobs.com/2015/01/27/auschwitz-70-ans-apres-donner-tort-a-marceline-loridan-257335.

51. Another obvious example of Holocaust internationalism is the non-Jewish Auschwitz survivor Charlotte Delbo, who linked her experiences nonreductively to events in Algeria, Greece, and Argentina, and also condemned Soviet terror. On Delbo, see my *Multidirectional Memory*, chap. 7.

52. For the importance of 1968 and in particular the Vietnam War in the globalization of Holocaust memory, see also Berthold Molden, "Vietnam, the New Left and the Holocaust: How the Cold War Changed Discourse on Genocide," in *Memory in a Global Age*, ed. Aleida Assmann and Sebastian Conrad (Basingstoke, UK: Palgrave Macmillan, 2010), 79–96.

53. The text of "On Treatment of Civilians" makes it clear that Loridan testified alone in Copenhagen. It includes transcripts of the film excerpts screened—excerpts that include the avowal that the Vietnamese will "never forget" what they have suffered. As Enzo Traverso writes, "The comparison between Nazi violence and U.S. imperialism was a commonplace of the antiwar movement," and in the Russell Tribunal, "Memory was mobilized to fight the executioners of the present, not to commemorate the victims of the past." I would add, however, that it was not very common to have an actual victim of the Nazis testifying in the way that Loridan did. See Traverso, *Left-Wing Melancholia: Marxism, History, and Memory* (New York: Columbia University Press, 2016), 13.

54. See Cathy Caruth, "Trauma and Experience: Introduction," in *Trauma: Explorations in Memory*, ed. C. Caruth (Baltimore: Johns Hopkins University Press, 1995), 10.

55. Marceline Loridan-Ivens, *Ma vie balagan*, written in collaboration with Elisabeth D. Inandiak (Paris: Robert Laffont, 2008), 173; my translation. In the last years of her life, Loridan-Ivens published two additional memoirs: *But You Did Not Come Back*, tr. Sandra Smith (New York: Grove Press, 2016 [French original: 2015]); and *L'amour après*, with Judith Perrignon (Paris: Grasset, 2018). In the latter volume, Loridan-Ivens uses the metaphor of the "valise d'amour," a suitcase holding love letters, yet another iteration of the trope of the suitcase.

56. The trope of the suitcase as *lieu de mémoire* is of course not limited to Loridan-Ivens. Such suitcases play a significant role in Holocaust commemoration. They are, for instance, displayed at various camps and museums and used in pedagogical projects such as *What We Carry*, which combines videotaped survivor testimony and the presentation of authentic artifacts carried in suitcases. See the project website: www.whatwecarry.org. Another innovative deployment of the suitcase as a figure of multidirectional memory can be found in the Turkish writer Menekşe Toprak's short story "Velizdeki Mektup," which recounts the "inheritance" of Germany's National Socialist history by a Turkish-German immigrant girl. See Menekşe Toprak, *Velizdeki Mektup* (Istanbul: YKY, 2007). The story has been translated into English as "The Letter in the Suitcase" by Yasemin Yildiz, *Massachusetts Review* 58.3 (2017): 429–41.

57. See Charlotte Delbo, *Days and Memory*, tr. Rosette Lamont (Evanston, IL: Marlboro Press / Northwestern, 2001).

58. See the reproduction of the image in Berthet, *La voix manquante*, 223.

59. See Hervé Hamon and Patrick Rotman, *Les porteurs de valises: La résistance française à la guerre d'Algérie* (Paris: Albin Michel, 1979).

60. Sergent's comments can be found in Dauman, dir., *Un été + 50*.

CHAPTER 6: "GERMANY IS IN KURDISTAN"

1. See Bilgin Ayata, "Kurdish Transnational Politics and Turkey's Changing Kurdish Policy: The Journey of Kurdish Broadcasting from Europe to Turkey," *Journal of Contemporary European Studies* 19.4 (2011): 523–33; "The Politics of Displacement: A Transnational Analysis of the Forced Migration of Kurds in Turkey and Europe" (PhD diss., Johns Hopkins University, 2011); and Ayata and Deniz Yükseker, "A Belated Awakening: National and International Responses to the Internal Displacement of Kurds in Turkey," *New Perspectives on Turkey* 32 (2005): 5–42.

2. While the Marxist-Leninist PKK has been known as famously authoritarian and guided by a cult of personality centered on its leader Abdullah Öcalan, the party has undergone significant changes in recent years. After Öcalan's arrest by the Turkish state in 1999, he shifted his political philosophy, and since then the Kurdish movement has been experimenting with forms of "democratic confederalism" based on the writings of the anarchist Murray Bookchin. See Rafael Taylor, "The New PKK: Unleashing a Social Revolution in Kurdistan," *Roar Magazine*, August 17, 2014, http://roarmag.org/2014/08/pkk-kurdish-struggle-autonomy/.

3. The bodies were allegedly dumped in an unmarked mass grave. According to PKK witnesses, Ronahî's body was discovered naked and mutilated. See "'Ich habe mich für die Befreiung der Menschheit der PKK angeschlossen,'" *RedGlobe*, October 24, 2014, http://www.redglobe.de/naher-mittlerer-osten/kurdistan/9995-ich-bin-sozialistin-und-habe-mich-fuer-die-befreiung-der-menschheit-der-pkk-angeschlossen; the article is described as a translation from a Kurdish newspaper, but no source is given. The Turkish state contests this account.

4. On Germans, including Wolf, who joined the PKK, see Klaus Brinkbaumer and Georg Mascolo, "Die verlorene Brigade," *Spiegel* 7 (2000): 58–64.

5. Astrid Erll, *Memory in Culture* (New York: Palgrave Macmillan, 2011), 138, 166. Also relevant to this chapter is Ann Rigney's work on memory of/in activism (although my example remains largely focused on the thematics of loss and violence that Rigney seeks to move beyond). See "Remembering Hope: Transnational Activism beyond the Traumatic," *Memory Studies* 11.3 (2018): 368–80.

6. See the article in *RedGlobe* cited in note 3 above.

7. "Monumental Tomb in Van named after German Activist Andrea Wolf," *Firat News*, September 15, 2013, http://en.firatnews.com/news/news/monumental-tomb-in-van-named-after-german-activist-andrea-wolf.htm.

8. See "Demolition Order for the Monumental Tomb Named after Andrea Wolf," *Firat News*, September 21, 2013, http://en.firatajans.com/news/news/demolition-order-for-the-monumental-tomb-named-after-andrea-wolf.htm.

9. See the 160-page, self-published memorial book *Im Dschungel der Städte, in den Bergen Kurdistans: Leben und Kampf von Andrea Wolf*, ed. Die Redaktionsgruppe, 2nd ed. (Berlin: Informationsstelle Kurdistan and AWI 1992–Literaturversand, 1999). This book includes a text from Wolf's mother, Lilo Wolf; photos of Wolf from all eras of her life; and extensive exchanges of letters between Wolf and various comrades in the radical left and Kurdish movements. A flyer from October 2013 advertises an event in Hamburg called "The View from the Mountains" on the fifteenth anniversary of Wolf's death, which was to take place in the "Tatort Kurdistan Café." The text of the flyer asks: "Who was Andrea? What did she want? What does that have to do with us?" In the Georg-von-Rauch-Haus in Berlin, one of the city's oldest squats, the inner courtyard was named "Ronahî-Platz" and a large mural was painted "In Memory of Andrea Wolf" by "a few artistically inclined Internationalists." See the Indymedia report at http://de.indymedia.org/2011/09/316315.shtml. Flyers posted next to the murals in the courtyard indict the "imperialist cronyism between Turkey and Germany" and declare that "Andrea recognized the international character of domination and exploitation and had drawn the consequences" from that recognition.

10. See *Affaire Wolf-Sorg c. Turquie*, June 8, 2010. See also "European Court Convicts Turkey for Inadequate Investigation," *Hürriyet Daily News*, http://www.hurriyetdailynews.com/default.aspx?pageid=438&n=echr-convicts-turkey-for-inadequate-investigation-on-ex-pkk-terrorist—2010-09-24.

11. Thomas Seibert, "Der ISIS and die Front-Frauen," *Tagesspiegel*, October 17, 2014, http://www.tagesspiegel.de/politik/kampf-um-kobane-der-is-und-die-front-frauen/10856460.html. For an informed view of women in the Kurdish movement, see Necla Acik, "Kobane: The Struggle of Kurdish Women against Islamic State," *openDemocracy*, October 22, 2014, https://www.opendemocracy.net/arab-awakening/necla-acik-kobane-struggle-of-kurdish-women-against-islamic-state.

12. See Amberin Zaman, "How a German Doctor Became a PKK Hero," *Al-Monitor*, November 17, 2014, http://www.al-monitor.com/pulse/originals/2014/11/turkey-syria-pkk-pyd-legend-doctor-medya.html#.

13. The origin of Wolf's nom de guerre is mentioned in Hito Steyerl's film *November*. On the suicide of Ronahî (Bedriye Tas), see Michael Schwelien, "Hat das Verbot die PKK noch gestärkt?," *Die Zeit*, April 1, 1994, http://www.zeit.de/1994/14/hat-das-verbot-die-pkk-noch-gestaerkt.

14. One obvious analogue to the case of Wolf/Ronahî is the better-known case of Che Guevara. See Paul J. Dosal, "San Ernesto de la Higuera: The Resurrection of Che Guevara," in *Death, Dismemberment, and Memory: Body Politics in Latin America*, ed. Lyman L. Johnson (Albuquerque: University of New Mexico Press, 2004), 317–41; 318.

15. In addition to her ongoing work on globalization, Steyerl made early contributions to antiracist German discourses on migration and postcoloniality, but she also resists the ethnicization of politics and the way she was—as a woman of color—"put into all sorts of absurd identity categories." Because she felt unable to "tell (hi)stories outside the mainstream" in the German context, she decided after her first film, *Die leere Mitte* (1998), to address her work to "international" art publics. One sign of that changed address is the language of narration, which shifts from German in the first film to English in the works I will consider. At the same time, as I will argue, the German national context continues to be an important frame of implication in her Andrea Wolf project. See her comments in Noa Ha and Hito Steyerl, "Berlin 1998–2017: Von der leeren zur kolonialen Mitte," in "Geschichte Schreiben," ed. Manuela Bauche and Sharon Dodua Otoo, special issue, *Neue Rundschau* 129.2 (2018): 108–16; citations from 110. See also Hito Steyerl and Encarnación Gutiérrez Rodriguez, eds., *Spricht die Subalterne deutsch? Migration und postkoloniale Kritik* [Can the subaltern speak German? Migration and postcolonial critique] (Münster: Unrast, 2003).

16. Hito Steyerl, "A Thing like You and Me," in *Hito Steyerl*, exhibition catalogue, with texts by Pablo Lafuente, Hito Steyerl, and Maria Mühle (Høvikodden, Norway: Henie Onstad Art Centre, 2010), 61–71. See also Charity Scribner's discussion of "postmilitant culture" in *After the Red Army Faction: Gender, Culture, and Militancy* (New York: Columbia University Press, 2015).

17. See Cihan Tekay, "In Memory of Suphi Nejat Ağırnaslı," Jadaliyya, October 16, 2014, http://reviews.jadaliyya.com/pages/index/19651/in-memory-of-suphi-nejat-agirnasli. See also Étienne Balibar's short statement in solidarity with Kobanê,

where he observes: "Forms of solidarity, self-management and self-determination are developing, straddling the border, which confer on the resistance the character not only of a nationalist struggle, but that of a democratic experiment." See Balibar, "For the Resistance in Kobane," tr. David Broder, *Verso* (blog), November 3, 2014, http://www.versobooks.com/blogs/1739-etienne-balibar-for-the-resistance-in-kobane. Other sources on internationalism in the Kurdish struggle include the short documentaries *Our War*, dir. Benedetta Argentieri, Bruno Chiaravalloti, and Claudio Jampaglia (PossibleFILM, 2016); and Vice International, *Foreigners Fighting ISIS in Syria: The War of Others* (Vice, 2016).

18. Some commentators have likened the struggle in Rojava to the Spanish Civil War, perhaps the most significant attempt to create a revolutionary form of direct democracy that attracted internationalist solidarity. As David Graeber notes, however, Rojava has not (yet) attracted the same level of internationalist support as the Spanish struggle. See his "Why Is the World Ignoring the Revolutionary Kurds in Syria?," *The Guardian*, October 8, 2014, http://www.theguardian.com/commentisfree/2014/oct/08/why-world-ignoring-revolutionary-kurds-syria-isis?CMP=twt_gu.

19. This dimension of the film has not received much commentary. I have in mind the film's inclusion through different means of figures such as a soldier who fought for Germany in World War I and was later persecuted during National Socialism; Friedrich Hollaender, a Jewish songwriter who had to flee the Nazis, but who also wrote racist/colonialist songs; and the protesting construction workers, at once marginalized by transnational capitalism's use of migrant labor and racist in their account of their situation.

20. Although viewers and critics often assume the voice-over narration is by Steyerl, the voice is identified in the closing credits as that of Hatice Ayten.

21. Hito Steyerl, "In Defense of the Poor Image," in *The Wretched of the Screen* (Berlin: Sternberg Press / e-flux, 2012), 32–33.

22. See Ayata, "Politics of Displacement," for an account of the dialectic between state-initiated displacement and transnational activism.

23. Bilgin Ayata, "Kurdish Transnational." The first quotation is from p. 525; the second comes from a journalist Ayata cites and is found on p. 530.

24. The quotation is from T. J. Demos's fine reading of Steyerl's work in *The Migrant Image: The Art and Politics of Documentary during Global Crisis* (Durham, NC: Duke University Press, 2013), 78.

25. Skeptical accounts of such internationalist connections tend to denigrate the idealizing, imaginary identifications of German students with revolutionary movements elsewhere, but Quinn Slobodian and others have uncovered grounded histories of interpersonal exchange. See Slobodian, *Foreign Front: Third World Politics in Sixties West Germany* (Durham, NC: Duke University Press, 2012); and Niels Seibert, *Vergessene Proteste: Internationalismus und Antirassismus, 1964–1983* (Münster: Unrast, 2008).

26. See Hito Steyerl, "*November*: A Film Treatment," *Transit* 1.1 (2004): 2.

27. Jeremy Varon, *Bringing the War Home: The Weather Underground, the Red Army Faction, and Revolutionary Violence in the Sixties and Seventies* (Berkeley: University of California Press, 2004), 15.

28. Lori Allen, "The Polyvalent Politics of Martyr Commemorations in the Palestinian Intifada," *History and Memory* 18.2 (2006): 107–38; 114, 118, 117.

29. In another essay on Palestine, Allen addresses the "politics of immediation"—direct appeals to human rights via images of suffering that produce highly charged affects. No doubt such a politics exists in the Kurdish case as well, but Steyerl's investigation of Wolf's story deliberately contests immediation. See Lori Allen, "Martyr Bodies in the Media: Human Rights, Aesthetics, and the Politics of Immediation in the Palestinian Intifada," *American Ethnologist* 36.1 (2009): 161–80.

30. Dziga Vertov, *Kino-Eye: The Writings of Dziga Vertov*, ed. Annette Michelson, tr. Kevin O'Brien (Berkeley: University of California Press, 1984), 52. Vertov's brother and cameraman, Mikhail Kaufman, comments that montage allows us to "conjoin" what has been "torn apart both temporally and physically," in "An Interview with Mikhail Kaufman," *October* 11 (Winter 1979): 62.

31. See Nora M. Alter, *Chris Marker* (Urbana: University of Illinois Press, 2006), 75.

32. Godard's self-reflexive reuse of his own work recalls Steyerl's own strategy of using the early martial arts film in *November*. That similarity calls into question to some degree the distance Steyerl is trying to establish between her postrevolutionary aesthetic and *Loin du Vietnam*'s revolutionary aesthetic.

33. Steyerl, "A Thing like You and Me," 61, 71.

34. Hito Steyerl, "Missing People: Entanglement, Superposition, and Exhumation as Sites of Indeterminacy," in *The Wretched of the Screen* (Berlin: Sternberg Press / e-flux, 2012), 153. Although unmentioned, the influence of Bruno Latour and the flat ontologies of his actor-network theory seems present here.

35. In a largely appreciative review of Steyerl's critical writings, Tony Wood makes a related point: "The appeal to the object's inert potential arguably relies on a reification of the subject-object split, whereas it would surely make more sense to retain a sense of the mutually interwoven, fundamentally mediated character of both." See Tony Wood, "Reserve Armies of the Imagination," *New Left Review* 82 (2013): 142.

36. In a published film treatment, this sequence continues with an even more significant indictment: "There is not only the history of Kurds and also Turks in Germany, but also the history of the circulation of weapons of mass destruction from Germany into Iraq. The chemical weapons used against the Kurds were supplied by a German company. . . . More than 5000 people died when gas was used against the village of Halabja in 1987." See Steyerl, "Film Treatment," 12.

37. This quotation is from Lockheed Martin's website: http://www.lockheedmartin.com/us/who-we-are/global/germany.html.

38. These shots also recall contemporary forms of witnessing political violence via cell phone. See the video opinion piece about the Rohingya by Matthew F. Smith, Taimoor Sobhan, and Japhet Weeks, "Capturing Their Genocide on Their Cellphones," *New York Times* August 27, 2018, https://www.nytimes.com/video/opinion/100000006035884/capturing-their-genocide-on-their-cellphones.html.

39. This text describes the Art Institute's "Focus" exhibit on Steyerl in 2012–13. The curators also write, "While her subjects vary widely, her work is consistently based on the premise that we are always implicated, consciously and unconsciously, in the stories that we tell." See http://www.artic.edu/exhibition/focus-hito-steyerl.

40. In 2017, Steyerl was in fact named the most influential person in the art world by the British magazine *ArtReview* in their Power 100 list: https://artreview.com/power_100/.

41. For further discussion of Steyerl's relation to her modernist predecessors, see Pablo Lafuente, "For a Populist Cinema: On Hito Steyerl's *November* and *Lovely Andrea*," *Afterall: A Journal of Art, Context, and Enquiry* 19 (2008): 64–70; and Marit Paasche, "The New Protagonist: On the Films of Hito Steyerl," in *Urban Images: Unruly Desires in Film and Architecture*, ed. Synne Bull and Marit Paasche (Berlin: Sternberg Press, 2011), 23–33.

42. In Kerstin Stakemeier's reading, Steyerl's films maintain solidarity as a virtue but reject the way organized political parties like the PKK have channeled it. See Stakemeier, "Minor Findings and Major Tendencies," *Afterall: A Journal of Art, Context, and Enquiry* 19 (2008): 54–63.

43. A report on Austrian radio (ORF) describes Steyerl traveling to Suruç after a talk in Istanbul in autumn of 2014 in order to work with local artists engaged with refugees from Kobanê and mentions that Steyerl's interest in the Kurdish question grew out of her Wolf project. See "Hito Steyerl über Kunst and Krieg," http://oe1.orf.at/artikel/389338.

44. Önder Çakar, Rojava Film Commune, and Hito Steyerl, "I Don't Have Time!," *e-flux journal* 86 (November 2017): n.p.; Hito Steyerl and Rojava Film Commune, "The Color of Women: An Interview with YPJ Commanders Dilovan Kobani, Nirvana, Ruken, and Zerin," *e-flux journal* 86 (November 2017): n.p., http://www.e-flux.com/journal/86/.

45. After identifying as socialist, the Combahee River Collective Statement continues: "We are not convinced, however, that a socialist revolution that is not also a feminist and antiracist revolution will guarantee our liberation." Reproduced in Keeanga-Yamahtta Taylor, ed., *How We Get Free: Black Feminism and the Combahee River Collective* (Chicago: Haymarket Books, 2017), 19–20.

46. See Alain Badiou, *Ethics: An Essay on the Understanding of Evil*, tr. Peter Hallward (New York: Verso, 2001), ch. 4.

47. Bruno Bosteels, *Badiou and Politics* (Durham, NC: Duke University Press, 2011), 29.

48. In more recent work, Badiou has dispensed with the importance of naming, but it seems to me that it remains an important part of the work of fidelity for Steyerl. See ibid., 211.

CONCLUSION: TRANSFIGURING IMPLICATION

1. See https://www.tate.org.uk/art/art-terms/f/figurative-art.

Index

Abstract (Steyerl), 190, *191*, 192
Abu Ghraib scandal, 4
"Academic Freedom and the ASA's Boycott of Israel" (Butler), 232n48
Achcar, Gilbert, 228n9
Acik, Necla, 240n11
aesthetics: affect and, 26–27, 60; of implication, 22–23, 90–91, 100–101, 104–11; of internationalism, 163–86; modes of address and, 24, 200, 219n18; narratology and, 88–91, 96–104; privilege and, 25; remediation and, 27, 165–66, 169–86, 190, 193; serial projects and, 23, 26–27; temporality and, 96–104
affect, 25; aesthetic projects and, 26–27, 68–75; image juxtaposition and, 129–31, 134–36, 140–42; implication and, 118–25; long-distance solidarity and, 25, 140–41; nationalism and, 16–17, 118–25, 227n2, 228n7. *See also* axis of political affect (of multidirectional memory)
An Affective State (Parkinson), 214n15
affirmative internationalism, 153, 193–97
African Immanuel Essemblies Brass Band, 112
African National Congress (ANC), 88

After Evil (Meister), 221n46
After the Red Army Faction (Scribner), 240n16
Against Purity (Shotwell), 212n50
Ağırnaslı, Suphi Nehat, 174–75
Agnotology (Proctor and Schiebinger), 214n13
Alexander, Jeffrey, 233n12
Alexander, Michelle, 65
Algeria, Year Zero (Loridan and Sergent), 163–64, 175
Algerian War, 127–28, 130, 153, 159–63, 169
Allen, Lori, 183, 242nn28–29
Ambiguities of Witnessing (Sanders), 223n11
American Studies Association, 122
"Amnesty or Impunity?" (Mamdani), 224n16
Anderson, Benedict, 25, 90, 95–96, 99
Anderson, Perry, 154–55
Anielewicz, Mordechai, 129
animation, 97–99
Anthropocene, 11–12, 201
anthropocentrism, 74–75, 104
Anti-Defamation League, 128
Antigua, 24, 68–80
anti-imperialism, 153–58
antiracism, 5–6
"Apartheid" (Makdisi), 230n28
apartheid (South African), 11, 96–104

The Arabs and the Holocaust (Achcar), 228n9
Araujo, Ana Lucia, 217n4
"The Architecture of Erasure" (Makdisi), 230n28
Arch of Titus, 87
Arc/Procession (Kentridge), 87–91, *88*, 99, 102–3, 111–17
Arendt, Hannah, 1, 18, 23, 35, 44–45, 49–50, 83, 108, 142, 215n22, 228n7
Argentina, 91
Armenian genocide, 28
Art Institute of Chicago, 191–93, 243n39
Auschwitz-Birkenau, 131, 153, 159–60, 168–70, 235n29
Auster, Paul, 101–2
avant-garde, 104–6
axis of comparison (of multidirectional memory), 124–25, *125*, 128–34
axis of political affect (of multidirectional memory), 124–25, *125*, 134
Ayata, Bilgin, 180
Azoulay, Ariella, 141, 231n40, 232nn44–45

Bach, Johann Sebastian, 114
Badiou, Alain, 196–97
Badiou and Politics (Bosteels), 244n47
Bakhtin, Mikhail, 95–96, 224n20
Balibar, Étienne, 240n17
Barbuda, 75–80
Barkan, Elazar, 60–61, 71–72, 217n5
Bashir, Bashir, 121–22
BDS movement, 118–22, 143–44
Beckmann, Max, 97
Being a Character (Bollas), 211n44
Beloved (Morrison), 65–66
The Beneficiary (Robbins), 56, 211n43, 232n50

beneficiary figure, 13–15; definition of, 211n43; global inequality and, 17, 48–49; human rights discourses and, 31–32; the Nakba and, 141–44; perpetrator and, 210n39; responsibilities of, 20–21, 143; Rwandan genocide and, 15–17; slavery and, 17, 24, 81–82; temporality and, 32; theorization of, 20, 31–32, 55–58
Benjamin, Walter, 78, 87–88, 90, 95–96
Bentham, Jeremy, 154
Berlant, Lauren, 10, 209n23
Berthet, Frédérique, 235n29
Berto, Juliet, 185
Best, Stephen, 65–67, 80
Bethell-Codrington, Christopher, 75–76, 78
Betty's Hope, 76
Bevernage, Berber, 9, 52–53
"Beyond Nuremberg" (Mamdani), 207n14
Bhabha, Homi, 115, 117
biopower, 53–54, 77, 214n11
The Birch-Tree Meadow (Loridan-Ivens). See *La petite prairie aux bouleaux* (Loridan-Ivens)
Bitter Fruit (Dangor), 98
Black Atlantic, 9–10, 74–75
Black Lives Matter, 2–5, 7, 205n3
"Black Power Incarcerated" (Whitehorn), 214n10
Black Skin, White Masks (Fanon), 70
Bland, Sandra, 7
Bollas, Christopher, 211n44
Bosteels, Bruno, 196
Bourdieu, Pierre, 211n45
Boyd, Rekia, 11
Bramen, Carrie Tirado, 19
Braude, Claudia, 110
"British Fortunes and Caribbean Slavery" (Petley), 220n30

Broeck, Sabine, 219n18
The Broken Voice (Eaglestone), 212n47
Brown, H. Rap, 209n24
Brown, Mike, 11
Brown, Wendy, 71
Burdens of Political Responsibility (Schiff), 210n30
Butler, Judith, 26, 130–31, 143–45, 231n32
But You Did Not Come Back (Loridan-Ivens), 238n55
bystanders, 40–41, 50. See also beneficiary figure

Calvino, Italo, 101–2
"Campo Fiori" (Miłosz), 125–26
capitalism, 11–12, 68–80, 108–9, 192–93, 201. See also colonialism; slavery
carceral state, 39–40, 46, 132, 219n21
Card, Claudia, 214n9
Caricom Reparations Commission, 208n21
Caruth, Cathy, 169
"The Case for Reparations" (Coates), 208n21
Castro, Fidel, 149–50, 185, 233n4
Celan, Paul, 113–15
Césaire, Aimé, 108
A Child at Gunpoint (Raskin), 231n37
Chronicle of a Summer (Rouch and Morin), 26, 154, 160–63, 166–69, 236n42
chronotopes, 95–97, 224n18
Churchill, Caryl, 124–25
circulation, 163–64
Cities of the Dead (Roach), 219n21
Citizen (Rankine), 205n4
Civil Obedience (Lazzara), 212n50
climate change, 12
Closing the Books (Elster), 223n8
Coates, Ta-Nehisi, 59, 208n21

Cobb, Jelani, 7, 207n17
Codrington family, 75–81, 219n16
Coetzee, J. M., 98
Cohen, Stanley, 95, 208n19
Cohn-Bendit, Daniel, 3, 206n5
collective responsibility, 2, 12, 18–21, 25–26, 35, 42–53, 83, 191, 201
"Collective Responsibility" (Arendt), 46–47
colonialism, 14, 26–27, 68–75, 108, 141–44, 150, 154–58, 212n48. See also slavery; tourism
The Color of Law (Rothstein), 209n26
Columbus, Christopher, 69
Combahee River Collective, 22–23, 34–41, 45–46, 48–49, 53, 56, 194, 200, 243n45
"Combahee River Collective Statement" (Smith, Smith, and Frazier), 35–36
Community and Conscience (Shimoni), 222n6
competition, 25–26, 134–40
complex implication, 8, 24–25, 40–41, 90–91, 110, 123–25, 140, 163, 200–201, 220n23
Complicities (Sanders), 205n2
complicity, 13–14, 51–52, 90–91, 212n50
Complicity (Kutz), 209n28
Concentrationary Cinema (Pollock and Silverman), 235n33
concentration camps, 37–41, 46, 48–49, 53–55, 125–28, 132. See also specific camps
Congo, 160
consent, 42, 54, 214n13
Contemporary Jewish Writing in South Africa (Braude), 226n38
Contested Land (Roberts), 228n9
Cooper, Anna Julia, 35–36
cosmopolitanism, 31–32, 43, 157, 168–69. See also internationalism

248   Index

Country of My Skull (Krog), 114
Cover, Robert, 94, 223n9
Craps, Stef, 228n13
Crawford, John, 207n17
Crenshaw, Kimberlé, 35–37, 213n4
criminal guilt, 18, 50, 141–42, 210n39
critical internationalism, 153
Croombs, Matthew, 233n5
Crownshaw, Richard, 209n26
Crush, Jonathan, 108, 226n36
Cuba, 150, 183
"Cultural Memory Studies in the Age of the Anthropocene" (Crownshaw), 209n27

Dangor, Achmat, 98
Danner, Mark, 4
Dauman, Florence, 235n28
death, 113–14
The Debt (Robinson), 217n3
decentering, 139–40
decolonization processes, 159–64
Delbo, Charlotte, 169, 237n51
Deleuze, Gilles, 40–41
"Demarginalizing the Intersection of Sex and Race" (Crenshaw), 213n4
descendant figure, 13–15, 24; implication and, 63–68, 78–80, 141–44; justice and, 59, 80; legacies and, 63–68; slavery and, 59, 70–75, 78–80. *See also* Codrington family; colonialism; slavery
detachment, 33–34, 50
"Deterritorialising the Holocaust" (Parr), 231n38
diasporas: African, 65; exilic experience and, 99–100; Jewish, 17–19, 24, 120; Kurdish, 178–81; long-distance solidarity and, 25
Die leere Mitte (Steyerl), 176, 240n15

Die Schuldfrage (Jaspers), 42, 44
differentiation (logic of), 134–40
DiIorio, Sam, 235n28
Dink, Hrant, 3
Discipline and Punish (Foucault), 214n11
disembedded subjects, 90–91, 101, 111–17
Disgrace (Coetzee), 98
disidentification, 6, 207n12
Disidentifications (Muñoz), 207n12
dislocation, 178–81
Dodington Park, 75
Dorfman, Ariel, 114
Dostoevsky paradigm, 53–55
Draper, Nicholas, 60, 66–67, 75–80
Drawings for Projection (Kentridge), 24, 97–98, 101–17
The Drowned and the Saved (Levi), 37–41
Du Bois, W. E. B., 126–28, 132, 137, 139, 229n17
Dubow, Jessica, 225n33
Duranti, Marco, 234n19
Duras, Marguerite, 127, 130, 162–63
Dziga Vertov Group, 184

Eaglestone, Robert, 212n47
Eastwood, Clint, 93
Ebony and Ivy (Wilder), 217n3
Eckstein, Soho. *See* Kentridge, William
e-flux (journal), 194
Egypt, 133
Eichmann, Adolf, 45, 161
Eichmann in Jerusalem (Arendt), 228n7
Eisenstein, Sergei, 106, 185–86
Eisler, Hanns, 184
Elster, John, 223n8
emancipation (from slavery), 63, 67
Enwezor, Okwui, 225n29

Epistemology of the Closet (Sedgwick), 214n13
equation (logic of), 129–32, 134–37, 150, 155, 230n22, 231n32
The Era of Transitional Justice and Beyond (Gready), 223n11
Erll, Astrid, 172, 235n31
The Ethics of Storytelling (Meretoja), 224n22
European Convention on Human Rights, 173
European Court of Human Rights, 173, 190
event, the, 195–97
"Exodus" (Anderson), 227n3
Experiencing Fiction (Phelan), 224n22
extermination camps, 132
extimacy, 79
Eyerman, Ron, 65

Fanon, Frantz, 70
Faster, Pussycat! Kill! Kill! (Meyer), 178, 184
Felix in Exile (Kentridge), 99–101
feminism, 35–37, 56–58, 176–77
fidelity, 195–97
The Figural Jew (Hammerschlag), 206n5
Finkelstein, Norman, 128
Finkielkraut, Alain, 206n5
Foreign Front (Slobodian), 241n25
forgetting, 25–26
"Forms of Time and of the Chronotope in the Novel" (Bakhtin), 224n20
Forti, Simona, 20, 23, 35, 53–55, 200, 214n13
Foucault, Michel, 40, 53–54
Frames of War (Butler), 130
Fraser, Nancy, 21–22, 81–83, 138, 140, 211n45
Frazier, Demita, 36

Freedom Dreams (Kelley), 217n4
Freedom Time (Wilder), 234n17
From #BLACKLIVESMATTER to Black Liberation (Taylor), 205n3
"From Codrington to Codrington" (documentary), 76
"Fugitive Justice" (Best and Hartman), 216n1
Fullbrook, Mary, 216n25
Futures Past (Koselleck), 222n12

Galloway, George, 129–30
Garner, Eric, 7
Garrel, Maurice, 149
Garvey, Marcus, 65
Gaza, 123–25, 128–34, 228n14
Gehry, Frank, 192–93
gender, 5, 35–37, 56–57. *See also* intersectionality
genealogical implication, 60, 75–81
Genealogy of Morals (Nietzsche), 53–54
General Dynamics, 192–93
The Generation of Postmemory (Hirsch), 210n33
genocide, 15–17, 117; Armenian, 28
German Autumn (1977), 181
Gikandi, Simon, 75
Gilroy, Paul, 9–10
global warming, 74
Godard, Jean-Luc, 149–50, 156, 164, 183–85, 190–91, 242n32
Goethe, Johann Wolfgang von, 114
Goldberg, Amos, 121–22
Goldberg, David Theo, 229n20
Goldstone, Richard, 123–24
Gordimer, Nadine, 89–90, 98, 222n4
"Governing European Subjects" (Yildiz), 224n18
Governing the World (Mazower), 234n13
Graeber, David, 241n18

Gramsci, Antonio, 89, 222n5
Gray, Freddie, 7, 11
"The Gray Zone" (Levi), 12, 214n12
gray zones, 12–13, 22, 37–41, 46, 53–55, 60–61, 80, 139, 214n8
Gready, Paul, 94
"Groping through Gray Zones" (Card), 214n9
The Guardian, 129
Guevara, Che, 185, 240n14
guilt: collective, 47; criminal, 34–35, 42–44, 47, 50, 61, 141–42, 210n39; implicated subjects and, 45–49; nationalism and, 42–49; political, 43–47, 49, 141, 188; responsibility as opposed to, 20–21, 35, 41–51, 216n26; victim-perpetrator imaginary and, 41–49
The Guilt of Nations (Barkan), 60–61
gun violence, 12

Haider, Asad, 213n6
Hall, Catherine, 60, 66–67, 75–80
Hammerschlag, Sarah, 206n5
Handspring Puppet Company, 116
Harris, Cheryl I., 221n42
Hartman, Saidiya, 65, 80, 208n22, 218n8
Haski, Pierre, 237n49
Hatzair, Hashomer, 129
haunting, 62–63, 109–10, 113–14
Haunting Legacies (Schwab), 210n33
Hegel, Georg Wilhelm Friedrich, 70
heroes, 186–97
Heshel's Kingdom (Jacobson), 110
Hiroshima mon amour (Resnais and Duras), 162
Hirsch, Marianne, 14, 62, 210n33
"History as the Main Complaint" (Dubow and Rosengarten), 225n33
Hollaender, Friedrich, 241n19
Holocaust: Germans as beneficiaries of, 17; human rights discourses and, 42–49, 138–40, 234n19; implication in, 11, 25, 37–41, 53–55; internationalism and, 149–54, 163–69; Kentridge's allusions to, 109–10, 113–17; memory work and, 57–58, 127–40, 152–53, 157, 181; postmemory generation and, 14, 62, 123–25; responsibility for, 17–18, 34, 42–49; suitcases and, 169–70; Warsaw Ghetto and, 124–34; witnessing and, 159–63, 167
"Holocaust Memory and the Critique of Violence" (Craps), 228n13
Hope and Memory (Todorov), 213n51
"How a German Doctor Became a PKK Hero" (Zaman), 240n12
How to Accept German Reparations (Slyomovics), 218n6
How We Get Free (Taylor), 213n5
How Yukong Moved the Mountains (Ivens and Loridan-Ivens), 164, 167, 175
Human Rights and Memory (Levy and Sznaider), 157
human rights discourses, 14–16, 24, 31–50, 57–58, 68–75, 91–96, 138–42, 153–58, 168–69, 173, 216n1
Hurston, Zora Neale, 65
Huyssen, Andreas, 225n32
hyperobjects, 74

"I am Trayvon Martin," 2–3
identification, 2–4, 12, 25, 47–50, 81, 121–22, 150, 156–58, 186–97
identity politics, 35–36
ideological implication, 118–25
imagined communities, 99, 155, 197
"Imagining Humanity" (Schwenkel), 236n38
Immler, Nicole, 62

implicated subjects: affect and, 118–25; agency of, 51–53, 55–58; beneficiary figure and, 15–17, 31–32, 43, 201; complicity and, 13–14, 25, 51–52, 107; definitions of, 1, 8, 13, 199; guilt and, 41–49; historical dynamics of, 8–10; human rights discourse and, 14–16, 154–58, 216n1; impurity of, 53–55, 199–200; inequality and, 31–33; internationalism and, 149–54, 171–97; intersectionality and, 34–37, 48–49; justice and, 1–2, 8–9, 11–12, 19–20, 60–63, 104–11, 221n46; legacies and, 63–68; memory and, 118–25, 175–76; political actions of, 152–54, 169–70, 179–97, 200–204; race and, 68–75; slavery and, 59–60, 72–84; solidarity and, 32–33, 35–37; spatiality of, 37–41; structural violence and, 2–11, 49–53; victim-perpetrator dichotomy and, 1–2, 6–8, 21–22, 33–34, 37–41, 46, 53–55, 57–58, 80–84, 173–75; vocabulary absences and, 1–2, 7. *See also* beneficiary figure; guilt; haunting; justice; legacies; memory; race and racism; responsibility; solidarity

implication: aesthetic dimensions of, 23–24, 60, 68–75, 90; affect and, 118–25; complex, 8, 24–25, 40–41, 110, 123–25, 140, 163, 200, 220n23; complicity and, 13–14, 51–52, 90–91, 107; definitions of, 19, 79; descendant figure and, 70–75; embeddedness and, 111–17; the event and, 196–97; flat ontologies and, 187–88; genealogical, 58, 60, 75–81; gray zones and, 37–41, 46; guilt and, 45–49; identification and nonidentification responses and, 2–7, 12; impurity and, 53–55, 173–76; internationalism and, 26–27; legacies and, 63–68, 72–80; narratology of, 96–104; nationalism and, 163–97; privilege and, 5–6, 37–41; restitution and, 60–63; solidarity efforts and, 3, 32–33; structural inequality and, 1–2, 60, 75–81; temporality of, 8–11, 16–17, 25, 27, 32, 49–53, 55, 78–80, 200–204; walking alongside as, 114–17. *See also* justice; memory; responsibility

indigenous peoples, 4
individualism (limitations of), 7
Inheritance Trouble (Rothberg and Yildiz), 211n42
Inside Out West (program), 76
internationalism, 13; aesthetic projects and, 26–27; affirmative v. critical versions of, 153, 156–58, 196–97; Holocaust and, 159–69; human rights discourses and, 31–33; implication and, 26–27, 149–54, 187–97; socialism and, 154–58, 172; solidarity and, 171–75, 181–86, 194–97
intersectionality, 5, 22–23, 34–37, 48–49, 55–58, 194, 213n4, 215n23
"Intersectionality and Its Discontents" (Nash), 213n4
In the Shadow (Rabinbach), 214n16
In the Wake (Sharpe), 208n22
Invictus (Eastwood), 93–94
Iraq War, 4, 189
ISIS, 28, 173–75
Israel/Palestine crisis, 11, 17–19, 25, 117–25, 128–45, 183
Israel's Holocaust and the Politics of Nationhood (Zertal), 228n9
Istanbul Biennial, 192

"Is the Museum a Battlefield?" (Steyerl), 192, 196–97
Ivens, Joris, 26, 149, 152, 164, 166–68, 190–92

Jacobson, Dan, 110
"Jamaica Calls for Britain to Pay Billions of Pounds in Reparations for Slavery" (Mason), 208n21
Jaspers, Karl, 18, 23, 35, 42–45, 49–50, 83, 141–42, 188, 210n39
Jews and Jewishness: implication and, 110, 134–44; Israel/Palestine crisis and, 118–25; long-distance nationalism and, 118–25; racialization of, 123–28; in South Africa, 98, 108–11; Warsaw Ghetto and, 123–28. *See also* diasporas; Holocaust; Israel/Palestine crisis
Jim Crow, 4, 9, 65
Johannesburg, 2nd Greatest City after Paris (Kentridge), 102–3, 105, 116
Johnson, Walter, 218n8
Journey to the Moon (Kentridge), 102
The Judicial Imagination (Stonebridge), 215n19
July's People (Gordimer), 222n5
justice: abnormal, 82–83, 138; descendants and, 59, 80; distribution/recognition/representation axes and, 21–22; human rights discourses and, 15–16, 24, 31–32, 92–93, 138–40; implicated subjects' role in, 1–2, 11–12, 19–20, 141–44; inequality and, 81–84; memory and, 11; pedagogy of, 161–63; political communities and, 49–53; reconciliation and, 16; reflexive, 138; responsibility for, 18–21, 23, 35, 41–53, 55–60, 200–204; restitution and, 59–63, 80–84, 221n46; temporality and, 52–53, 59, 61–62; transitional, 15–16, 32, 43–44, 90–96, 104–11. *See also* colonialism; human rights discourses; slavery; solidarity

Kaufman-Osborn, Timothy, 4, 13
Kelley, Robin D. G., 217n4
Kentridge, William, 24; alter egos of, 91, 97, 99–111, 115–16, 190, 199; ethics of, 114–17; family of, 222n6; formal experimentation of, 23–24, 90–91, 97–102, 104–6, 112, 223n10; implication and, 24–25, 32, 139–41; the interregnum and, 87–91; multidirectional memory and, 91, 104–11; narratology and, 96–104, 111–17
Kerner Commission Report, 10–11
Ketcham, Diana, 226n39
Kincaid, Jamaica, 24, 60, 68–78, 80, 83, 100, 199–200, 219n16, 219n18
King, Martin Luther, Jr., 89
King, Oona, 129
"Kobane" (Acik), 240n11
Kohl, Helmut, 17
Koselleck, Reinhart, 222n12
Krauss, Rosalind, 97, 101, 226n35
Krog, Antjie, 114–15
Ku Klux Klan, 127
"Kurdish Transnational Politics and Turkey's Changing Kurdish Policy" (Ayata), 238n1
Kurdistan, 11, 27–28, 171–86, 201
Kushner, Tony, 145
Kutz, Christopher, 209n28

Lacan, Jacques, 79
LaCapra, Dominick, 221n39
La Chinoise (Godard), 150, 185

L'amour après (Loridan-Ivens), 238n55
La petite prairie aux bouleaux (Loridan-Ivens), 164, 168
The Last Utopia (Moyn), 156
Law of Return (Israeli), 120
Lazzara, Michael, 212n50
Léaud, Jean-Pierre, 185
Lebron, Christopher, 205n3
Lee, Bruce, 184
legacies: collective responsibility and, 20–21; definitions of, 63–64; haunting, 62–63; implicated subjects as inheritors of, 1–6, 75–80; memory and, 76–77; of slavery, 4, 18, 25, 59–60, 63–68
Legacies of British Slave Ownership project, 24, 60, 66–67, 75–80, 83
The Legacy of Abused Children (Schechner), 134–35, *135–36*, 136–37, 139–40, 144, 193
legalism (discursive), 7, 14–15, 18, 20–21, 43–44, 47–50
Le juif imaginaire (Finkielkraut), 206n5
Lelouch, Claude, 149
L'enfant juif de Varsovie (Rousseau), 231n37
"Les deux ghettos" (Duras), 127, 130, 162
Lettre de Siberie (Marker), 233n3
Levi, Neil, 206n5
Levi, Primo, 12–13, 22–23, 35, 37–41, 46, 48–49, 53–55, 139
Levinas, Emmanuel, 115, 117
LeVine, Mark, 133
Levitsky, Steven, 118–22, 144
Levy, Daniel, 154, 157–58, 163
Loin du Vietnam (Marker, et al.), 149–56, 162, 164, 168, 176, 181, 183–85, 190–91
"*Loin du Vietnam*" (Croombs), 233n5
long-distance solidarity, 12, 17–19, 25–27, 32–33, 149–54, 164–69, 171–75, 181–86
Loridan-Ivens, Marceline, 23, 26, 33, 139, 149–70, 175–76, 180–81, 190–92, 196–97, 201, 235n30
Lose Your Mother (Hartman), 208n22, 218n8
Lübecker Totentanz (Notke), 113
Luft, Aliza, 208n18
Lugones, María, 159, 170
lustration, 44, 92
Lyotard, Jean-François, 138

Makdisi, Saree, 120, 229n20
Making All Black Lives Matter (Ransby), 205n3
The Making of Black Lives Matter (Lebron), 205n3
Making Whole What Has Been Smashed (Torpey), 217n4
Maltz-Leca, Leora, 103, 223n10
Mamdani, Mahmood, 16, 24, 44, 57, 207n14, 215n17
Mandela, Nelson, 88, 93
Man with a Movie Camera (Vertov), 183
"Many Billions Gone" (Westley), 217n4
"Marceline Loridan a filmé la Chine de Mao" (Haski), 237n49
Marker, Chris, 149, 151, 156, 165, 184, 233n3
Martin, Trayvon, 2–11, 27, 201, 205n4, 206n11
Martinique, 70
"Martyr Bodies in the Media" (Allen), 242n29
Martyr Ronahî. *See* Wolf, Andrea
Masilo, Dada, 112
Mason, Rowena, 208n21
Ma vie balagan (Loridan-Ivens), 26–27, 169–70

Maxwell, Bill, 205n4
May '68 and Its Afterlives (Ross), 233n10
Mazower, Mark, 234n13
McGlothlin, Erin, 62, 210n33
Mediation, Remediation, and the Dynamics of Cultural Memory (Erll and Rigney), 235n31
Meister, Robert, 14–16, 21, 24, 31–32, 93, 221n46, 222n47, 224n15
Mémorial de la Shoah, 169
memory, 11; aesthetics of, 25; collective responsibility for, 56–57; comparison axis and, 124–25; conflicts in, 118–20, 122–25; forgetting and, 25–26; human rights discourses and, 156–58; implication and, 34, 118–25, 175–76; internationalism and, 157–58; martyrdom and, 171–74, 181–97; multidirectional, 20, 91, 104–11, 114–28, 233n12; plurimedial constellation of, 172; political affect axis of, 124–25, 159–63; postmemory and, 14, 62, 123–25, 159–63, 201; remediation and, 27, 165–66, 169–86, 190, 193; restitution and, 60–63. *See also* implicated subjects; justice; legacies; solidarity
"Memory Citizenship" (Rothberg and Yildiz), 215n22
A Mercy (Morrison), 66
Meretoja, Hanna, 224n22
Meyer, Russ, 178, 184
migration and migrants, 4, 62, 114, 121, 176, 215n22
Miller, Philip, 116
Mills, Charles, 34
Mine (Kentridge), 102, 105–11, *107–9*, 112, 116
"The Miner's Ear" (Morris), 226n36

"Minor Findings and Major Tendencies" (Stakemeier), 243n42
"Missing People" (Steyerl), 187, 190
Mistaken Identity (Asad), 213n6
Modernist Form and the Myth of Jewification (Levi), 206n5
Modern Language Association, 122
Molden, Berthold, 237n52
More Sweetly Play the Dance (Kentridge), 111–17, 226n40, 227n45
Morin, Edgar, 26, 154, 160–64, 166–67
Morris, Rosalind C., 226n36
Morrison, Toni, 65–66
Morris-Suzuki, Tessa, 79, 212n50
Morton, Timothy, 74
mourning, 10
Moyn, Samuel, 24, 31–32, 35–36, 43, 57, 156, 158, 234n19
multidirectional memory: Loridan-Ivens and, 159–60; map of, *125*; race and racialization and, 126–27; remediation and, 27, 165–66, 169–86, 190, 193; solidarity and, 127–45; theorization of, 20, 25–26, 91, 104–11, 114–25, 233n12
Multidirectional Memory (Rothberg), 25, 122, 126, 212n48
Muñoz, José, 207n12
Muslim ban, 4
My Life and Ethiopia's Progress (Selassie), 89

Nakba, 128–44
Napoleon Bonaparte, 47
narratives: fetishism of, 94, 100–101, 104; of implication, 96–104; of progress, 87–91, 111–17, 224n15; of transitional justice, 90–104; of violence and violation, 92–93
Nash, Jennifer C., 213n4

nationalism, 49–53, 95–96, 99, 110; affect and, 17–18, 118–25, 227n2, 228n7; citizenship and, 120–21; implication and, 163–97; internationalisms and, 157–58; long-distance, 16–17, 25, 118–25
Nation-State Bill (Israeli), 121
"Nazi Photographs in Post-Holocaust Art" (Hirsch), 230n27
negative solidarity, 45–46
"The Negro and the Warsaw Ghetto" (Du Bois), 126–27
neocolonialism, 72, 78
neoliberalism, 14–15, 95–96, 224n18
New Demons (Forti), 20
New Left, 184–85
"The New PKK" (Taylor), 238n2
newspapers, 99–100
Nietzsche, Friedrich, 53–54
Night and Fog (Resnais), 162, 184
Nixon, Rob, 225n31
"No ban on stolen land," 5
Nolan, Mary, 234n13
"Nomos and Narrative" (Cover), 223n9
None to Accompany Me (Gordimer), 98
nonidentification, 2–3, 5, 6, 25, 27, 48, 50, 206n11
The Nose (opera), 104
Nothing Ever Dies (Nguyen), 236n38
Notke, Bernt, 113
"Novel Truths" (Grady), 223n11
November (Steyerl), 173–88, *189*, 196–97
Nuremberg trials, 42–44, 92, 94

obedience, 53–55, 212n50
object-oriented ontology (OOO), 187–88
Öcalan, Abdullah, 238n2
October (Eisenstein), 185
"One Track Minds" (Slaughter), 219n18

"On Failing to Make the Past Present" (Best), 66
"On Postcolonial Narratology" (Prince), 223n9
"On the Concept of History" (Benjamin), 211n45
On the Mines (Goldblatt and Gordimer), 225n29
Ophir, Adi, 131
The Order of Evils (Ophir), 131–32

Palestinians, 121, 123–24, 128–36, 140–42, 144, 183
palimpsests, 98–101, 104, 110–11
Parkinson, Anna, 214n15
Parr, Adrian, 231n38
Parting Ways (Butler), 143–44
passivity, 53–54
The Past within Us (Morris-Suzuki), 212n50
Patterson, Orlando, 64
perpetrators, 8; human rights discourses and, 14–16, 33; imaginary of, 7, 51–55; implicated subject figure and, 1, 6, 21–22, 25–26, 33–34, 46, 173–76; multidirectional memory and, 118–25, 181; purification of, 139–40; reckonings with, 10, 13; restitution and, 60–61. *See also* guilt; implication; victims
Perpetual War (Robbins), 212n49
perpetuators, 17, 25–26, 120, 142–43, 145
Petley, Christer, 220n30
Phelan, James, 96
Pick, Daniel, 208n19
Pienaar, Francois, 93
PKK (Kurdistan Workers' Party), 28, 171–82, 185–86, 192, 238n1
Plato, 117, 227n43
political guilt, 43–47, 49, 141, 188

Political Reconciliation (Schaap), 215n16
"Politics, Identification, and Subjectivization" (Rancière), 206n5
The Politics of Aesthetics (Rancière), 230n25
"The Politics of Displacement" (Ayata), 238n1
"The Polyvalent Politics of Martyr Commemorations in the Palestinian Intifada" (Allen), 242n28
"A Poor Christian Looks at the Ghetto" (Miłosz), 125–26
poor image, 178–79, 186–87
Portage (Kentridge), 111
postmemory, 14, 62, 123–25, 201
Power/Knowledge (Foucault), 214n11
The Price of Emancipaton (Draper), 66
Prison Notebooks (Gramsci), 89
privilege, 5–6; aesthetics and, 25; misrecognition and detachment and, 33–34
"Privilege of Unknowing" (Sedgwick), 214n13
Procession (Kentridge), 111
profiling (by police), 4, 7–8
progress narratives, 87–91
"Projected Memory" (Hirsch), 231n37
Puar, Jasbir, 48–49, 215n23
purification, 95–96, 138–40, 173–76, 216n1. *See also* guilt; human rights discourses; justice

"Quest for Justice" (Stone), 229n19
The Question of German Guilt (Jaspers), 42, 44

Rabinbach, Anson, 44–45
race and racism: antiracism and, 5–6; apartheid and, 24, 87–96; feminism and, 35–37; gender and, 5, 35–37, 56–57; immigration and, 4; Israel/Palestine crisis and, 124–25; memory and, 123–28; misrecognition and, 34; multidirectionality and, 126–27; slavery and, 4, 24, 52, 61–62, 64–75; urban uprisings and, 10–11. *See also* Holocaust; intersectionality; Israel/Palestine crisis; Jews and Jewishness; slavery
Race and the Epistemologies of Ignorance (Sullivan and Tuana), 214n13
Radstone, Susannah, 139–41
RAF (Red Army Faction), 172, 181
Rancière, Jacques, 117, 130, 206n5
Rankine, Claudia, 205n4
Ransby, Barbara, 205n3
Rapoport, Nathan, 126, 129
Raskin, Richard, 231n37, 232n41
Reading People, Reading Plots (Phelan), 224n22
recognition (politics of), 81
"Reconciliation and Remembering" (Rigney), 217n5
reflexive justice, 138
The Refusal of Time (Kentridge), 112
Refuse the Hour (Kentridge), 112
remediation, 27, 165–66, 169–70, 173–75, 178–86, 190, 193
reparations, 9–10, 56–57, 59, 61, 80–84, 92, 208n21, 216n27
Reparations for Slavery and the Slave Trade (Araujo), 217n4
Report of the National Commission on Civil Disorders (Kerner Commission Report), 10–11
"Reserve Armies of the Imagination" (Wood), 242n35
Resnais, Alain, 149, 184
responsibility: Arendt on, 1, 18, 45–49; collective, 18–21, 25–26, 42–49, 56–58, 83; collective action in

remediation of, 51–53; guilt and, 20–21, 35, 41–51, 216n26; implication's temporality and, 8–9, 59–60; for justice, 18–21, 23, 49–53, 81–82, 143, 200–204; memory and, 26; political communities and, 45–53, 56–58, 142–44, 195–97, 200–204; temporality and, 8–9, 17–18, 201; Young on, 14

Responsibility for Justice (Young), 23, 49, 51–52

restitution, 59–63, 80–84, 221n46

Rice, Tamir, 7, 207n17

Ricoeur, Paul, 73

Rigney, Ann, 218n5, 235n31

"The Rise and Fall of Internationalism" (Nolan), 234n13

Riva, Emmanuelle, 162

Roach, Joseph, 219n21

Robbins, Bruce, 16–17, 21, 24, 31–32, 43, 55–58, 72, 144–45, 158, 210n39

Roberts, Jo, 228n9

Robinson, Randall, 217n3

Robinson, William, 128–29, 131–34, 137, 229n19, 230n29

"'The Rock'" (Krauss), 225n25

Rojava, 28, 174, 194

Rojava Film Commune, 194–95

ROJ-TV, 180

Rosengarten, Ruth, 225n33

Ross, Fiona, 163

Ross, Kristin, 156

Rothstein, Richard, 209n26

Rouch, Jean, 26, 154, 160–64, 166–67

Rousseau, Frédéric, 231n37

Russell International War Crimes Tribunal, 152, 237n53

Rwanda, 16, 114

Sanders, Bernie, 208n21

Sanders, Mark, 205n2, 227n46

Santner, Eric, 90–91, 100–101

Sanyal, Debarati, 13, 209n28, 210n32, 213n51

Schaap, Andrew, 214n16

Schechner, Alan, 134–37, 139–41, 144, 193, 199, 232n41

Schiff, Jade Larissa, 210n30

Scholem, Gershom, 228n7

Schwab, Gabriele, 14, 62, 210n33

Schwarz-Bart, André, 134

Scott, David, 220n30

Scribner, Charity, 240n16

Second Generation Holocaust Literature (McGlothlin), 210n33

Sedgwick, Eve Kosofsky, 42

Segev, Tom, 228n9

Sehît Ronahî. *See* Wolf, Andrea

Selassie, Haile, 88–89, 222n4

Şenocak, Zafer, 18

Sergent, Jean-Pierre, 163, 166, 169–70

serial project, 23, 26–27

settler colonialism. *See* colonialism

7 Fragments for Georges Méliès (Kentridge), 102

Seven Jewish Children (Churchill), 124–25

The Seventeenth Parallel (Loridan-Ivens and Ivens), 26, 165–69, 175, 236n42

The Seventh Million (Segev), 228n9

sexual harassment, 12

sexuality, 49

Shadow Procession (Kentridge), 111–12

Shakur, Assata, 183

Sharpe, Christina, 73, 208n22

Shimoni, Gideon, 222n6

Shotwell, Alexis, 212n50

Sites of Slavery (Tillet), 217n4

Six-Day War, 129

Six Drawing Lessons (Kentridge), 115, 117

Slaughter, Joseph, 219n18

slavery: apartheid and, 24; archives of, 77–80; beneficiary figure and, 17, 24; Black Atlantic concept and, 9–10; capitalism and, 66–80, 108–9; collective responsibility and, 18; colonialism and, 68–75; descendants of, 70–75; implication in, 57–58, 78–80; Kentridge's renderings of, *108*; legacies of, 4, 24, 58, 63–68, 75–80; reparations for, 9–10, 80–84; responsibility for, 59–60; restitution and, 60–63, 80–84; South African, 108–9; temporality of, 61–62, 68–75; Young on, 52
Slavery and Social Death (Patterson), 64
Slobodian, Quinn, 241n25
SLON collective, 149–54, 156, 194, 232n1, 233n7
Slow Violence and the Environmentalism of the Poor (Nixon), 225n31
Slyomovics, Susan, 218n6
A Small Place (Kincaid), 24, 60, 68–78, 80, 83
A Small Town near Auschwitz (Fullbrook), 216n25
Smith, Barbara, 36
Smith, Beverly, 36
Smith, William Gardner, 162–63
Sobriety, Obesity and Growing Old (Kentridge), 103, *105*, 116
socialism, 153–60, 172, 243n45
solidarity: across victim-beneficiary divide, 21, 60–61, 80–84; competition and, 25–26; identification and, 3–4, 48–49; implication and, 27; intersectionality and, 35–37; long-distance, 12, 127–28, 149–54, 164–69, 179–86; multidirectional memory and, 20, 127–45; negative, 45–46; vulnerability and, 27–28
Some of My Best Friends Are Zionists (Robbins), 144–45
sound (in films), 166–67, 169–70
South Africa: Jewishness in, 98, 108, 110–11; race and apartheid in, 24–25; transitional justice in, 91–96
Soviet Union, 155
spatiality, 39–41
Spricht die Subalterne deutsch? (Steyerl and Rodriguez), 240n15
Stakemeier, Kerstin, 243n42
States of Denial (Cohen), 208n19
Stereoscope (Kentridge), 103
Steyerl, Hito, 23, 27, 33, 152–53, 158, 170–86, 199, 201, 240n15
Stoler, Ann Laura, 208n19
Stone, Judith, 229n19
Stonebridge, Lyndsey, 215n19
The Stone Face (Smith), 162–63
Strike (Eisenstein), 106
Stroop Report, 135, 141
structural implication, 60, 75–81
"The Struggle for Transformation in South Africa" (Clarke and Bassett), 223n7
suitcases, 169–70, 238n56
surrogation, 72, 219n21
Sznaider, Natan, 154, 157–58, 163

Taub, Naomi, 227n2
Taylor, Keeanga-Yamahtta, 205n3
Taylor, Rafael, 238n2
Teitel, Ruti, 90, 92–94, 98
Teitelbaum, Felix. *See* Kentridge, William
temporality: aesthetics of, 96–104; continuity and, 94–96; domination and, 53–58; genealogy and structure and, 24, 62–63; haunting dynamics and, 62–63;

human rights discourses and, 14–16; imaginations of, 95–96; implication's dynamics and, 8–11, 16–17, 32, 55–58, 78–80, 200–204; justice and, 52–53, 59; legacies and, 63–68; memorialization and, 56–58; narratology and, 94–104; presentism and, 26; responsibility and, 8–9, 17–18, 42–53, 59–60, 201; of slavery, 61–62, 68–75; thick time and, 91, 97, 104, 225n24

Tenenboim-Weinblatt, Keren, 231n35
terrorist label, 178–79, 181, 188–89, 201
testimony, 26–27, 166, 169–70
"Theses on the Philosophy of History" (Benjamin), 220n22
thick time, 91, 97, 104, 225n24
"A Thing Like You and Me" (Steyerl), 186–87, 190
"Thinking about Denial" (Hall and Pick), 208n19
Third International, 155
Tillet, Salamishah, 217n4
"Todesfuge" (Celan), 113–15
Todorov, Tzvetan, 213n51
Toprak, Menekşe, 238n56
Torpey, John, 217n4
"Total Cinema" (DiIorio), 235n28
tourism, 24, 74–75, 78–80, 199
"Toward a Dynamic Theory of Action at the Micro Level of Genocide" (Luft), 208n18
transitional justice, 15, 32, 43–44, 90–111, 224n15
transmission belt effects, 35–37, 55, 200
trauma, 33, 159–60, 166; justice and, 83–84; long-distance solidarity and, 26–27, 163–69; slavery as, 59–60, 64, 80–81; transitional justice and, 91–96
traumatic realism, 100–101, 104, 212n48
Traumatic Realism (Rothberg), 212n48
traveling images, 173–75, 186–87, 190
Traverso, Enzo, 237n53
Treblinka, 125, 132
"The Trial of Israel's Campus Critics" (Goldberg and Makdisi), 229n20
Triumph and Laments (Kentridge), 111, 116
Trump, Donald, 4
Truth and Reconciliation Commission of South Africa Report, 90
Turkey, 27, 171, 173, 180, 188, 192

"(Un)Civil Engineering" (Enwezor), 225n29
Un été + 50 (Dauman), 235n28
UN Human Rights Commission, 123–25
Universal Declaration of Human Rights, 156, 234n19

Varda, Agnès, 149
"Velizdeki Mektup" (Toprak), 238n56
Vertov, Dziga, 183–84, 186
victims: human rights discourses and, 14–16, 33; imaginary of, 7–8, 51–55; implicated subject figure and, 1, 6, 21–22, 33–34, 46, 173–76; multidirectional memory and, 124–25, 135–36; purification of, 139–40; reckonings of, 10; restitution and, 60–61; solidarity and, 21
Vietnam, 11, 26–27, 149–54, 159, 164–69, 180, 184
"Vietnam, the New Left, and the Holocaust" (Molden), 237n52

Visualizing the Holocaust (Bathrick, Prager, and Richardson), 230n27
vulnerability, 27–28, 143

Walcott, Derek, 74
Warsaw Ghetto, 124–34, 140–45, 162, 199
Warsaw Ghetto Uprising (Rapoport), 126
Washington Post, 118, 120–22, 144
Waugh, Thomas, 233n2
"We are all Trayvon Martin," 2–3, 3, 5
"We are not Trayvon Martin," 4–8, 22–23, 25, 27, 48, 150, 199, 206n11
Westley, Robert, 217n4
"We Will Get through This Together" (Tenenboim-Weinblatt), 231n35
Weyl, Glen, 118–22, 144
"When Light Becomes White" (Broeck), 219n18
Whitehorn, Laura, 214n10
"Whiteness as Property" (Harris), 221n42
white supremacy, 7, 205n3
"Why Is the World Ignoring the Revolutionary Kurds in Syria?" (Graeber), 241n18

Wiesel, Elie, 107
Wieviorka, Annette, 161
Wilder, Craig, 217n3
Wilder, Gary, 234n17
William Kentridge, Nalini Malani (Huyssen), 225n32
"Without Exception" (Berlant), 209n23
witness, 159–64, 167, 181–86
Wolf, Andrea, 27, 171–97, 199, 238n4
Wolf, Lilo, 239n9
A Woman Named Solitude (Schwarz-Bart), 134
Wood, Tony, 242n35
The World and Africa (Du Bois), 127
"Writing on the Wall" (Ketcham), 226n39

YAJK (PKK division), 172
Yildiz, Yasemin, 211n42
Young, Iris Marion, 14, 23, 35, 49–51, 54–55, 136–37, 143, 151–52, 216n26

Zaman, Amberlin, 240n12
Zertal, Idith, 129
Zimmerman, George, 4–8, 10, 27, 47
Zionism, 118–25, 129, 143–44

Cultural Memory in the Present

Hans Ruin, *Being with the Dead: Burial, Sacrifice, and the Origins of Historical Consciousness*
Eric Oberle, *Theodor Adorno and the Century of Negative Identity*
David Marriott, *Whither Fanon? Studies in the Blackness of Being*
Reinhart Koselleck, *Sediments of Time: On Possible Histories*, translated and edited by Sean Franzel and Stefan-Ludwig Hoffmann
Devin Singh, *Divine Currency: The Theological Power of Money in the West*
Stefanos Geroulanos, *Transparency in Postwar France: A Critical History of the Present*
Sari Nusseibeh, *The Story of Reason in Islam*
Olivia C. Harrison, *Transcolonial Maghreb: Imagining Palestine in the Era of Decolonialization*
Barbara Vinken, *Flaubert Postsecular: Modernity Crossed Out*
Aishwary Kumar, *Radical Equality: Ambedkar, Gandhi, and the Problem of Democracy*
Simona Forti, *New Demons: Rethinking Power and Evil Today*
Joseph Vogl, *The Specter of Capital*
Hans Joas, *Faith as an Option*
Michael Gubser, *The Far Reaches: Ethics, Phenomenology, and the Call for Social Renewal in Twentieth-Century Central Europe*
Françoise Davoine, *Mother Folly: A Tale*
Knox Peden, *Spinoza Contra Phenomenology: French Rationalism from Cavaillès to Deleuze*
Elizabeth A. Pritchard, *Locke's Political Theology: Public Religion and Sacred Rights*
Ankhi Mukherjee, *What Is a Classic? Postcolonial Rewriting and Invention of the Canon*
Jean-Pierre Dupuy, *The Mark of the Sacred*
Henri Atlan, *Fraud: The World of* Ona'ah
Niklas Luhmann, *Theory of Society, Volume 2*
Ilit Ferber, *Philosophy and Melancholy: Benjamin's Early Reflections on Theater and Language*
Alexandre Lefebvre, *Human Rights as a Way of Life: On Bergson's Political Philosophy*
Theodore W. Jennings, Jr., *Outlaw Justice: The Messianic Politics of Paul*

Alexander Etkind, *Warped Mourning: Stories of the Undead in the Land of the Unburied*
Denis Guénoun, *About Europe: Philosophical Hypotheses*
Maria Boletsi, *Barbarism and Its Discontents*
Sigrid Weigel, *Walter Benjamin: Images, the Creaturely, and the Holy*
Roberto Esposito, *Living Thought: The Origins and Actuality of Italian Philosophy*
Henri Atlan, *The Sparks of Randomness, Volume 2: The Atheism of Scripture*
Rüdiger Campe, *The Game of Probability: Literature and Calculation from Pascal to Kleist*
Niklas Luhmann, *A Systems Theory of Religion*
Jean-Luc Marion, *In the Self's Place: The Approach of Saint Augustine*
Rodolphe Gasché, *Georges Bataille: Phenomenology and Phantasmatology*
Niklas Luhmann, *Theory of Society, Volume 1*
Alessia Ricciardi, *After La Dolce Vita: A Cultural Prehistory of Berlusconi's Italy*
Daniel Innerarity, *The Future and Its Enemies: In Defense of Political Hope*
Patricia Pisters, *The Neuro-Image: A Deleuzian Film-Philosophy of Digital Screen Culture*
François-David Sebbah, *Testing the Limit: Derrida, Henry, Levinas, and the Phenomenological Tradition*
Erik Peterson, *Theological Tractates*, edited by Michael J. Hollerich
Feisal G. Mohamed, *Milton and the Post-Secular Present: Ethics, Politics, Terrorism*
Pierre Hadot, *The Present Alone Is Our Happiness, Second Edition: Conversations with Jeannie Carlier and Arnold I. Davidson*
Yasco Horsman, *Theaters of Justice: Judging, Staging, and Working Through in Arendt, Brecht, and Delbo*
Jacques Derrida, *Parages*, edited by John P. Leavey
Henri Atlan, *The Sparks of Randomness, Volume 1: Spermatic Knowledge*
Rebecca Comay, *Mourning Sickness: Hegel and the French Revolution*
Djelal Kadir, *Memos from the Besieged City: Lifelines for Cultural Sustainability*
Stanley Cavell, *Little Did I Know: Excerpts from Memory*
Jeffrey Mehlman, *Adventures in the French Trade: Fragments Toward a Life*
Jacob Rogozinski, *The Ego and the Flesh: An Introduction to Egoanalysis*
Marcel Hénaff, *The Price of Truth: Gift, Money, and Philosophy*
Paul Patton, *Deleuzian Concepts: Philosophy, Colonialization, Politics*
Michael Fagenblat, *A Covenant of Creatures: Levinas's Philosophy of Judaism*
Stefanos Geroulanos, *An Atheism That Is Not Humanist Emerges in French Thought*
Andrew Herscher, *Violence Taking Place: The Architecture of the Kosovo Conflict*
Hans-Jörg Rheinberger, *On Historicizing Epistemology: An Essay*
Jacob Taubes, *From Cult to Culture*, edited by Charlotte Fonrobert and Amir Engel
Peter Hitchcock, *The Long Space: Transnationalism and Postcolonial Form*
Lambert Wiesing, *Artificial Presence: Philosophical Studies in Image Theory*

Jacob Taubes, *Occidental Eschatology*
Freddie Rokem, *Philosophers and Thespians: Thinking Performance*
Roberto Esposito, *Communitas: The Origin and Destiny of Community*
Vilashini Cooppan, *Worlds Within: National Narratives and Global Connections in Postcolonial Writing*
Josef Früchtl, *The Impertinent Self: A Heroic History of Modernity*
Frank Ankersmit, Ewa Domanska, and Hans Kellner, eds., *Re-Figuring Hayden White*
Michael Rothberg, *Multidirectional Memory: Remembering the Holocaust in the Age of Decolonization*
Jean-François Lyotard, *Enthusiasm: The Kantian Critique of History*
Ernst van Alphen, Mieke Bal, and Carel Smith, eds., *The Rhetoric of Sincerity*
Stéphane Mosès, *The Angel of History: Rosenzweig, Benjamin, Scholem*
Pierre Hadot, *The Present Alone Is Our Happiness: Conversations with Jeannie Carlier and Arnold I. Davidson*
Alexandre Lefebvre, *The Image of the Law: Deleuze, Bergson, Spinoza*
Samira Haj, *Reconfiguring Islamic Tradition: Reform, Rationality, and Modernity*
Diane Perpich, *The Ethics of Emmanuel Levinas*
Marcel Detienne, *Comparing the Incomparable*
François Delaporte, *Anatomy of the Passions*
René Girard, *Mimesis and Theory: Essays on Literature and Criticism, 1959–2005*
Richard Baxstrom, *Houses in Motion: The Experience of Place and the Problem of Belief in Urban Malaysia*
Jennifer L. Culbert, *Dead Certainty: The Death Penalty and the Problem of Judgment*
Samantha Frost, *Lessons from a Materialist Thinker: Hobbesian Reflections on Ethics and Politics*
Regina Mara Schwartz, *Sacramental Poetics at the Dawn of Secularism: When God Left the World*
Gil Anidjar, *Semites: Race, Religion, Literature*
Ranjana Khanna, *Algeria Cuts: Women and Representation, 1830 to the Present*
Esther Peeren, *Intersubjectivities and Popular Culture: Bakhtin and Beyond*
Eyal Peretz, *Becoming Visionary: Brian De Palma's Cinematic Education of the Senses*
Diana Sorensen, *A Turbulent Decade Remembered: Scenes from the Latin American Sixties*
Hubert Damisch, *A Childhood Memory by Piero della Francesca*
José van Dijck, *Mediated Memories in the Digital Age*
Dana Hollander, *Exemplarity and Chosenness: Rosenzweig and Derrida on the Nation of Philosophy*
Asja Szafraniec, *Beckett, Derrida, and the Event of Literature*
Sara Guyer, *Romanticism After Auschwitz*

Alison Ross, *The Aesthetic Paths of Philosophy: Presentation in Kant, Heidegger, Lacoue-Labarthe, and Nancy*
Gerhard Richter, *Thought-Images: Frankfurt School Writers' Reflections from Damaged Life*
Bella Brodzki, *Can These Bones Live? Translation, Survival, and Cultural Memory*
Rodolphe Gasché, *The Honor of Thinking: Critique, Theory, Philosophy*
Brigitte Peucker, *The Material Image: Art and the Real in Film*
Natalie Melas, *All the Difference in the World: Postcoloniality and the Ends of Comparison*
Jonathan Culler, *The Literary in Theory*
Michael G. Levine, *The Belated Witness: Literature, Testimony, and the Question of Holocaust Survival*
Jennifer A. Jordan, *Structures of Memory: Understanding German Change in Berlin and Beyond*
Christoph Menke, *Reflections of Equality*
Marlène Zarader, *The Unthought Debt: Heidegger and the Hebraic Heritage*
Jan Assmann, *Religion and Cultural Memory: Ten Studies*
David Scott and Charles Hirschkind, *Powers of the Secular Modern: Talal Asad and His Interlocutors*
Gyanendra Pandey, *Routine Violence: Nations, Fragments, Histories*
James Siegel, *Naming the Witch*
J. M. Bernstein, *Against Voluptuous Bodies: Late Modernism and the Meaning of Painting*
Theodore W. Jennings, Jr., *Reading Derrida / Thinking Paul: On Justice*
Richard Rorty and Eduardo Mendieta, *Take Care of Freedom and Truth Will Take Care of Itself: Interviews with Richard Rorty*
Jacques Derrida, *Paper Machine*
Renaud Barbaras, *Desire and Distance: Introduction to a Phenomenology of Perception*
Jill Bennett, *Empathic Vision: Affect, Trauma, and Contemporary Art*
Ban Wang, *Illuminations from the Past: Trauma, Memory, and History in Modern China*
James Phillips, *Heidegger's Volk: Between National Socialism and Poetry*
Frank Ankersmit, *Sublime Historical Experience*
István Rév, *Retroactive Justice: Prehistory of Post-Communism*
Paola Marrati, *Genesis and Trace: Derrida Reading Husserl and Heidegger*
Krzysztof Ziarek, *The Force of Art*
Marie-José Mondzain, *Image, Icon, Economy: The Byzantine Origins of the Contemporary Imaginary*
Cecilia Sjöholm, *The Antigone Complex: Ethics and the Invention of Feminine Desire*
Jacques Derrida and Elisabeth Roudinesco, *For What Tomorrow . . . : A Dialogue*

Elisabeth Weber, *Questioning Judaism: Interviews by Elisabeth Weber*
Jacques Derrida and Catherine Malabou, *Counterpath: Traveling with Jacques Derrida*
Martin Seel, *Aesthetics of Appearing*
Nanette Salomon, *Shifting Priorities: Gender and Genre in Seventeenth-Century Dutch Painting*
Jacob Taubes, *The Political Theology of Paul*
Jean-Luc Marion, *The Crossing of the Visible*
Eric Michaud, *The Cult of Art in Nazi Germany*
Anne Freadman, *The Machinery of Talk: Charles Peirce and the Sign Hypothesis*
Stanley Cavell, *Emerson's Transcendental Etudes*
Stuart McLean, *The Event and Its Terrors: Ireland, Famine, Modernity*
Beate Rössler, ed., *Privacies: Philosophical Evaluations*
Bernard Faure, *Double Exposure: Cutting Across Buddhist and Western Discourses*
Alessia Ricciardi, *The Ends of Mourning: Psychoanalysis, Literature, Film*
Alain Badiou, *Saint Paul: The Foundation of Universalism*
Gil Anidjar, *The Jew, the Arab: A History of the Enemy*
Jonathan Culler and Kevin Lamb, eds., *Just Being Difficult? Academic Writing in the Public Arena*
Jean-Luc Nancy, *A Finite Thinking*, edited by Simon Sparks
Theodor W. Adorno, *Can One Live After Auschwitz? A Philosophical Reader*, edited by Rolf Tiedemann
Patricia Pisters, *The Matrix of Visual Culture: Working with Deleuze in Film Theory*
Andreas Huyssen, *Present Pasts: Urban Palimpsests and the Politics of Memory*
Talal Asad, *Formations of the Secular: Christianity, Islam, Modernity*
Dorothea von Mücke, *The Rise of the Fantastic Tale*
Marc Redfield, *The Politics of Aesthetics: Nationalism, Gender, Romanticism*
Emmanuel Levinas, *On Escape*
Dan Zahavi, *Husserl's Phenomenology*
Rodolphe Gasché, *The Idea of Form: Rethinking Kant's Aesthetics*
Michael Naas, *Taking on the Tradition: Jacques Derrida and the Legacies of Deconstruction*
Herlinde Pauer-Studer, ed., *Constructions of Practical Reason: Interviews on Moral and Political Philosophy*
Jean-Luc Marion, *Being Given That: Toward a Phenomenology of Givenness*
Theodor W. Adorno and Max Horkheimer, *Dialectic of Enlightenment*
Ian Balfour, *The Rhetoric of Romantic Prophecy*
Martin Stokhof, *World and Life as One: Ethics and Ontology in Wittgenstein's Early Thought*
Gianni Vattimo, *Nietzsche: An Introduction*
Jacques Derrida, *Negotiations: Interventions and Interviews, 1971–1998*, edited by Elizabeth Rottenberg

Brett Levinson, *The Ends of Literature: The Latin American "Boom" in the Neoliberal Marketplace*

Timothy J. Reiss, *Against Autonomy: Cultural Instruments, Mutualities, and the Fictive Imagination*

Hent de Vries and Samuel Weber, eds., *Religion and Media*

Niklas Luhmann, *Theories of Distinction: Re-Describing the Descriptions of Modernity*, edited and with an introduction by William Rasch

Johannes Fabian, *Anthropology with an Attitude: Critical Essays*

Michel Henry, *I Am the Truth: Toward a Philosophy of Christianity*

Gil Anidjar, *"Our Place in Al-Andalus": Kabbalah, Philosophy, Literature in Arab-Jewish Letters*

Hélène Cixous and Jacques Derrida, *Veils*

F. R. Ankersmit, *Historical Representation*

F. R. Ankersmit, *Political Representation*

Elissa Marder, *Dead Time: Temporal Disorders in the Wake of Modernity (Baudelaire and Flaubert)*

Reinhart Koselleck, *The Practice of Conceptual History: Timing History, Spacing Concepts*

Niklas Luhmann, *The Reality of the Mass Media*

Hubert Damisch, *A Theory of /Cloud/: Toward a History of Painting*

Jean-Luc Nancy, *The Speculative Remark: (One of Hegel's bon mots)*

Jean-François Lyotard, *Soundproof Room: Malraux's Anti-Aesthetics*

Jan Patočka, *Plato and Europe*

Hubert Damisch, *Skyline: The Narcissistic City*

Isabel Hoving, *In Praise of New Travelers: Reading Caribbean Migrant Women Writers*

Richard Rand, ed., *Futures: Of Jacques Derrida*

William Rasch, *Niklas Luhmann's Modernity: The Paradoxes of Differentiation*

Jacques Derrida and Anne Dufourmantelle, *Of Hospitality*

Jean-François Lyotard, *The Confession of Augustine*

Kaja Silverman, *World Spectators*

Samuel Weber, *Institution and Interpretation: Expanded Edition*

Jeffrey S. Librett, *The Rhetoric of Cultural Dialogue: Jews and Germans in the Epoch of Emancipation*

Ulrich Baer, *Remnants of Song: Trauma and the Experience of Modernity in Charles Baudelaire and Paul Celan*

Samuel C. Wheeler III, *Deconstruction as Analytic Philosophy*

David S. Ferris, *Silent Urns: Romanticism, Hellenism, Modernity*

Rodolphe Gasché, *Of Minimal Things: Studies on the Notion of Relation*

Sarah Winter, *Freud and the Institution of Psychoanalytic Knowledge*

Samuel Weber, *The Legend of Freud: Expanded Edition*

Aris Fioretos, ed., *The Solid Letter: Readings of Friedrich Hölderlin*

J. Hillis Miller / Manuel Asensi, *Black Holes / J. Hillis Miller; or, Boustrophedonic Reading*
Miryam Sas, *Fault Lines: Cultural Memory and Japanese Surrealism*
Peter Schwenger, *Fantasm and Fiction: On Textual Envisioning*
Didier Maleuvre, *Museum Memories: History, Technology, Art*
Jacques Derrida, *Monolingualism of the Other; or, The Prosthesis of Origin*
Andrew Baruch Wachtel, *Making a Nation, Breaking a Nation: Literature and Cultural Politics in Yugoslavia*
Niklas Luhmann, *Love as Passion: The Codification of Intimacy*
Mieke Bal, ed., *The Practice of Cultural Analysis: Exposing Interdisciplinary Interpretation*
Jacques Derrida and Gianni Vattimo, eds., *Religion*

Lightning Source UK Ltd.
Milton Keynes UK
UKHW012246080622
404111UK00005B/250